Equity and Energy

Westview Replica Editions

The concept of Westview Replica Editions is a response to the continuing crisis in academic and informational publishing. Library budgets for books have been severely curtailed. Ever larger portions of general library budgets are being diverted from the purchase of books and used for data banks, computers, micromedia, and other methods of information retrieval. Interlibrary loan structures further reduce the edition sizes required to satisfy the needs of the scholarly community. Economic pressures on the university presses and the few private scholarly publishing companies have severely limited the capacity of the industry to properly serve the academic and research communities. As a result, many manuscripts dealing with important subjects, often representing the highest level of scholarship, are no longer economically viable publishing projects--or, if accepted for publication, are typically subject to lead times ranging from one to three years.

Westview Replica Editions are our practical solution to the problem. We accept a manuscript in camera-ready form, typed according to our specifications, and move it immediately into the production process. As always, the selection criteria include the importance of the subject, the work's contribution to scholarship, and its insight, originality of thought, and excellence of exposition. The responsibility for editing and proofreading lies with the author or sponsoring institution. We prepare chapter headings and display pages, file for copyright, and obtain Library of Congress Cataloging in Publication Data. A detailed manual contains simple instructions for preparing the final typescript, and our editorial staff is always available to answer questions.

The end result is a book printed on acid-free paper and bound in sturdy library-quality soft covers. We manufacture these books ourselves using equipment that does not require a lengthy make-ready process and that allows us to publish first editions of 300 to 600 copies and to reprint even smaller quantities as needed. Thus, we can produce Replica Editions quickly and can keep even very specialized books in print as long as there is a demand for them.

About the Book and Authors

Equity and Energy: Rising Energy Prices and the Living Standards of Lower Income Americans

Mark N. Cooper, Theodore L. Sullivan, Susan Punnett, and Ellen Berman

Arguing that the energy price policies of the 1970s represented a major equity/efficiency trade-off and led to a dramatic deterioration in the living standard of lower income households, the authors of this book present a comprehensive data-based assessment of the plight of lower income households during the decade of 1973-1983. After a general review of the recessionary and inflationary impact of rising energy prices on the national economy, they present detailed empirical assessments of three trends adversely affecting lower income households: (1) the rising share of household energy expenditures as a percentage of household income and the failure of income transfer programs to offset losses in purchasing power; (2) the rapid increase in energy-related operating costs in lower income rental housing and the coincident decline in the quality of housing; and (3) the rapid increase in energy-related operating costs of local governments which strained local fiscal resources and led to a cutback in the provision of redistributive services (such as health, education, and welfare) and a shift toward regressive taxes. The authors conclude that damage to the national economy and to the living standards of lower income households remains severe; price trends of the 1980s, they emphasize, represent only slight moderations of earlier trends, while the vulnerability to future energy price shocks has been reduced very little. The need for effective policy responses is even greater now than in the first decade of the energy crisis.

Mark N. Cooper is research director of the Consumer Energy Council of America (CECA) and the author of *The Transformation of Egypt*. Theodore L. Sullivan and Susan Punnett are research associates at CECA and Ellen Berman is executive director.

Equity and Energy

Rising Energy Prices and the Living Standards of Lower Income Americans

Mark N. Cooper, Theodore L. Sullivan, Susan Punnett, and Ellen Berman

Westview Press / Boulder, Colorado

A Westview Replica Edition

Published in 1983 in the United States of America by
    Westview Press, Inc.
    5500 Central Avenue
    Boulder, Colorado 80301
    Frederick A. Praeger, President and Publisher

Library of Congress Cataloging in Publication Data
Main entry under title:
Equity and energy.
    Includes bibliographical references.
    1. Cost and standard of living--United States. 2. Inflation
(Finance)--United States--Effect of energy costs on. 3. Middle
classes--United States. 4. Poor--United States. I. Cooper, Mark N.
HD6983.E67   1983   339.4'7'0973   83-14642
ISBN 0-86531-999-5

Contents

Tables

xi

Figures

Acknowledgments

We are grateful to the Ford Foundation for providing the principle funding for the research embodied in this book. Research conducted with support from the Mississippi Legal Services Coalition and the National Consumer Law Center has also been included.

We are also grateful to the individuals who assisted in the research for the book: Robert Krinsky, Stefanie Brand, Smita Kumar, Julie Mencher, and Matthew Frey.

And for secretarial support in typing draft after draft of manuscript, we give our thanks to Tracie Wieland, Mary Beth Zimmerman, and Candace Smith.

1
Introduction:
A Decade of Despair

In the pell mell rush to analyze every aspect of the
energy "issue" in the turbulent aftermath of the 1973
Arab oil embargo, hundreds of major studies have been
written about the general implications of rising energy
prices -- for the economy, national security, the
environment, and alternative energy options.1/ In
retrospect, what is remarkable is that none of these
treatises devoted more than superficial attention to
that segment of society which has borne the greatest
brunt of the 400 percent increase in prices: low and
lower middle income households. This study seeks to
reverse that imbalance.

Rather than being another analysis of the general
economic impact of rising prices, this report is devoted
to a comprehensive analysis of the numerous direct and
indirect ways that rising energy prices have eroded the
living standard of lower income Americans. For them, it
has truly been a decade of despair.

To be sure, such a study is long overdue, but
because of a number of recent developments and the
unresolved nature of the price/impact problem, the need
for a study such as this is particularly pressing.
First, the economic issue has been largely resolved.
After a decade of honest debate, conflicting analyses,
and some self-serving obfuscation, it has become
overwhelmingly clear that rising energy prices have
wreaked havoc on our economy. Both the popular press
and more academic policy analyses have recently
recognized the awesome impacts that are caused by rising
energy prices.

As _Business Week_ magazine declared in its March 22,
1982 issue:

> Reeling from the twelvefold price increase from
> 1973 to 1981, the industrial nations -- nurtured on
> more than a century of cheap energy -- not only

2

went plummeting into two recessions but also suffered further as inflation rates soared to record
levels.2/

Several months later, in July 1982, the Atlantic
Institute joined with a number of scholars at Harvard
and MIT to reach a similar conclusion:

With oil so important in the economy, the two
oil shocks inevitably had to have a dramatic impact
upon the fortunes of an industrial world that had
become dependent upon this fuel. And these shocks
did have pervasive effects, both in that which can
be measured -- inflation, recession, and unemployment -- and that which cannot so easily be measured
-- eroding confidence and growing discontent.
These are the consequences we struggle with
today. The oil shocks appear to have ended the era
of high growth and full employment -- what has been
called the era of "flamboyant growthmanship." In
its place, they have initiated a new and uncertain
and uncomfortable era of "stagflation," a dual
visitation of high inflation and low growth.
Indeed, the two surges in oil prices clearly
have been a driving force behind today's stagflation. Curiously, though, some analysts have gone
into very considerable intellectual acrobatics to
deny this obvious reality, with the result that a
part of recent economic debate has been strangely
irrelevant.3/

Although there are some analysts who continue to
resist this conclusion, it is sufficiently clear and
well-documented to be taken as a basic fact of the
economic life of the 1970s. We can safely begin with
this conclusion as a premise -- rising energy prices
caused tremendous economic losses during the 1970s.
Given that, we can move on to examine what those losses
meant to specific subsets of the population. Our
analysis starts at the most logical place for social
impact analysis -- an assessment of the impact on the
most vulnerable group in society, lower income
households.
There is a second reason why the need for this study
is particularly pressing at this moment -- record energy
price increases remain a critical issue. Although
Americans would like to believe that energy price shocks
are behind us, that is decidedly not the case. Some,
such as the above-mentioned policy analysts at the
Atlantic Institute and Harvard, believe that future
price shocks will come from abroad in a similar form to
those in the 1970s. We are just as concerned about
price shocks that are domestic in origin because most of

the energy price increases suffered by Americans in the 1970s did originate domestically.4/ In 1982-83, strong efforts were made to have Congress raise energy prices significantly by accelerating the decontrol of natural gas5/ and/or imposing a fee on imported crude oil and/or by levying taxes on energy consumption in general.6/ These measures would have involved transfers of economic resources on a scale that rivaled those of the 1970s.

Whether domestic or foreign in origin, the threat of energy price shocks is not a thing of the past. Social impact analysis is urgently needed so that it may be used as a foundation for sound policy decisions, since these decisions can affect the likelihood or size of future price increases and can influence which sectors of the population will bear the burden.

There is a third reason why the need for this study is urgently pressing at this moment. The tremendous impact of the second (and larger) of the oil price shocks (1979-81) is only now becoming apparent and the data necessary to conduct a proper social impact analysis is finally becoming available.

As our analysis shows, lower income Americans have suffered through a decade of devastation in which energy prices eroded their living standard far more than the living standard of other segments of the population. In fact, the potentially disastrous impacts of a third or fourth oil price shock that analysts (such as Daniel Yergin in the Harvard/Atlantic Institute study) suggest could befall large numbers of middle class Americans have already afflicted lower income Americans in many very real and painful ways as a result of the first two energy price shocks (1973-75 and 1979-81).7/ This point cannot be stressed enough. What many careful and compassionate analysts fear may happen to the middle classes in the next oil price shock, because energy now claims a larger share of their income and plays a larger role in their consumption, has already happened to lower income Americans, because energy was already claiming a large part of their income and playing a large part in their consumption just prior to the first two energy price shocks. This is the harsh reality that is missing from the earlier studies. This is the reality of the decade of despair that we describe in this new study.

AN OVERVIEW OF THE RESULTS

We document that over the period from 1972 to 1982, energy prices took a huge bite out of the household income of lower income families -- far larger than that of the middle or upper classes. Further, we show that the loss of household purchasing power is only one of many ravages of rising energy prices. In this study we add two new dimensions to the analysis of the role that rising energy prices have played in eroding the living standard of lower income Americans. We suggest that rising energy prices have undermined the viability of the lower income rental housing stock and have robbed local governments of the resources necessary to provide lower income Americans with the public services on which they rely. When the various elements of the problem are integrated, they serve to portray a grim picture of extreme hardship.

Moreover, as we describe in Chapter 2, it should be stressed that we are not talking here about the plight of the poorest of the poor. Our analysis focuses on the bottom third of the income distribution scale -- roughly 23 million households with incomes below $10,000 in 1979. It is a very large and vulnerable population made up primarily of the poor and the near poor and the elderly and near elderly who are retired or disabled.

Indeed, as discussed in general terms in Chapters 2 and 3, rising energy prices pose basic moral and economic problems for American society -- the moral dilemma of how to ensure access to a basic necessity; the economic dilemma of how to sustain growth when the price of a vital commodity utterly disrupts economic activity.

After posing these issues in the early chapters, the remainder of the work demonstrates that the responses to these problems in the 1970s were disastrous for the lower income population.

As described in Chapters 4 through 6, the central problem that lower income households face is that they consume much less energy than non-lower income households, yet they are forced to devote a disproportion- ately larger share of their income to energy expendi- tures. Low income households (the poorest 13 percent of the population) consume about 25 percent less energy at home and lower middle income households (the next poorest 20 percent) consume about 15 percent less energy at home than non-lower income households (the richest 66 percent). Low income households consume about 75 per- cent less gasoline and lower middle income households consume about 50 percent less than non-lower income households.

Yet, over the period of 1972 to 1980, low income families saw their bills for direct household energy consumption (i.e., energy used in the home plus gasoline or diesel fuel used for private, personal transpor- tation) increase from 17.3 percent of their income to 36.6 percent. Lower middle income families saw their direct energy bills rise from 9.4 percent of their income to 19.2 percent. By contrast, the direct energy bills of non-lower income households increased from only 5.2 percent to 8.0 percent of their income.

This dismal record of the erosion of income of the lower income households can be expressed in a number of other ways as described in Chapter 6. The aggregate loss of purchasing power by lower income households due to rising prices for household energy was approximately $75 billion between 1972 and 1981. Direct energy assistance offset this loss by at most about $7 billion. General income maintenance programs delivered at most another $5 billion through increases in benefits that were caused by energy-price-induced inflation. Thus, income was anything but maintained and, if one listens to current rhetoric, that was the heyday of income maintenance.

This is not to imply that only the low and lower middle income groups suffered. The decade was difficult for all groups. However, even after income transfers are taken into account, it is clear that lower income groups bore a much heavier burden. The real purchasing power of low and lower middle income households, after energy expenditures and inflation are removed from income, declined by almost 19 percent between 1972 and 1979. This entire loss of real purchasing power can be attributed to rising energy prices. For the non-lower income population, the loss of purchasing power, after inflation and energy expenses are taken into account, was only 10 percent. Thus, the low and the lower middle income households lost twice as much in real purchasing power to spend on non-energy goods and services as the middle and upper income classes.

Policy analysts and policymakers have been fighting for almost a decade about these numbers. Our objective in this detailed analysis of these impacts is to lay to rest, once and for all, any doubts about the awesome magnitude of the impact of rising energy prices on the household budgets of lower income Americans. We hope that this study will dispel any lingering misimpressions about whether the income transfer programs, in their present form, can sufficiently mitigate the impact of rising energy prices on lower income households.

In this study we also explore two new fronts in the debate over energy and the lower income population. In Parts 3 and 4 we argue that rising energy prices have played a major part in disproportionately eroding the quality of life of the lower income population by causing a systematic deterioration of basic services on which that population depends -- specifically, rental housing and the provision of local public services. Unlike the estimate of lost household purchasing power, we cannot produce a specific impact estimate in this area. We make these assertions in a different framework from the household budget arguments. We offer the first specification of a hypothesis in the boldest terms that we can. We realize that different approaches and more

detailed analyses might modify the argument. We are
convinced, however, that they would not alter the basic
thrust of our conclusions.

The housing argument is laid out in Chapter 7.
Energy prices were a major factor contributing to the
collapse of the economic viability of the lower income
rental housing market. As operating costs were driven
up by energy prices, increased rents outstripped the
ability of lower income households to pay. The limited
ability of a community to meet the pressures of rising
shelter costs caused by rapidly increasing energy prices
poses an overall threat to the housing quality of the
entire community.

This is our version of the "rent gap" hypothesis
with the spotlight on energy. As rising energy prices
make housing unaffordable for the overall population of
the community, landlords find it generally more
difficult to replace lost income. Uncollectables mount,
but evictions lead to vacancies, not replacement
tenants, because those who can afford the rent are hard
to find. As individual units cease to generate income,
either because they are vacant or because rents go
uncollected, cutbacks in services may occur.

This threatening economic condition is compounded by
the fact that conservation investments have proven
difficult to implement in rental housing. Therefore,
rising energy prices are likely to place greater
pressure on the tenant community because conservation
investments are less likely.

We stress the fact that our explanation for the
mounting financial pressure on the lower income rental
market and the special problem that it creates is not
driven by good or bad intentions of landlords or
tenants. Rather, it assumes only the presence of
rational actors in a situation in which institutional
arrangements and economic constraints combine to create
and compound a social problem. Energy prices are one of
the major economic constraints.

Whether one believes that the other constraints on
the ability to collect rent are artificially imposed by
rent controls and/or the structure of income maintenance
programs and/or the simple fact that in a sluggish
economy the lower income population cannot maintain its
income, there is no doubt that massive pressures have
been placed on the housing market by rising energy
costs. Energy prices were pushing costs up from below
while the recessions caused by energy price shocks and
other factors were setting limits from above on the
ability to pay. The rental housing market was squeezed
in the middle.

We have examined data on the rental housing market
for both the public and private sectors, as discussed in
Chapter 8. In the private sector, in 1969, rents for

households in the bottom third of the income distribution were about $80 per month. Energy costs were approximately 14 percent of net operating expenses for rental units at that time. By 1979, the average rent for the poorest one-third of the population had risen to $200 per month and energy costs had jumped to 30 percent of net operating expenses. In fact, energy costs accounted for about 40 percent of the total increase in operating costs. When one component of costs increases that explosively, other aspects of the budget will suffer as well. This is the same logic applied above to households.

The rapid rise in operating costs resulted in two somewhat different forms of pressure on the rental market.

First, as operating costs rose faster than rent increases, landlords were squeezed. Expenditures by landlords to maintain and improve properties were cut back and the housing stock deteriorated. Ultimately, abandonments increased. Survey evidence shows a dramatic deterioration in the condition of lower income rental housing and a rapid jump in reports of abandoned buildings in lower income neighborhoods between 1973 and 1979 -- precisely the period of the energy price shocks.

Second, although rents did not rise as fast as operating costs, they did rise faster than the income of lower income households. The result was a squeeze on the economic resources of tenants. The most direct measure of this pressure can be seen in the rapid deterioration of housing stock over this period and from the fact that in 1980 almost two-thirds of all lower income households, compared to about one-half in 1973, were forced to devote 35 percent or more of their income to shelter costs (rent plus utilities).

In the public sector, the impact of rising energy prices was determined by a number of factors embedded in the financial structure of public housing. Utility costs were funnelled directly into subsidies but non-utility costs were not. As the aggregate level of subsidies rose, pressure mounted to hold costs down and non-utility expenditures were gutted. The quality and economic viability of public housing was undermined.

The data on increasing utility costs in public housing is even more extensive than in the private sector. In 1969, utility costs comprised 30 percent of operating expenses of public housing. By 1980, they had increased to almost 45 percent. Energy cost increases accounted for 44 percent of the increase in operating expenses during that period.

In Part 4, we analyze the impact of rising energy prices on public service delivery, and show that a similar dynamic process has eroded the living standard of lower income households by undermining public service

delivery. We have chosen to examine public services
because we believe that they rank as the fourth largest
component of the lower income population's consumption
-- after shelter, food and energy.

Our hypothesis for public services, as outlined in
Chapter 9, is similar to that for housing. It is our
contention that local governments were dealt a severe
blow by rising energy prices and that they have
compensated in ways that have disproportionately and
adversely affected lower income households. The
argument can be outlined as follows:

Energy prices contribute to increased fiscal stress.
Fiscal stress creates pressure to reduce services and
raise revenues. As measures are taken to relieve this
stress, low and lower middle income households are more
deeply affected than other groups for two primary
reasons.

First, locally provided public goods and services
constitute a larger share of their total consumption of
goods and services than they constitute for non-lower
income groups. Consequently, any service cutbacks will
affect them more than other groups.

Second, the actual cutbacks in services or increases
in revenues are not likely to be evenly distributed
among specific services or sources of revenue. Service
cutbacks are likely to be concentrated disproportionately in the area of redistributive services, of which
low and lower middle income households are disproportionately large consumers. We further hypothesize that,
within the political process of local finances, general
tax increases would occur in those areas where resis-
tance was weakest. Lower income households would be
least able to forestall the tax increases that affect
them most.

Again, we stress the fact that this explanation is
not driven by the good or bad intentions of local
government officials or local inhabitants. Rather, it
assumes only rational actors engaged in the enlightened
pursuit of their interests under difficult economic
circumstances and through specific political insti-
tutions. The results of these systemic factors and
structural processes are to the detriment of the lower
income population.

These simple hypotheses are well supported by the
data, as discussed in Chapter 10.

First, we observe a close correlation between
increases in the operating expenses of local governments
(defined as non-wage, non-salary, non-capital expenses)
and rising fuel prices. Since energy costs constitute
about 30 percent of operating expenses (thus defined)
and about 10 percent of total local government
expenditures, rising energy prices were certain to
create pressure on other expenditures.

At the local level, real expenditures for the four
redistributive services declined by an average of 2.3
percent per year between 1972 and 1979. For allocative
services, real expenditures increased by .3 percent per
year. Total real local spending increased at a rate of
.2 percent per year. In contrast, gross national
product (GNP) and personal income increased by about 2.5
percent real per year. Thus, not only were local
governments growing more slowly than the national
income, but redistributive services were shrinking at
the local level.

Local revenues were also dramatically restructured
during the period. Revenues derived from property taxes
declined from 61 to 49 percent of the total. Revenues
derived from sales taxes and user fees increased from 34
percent to 45 percent, while income taxes remained
relatively flat, going from 3 to 4 percent of the total.

It is interesting to note that concern over the "New
Federalism" has produced analyses which, for the most
part, predict behaviors by local governments similar to
those we observe have already occurred in the context of
energy. That is, in the face of sudden budget
imbalances and revenue needs, local governments will
rely heavily on increased sales taxes and, especially,
on conversion of many programs to those utilizing
service-based user charges as a primary funding source.
More importantly, local governments will maintain
certain services at the expense of redistributive
programs -- especially welfare.

The most ominous consequence from the point of view
of the lower income population is the fact that much of
the response to rising energy prices was to cushion the
blow by resorting to intergovernmental revenues. Yet,
the New Federalism threatens to reduce that revenue
source.

If one accepts, as we do, the argument that federal
energy price policy was a significant cause of the
economic problems and the fiscal stress placed on local
governments in the 1970s, then federal energy price
policy and the New Federalism would constitute a
devastating one-two punch to American local governments
and the low and lower middle income populations most
reliant upon them for services. Federal energy price
policy dealt the first blow by forcing local resources
out of redistributive areas, while intergovernmental
revenues partially filled the gap. The New Federalism
could deal the second blow by cutting back on the flow
of those revenues, leading almost certainly to a major
reduction of all redistributive services and reductions
in subsidies for allocative services as well. The net
effect would be a major, disproportionate increase in
the burden placed on low and lower middle income
households -- the same effect we have observed in the

rental housing market and the household budgets of the lower income population.

All of the above arguments and analyses are based on detailed survey evidence and other types of data that cover the period up until early 1981. In Chapter 11, we examine, with somewhat more aggregate and less detailed data, the impact of moderating oil prices in the period between early 1981 and early 1983. The basic conclusions we reach are that, measured either by household expenditures on energy or by the total national energy bill, the burden has not grown much lighter, the disproportionate burden on lower income households continues to grow worse, and prospects for quick relief are not very bright.

The reasons that the overall energy bill did not decline much are that petroleum product prices did not decline nearly as much as crude oil prices and that non-petroleum energy prices (electricity and natural gas) continued to increase sharply over the period. The reason that the burden shifted disproportionately onto lower income households is that the one form of energy which increased least in price (gasoline) accounts for a smaller share of the total lower income energy bill. The reasons that prospects for the decade ahead are not bright flows from the simple arithmetic of the first decade of the energy crisis. Even with the oil price decreases of 1982, the national energy bill, expressed as a percentage of GNP, had almost doubled since 1973. The energy expenditures of lower income households had at least doubled. It would take more than a decade of constant real energy prices and 5 percent real economic growth to return energy expenditures as a percentage of national or household income to their 1973 levels. Such a miraculous decade is hardly in prospect. Thus, the burden on lower income households is likely to remain especially onerous.

CONCLUSION

In light of the above discussion, the overall purpose of this study is to sharpen the understanding and empirical analysis of the equity impacts of rising energy prices. Our goals are to:

1. Refine the conceptual definition and discussion of the impact of rising energy prices on low and lower middle income households;

2. Establish the fundamental fact that those households bear a disproportionate burden due to rising energy prices;

3. Bring the most recent data to bear on the estimate of the magnitude of that burden; and

4. Initiate the analysis of several areas where a significant burden has been placed on the low and lower

middle income population -- areas that have been
previously overlooked or not studied in a systematic
fashion.

Part 1

Basic Issues

2
The Social Question

Changing patterns of energy consumption and the dynamic effects of rising energy prices on the economy and the national income distribution are undoubtedly among the most complex and trying issues that policymakers and policy analysts faced in the past decade. These issues are not only complex because of their technical nature, they are also politically trying because so much is at stake. As a society, we have lacked a basic framework to deal with them. The issues of energy pricing and supply burst upon the scene with such suddenness and fury as a result of the oil embargo of 1973 that the entire American frame of reference for thinking about energy was shattered. In many respects a viable set of definitions and concepts that would serve policymakers and average citizens has never been reconstructed.

We believe that, at the outset, it is of utmost importance to have a clear set of basic definitions and concepts in hand. Since the focus of the study is a social impact analysis, it is important to state at the outset that energy consumption and pricing are not treated as engineering or technical matters, nor are they considered as matters of simple economics. Rather, they are treated in a broader social context which, while encompassing both technical and economic considerations, places primary stress on social and equity concerns.1/

Because the study focuses on the social consequences of rising energy prices, it is also important to understand why the impact on the lower income population is a matter of primary social concern. This chapter presents the basic definition of the issue as applied in this study and describes the methodological approaches and conceptual framework that are dictated by that definition. We have coupled the conceptual and methodological discussions because we believe that basic definitional choices dictate methodological decisions.

15

THE SOCIAL ISSUE

It is obvious that energy price increases over the last decade imposed major hardships on all members of society, not just lower income Americans. Further, it is clear that the changes in consumption patterns made necessary by energy price increases were often extremely painful and disruptive for everyone, not just the lower income population. Nevertheless, the central hypothesis and argument of this study is that lower income Americans bore a disproportionate burden relative to other members of society. Rising energy prices placed a greater strain on their relatively limited resources and posed a greater threat to their relatively lower standard of living.

This is a matter which has received increasing attention over the past decade.2/ That attention stems from the interaction of two critical factors. First, energy is a vital necessity, essential for the mainte-nance of basic health, safety, and well-being. Second, energy prices have been escalating at unprecedented rates.

The combination of these two factors has meant that the portion of income devoted to energy expenditures by lower income households escalated dramatically over the decade as energy prices rose. Because energy is a vital necessity, it is extremely difficult to reduce consump-tion beyond certain minimum levels. As households begin to approach those minimum levels, they find it increas-ingly difficult to reduce consumption. No matter how high the price rises, they must pay the price in order to maintain their well-being. As a result, energy consumes an extremely large portion of their household budget and they are forced to struggle to find other commodities on which to cut back. In the limited budget of the lower income family, there is little fat to be cut and, consequently, rising energy prices erode their already meager living standard, threatening their basic health, safety, and well-being.

Based on this threat, it is possible to stipulate a direct and explicit moral obligation for society. One can assert that society must make a commitment to ensuring access to quantities of energy adequate for basic health, safety, and well-being, at a price that does not threaten the general living standard of the least advantaged members of society.

This study was conducted with the underlying assumption that the logical definition of energy as a vital necessity is correct and that the social consequences and the moral commitment implied by that definition are compelling.

The Historical, Political, and
Moral Background of the Issue

Toward the end of the decade of the 1970s, as policy
decisions were made to decontrol the price of energy and
permit it to rise to the extremely high levels set by
the foreign oil cartel,3/ it became apparent that
society could not just let prices rise and let economics
take its course. Society could not treat energy and
energy prices as mere technical/economic matters.
Commitments to intervene in the marketplace on both
the supply and demand sides were made because it was
believed that market forces could not solve the extremely varied and complex problems -- symbolized but not
fully described by a tripling of prices in a very short
period -- created by a radical restructuring of the
energy market.4/ Among the most basic commitments on
the demand side was a social equity commitment. Policymakers were convinced that energy is a vital necessity,
many of its uses not being discretionary, but critical
for the maintenance of basic health and well-being.
They concluded that society was obligated to exert
special efforts to ensure that those minimum quantities
of energy necessary for survival, health, and safety
were made available to every member of society.5/
Further, they concluded that rising energy prices should
not be allowed to erode disproportionately the living
standard of lower income households.
The most explicit statement of these policy
conclusions of the late 1970s can be found in the Crude
Oil Windfall Profit Tax Act of 1980:

1. Recent dramatic increases in the cost of primary
   energy sources have caused corresponding sharp
   increases in the cost of home energy;
2. Reliable data projections show that the cost of
   home energy will continue to climb at excessive
   rates;
3. The cost of essential home energy imposes a disproportionately larger burden on fixed income,
   lower income, and lower middle income households
   and the rising cost of such energy is beyond the
   control of such households;
4. Fixed income, lower income, and lower middle income households should be protected from disproportionately adverse effects on their incomes
   resulting from national energy policy;
5. Adequate home heating is a necessary aspect of
   shelter and the lack of home heating poses a
   threat to life, health, or safety;
6. Adequate home cooling is necessary for certain
   individuals to avoid a threat to life, health,
   or safety;

7. Low income households often lack access to energy supplies because of the structure of home energy distribution systems and prevailing credit practices; and

8. Assistance to households in meeting the burden of rising energy costs is insufficient from existing State and Federal sources.

It is the purpose of this title to make grants to States to provide assistance to eligible households to offset the rising costs of home energy that are excessive in relation to household income.6/

Although that Act is of no special relevance to this study -- i.e., we are not evaluating its specific concept, design, or execution -- it does provide a useful point of reference for a number of reasons. The Act is a landmark piece of legislation in many respects. It marked the culmination of an era for one of the most turbulent political and economic issues that has faced the United States since the Second World War -- energy prices. For many, it marked the end of the energy price debate -- although that may prove to be a mistaken conclusion. It remains the single largest piece of tax-raising legislation levied on a specific industry in the history of the country and, in principle, it committed one-quarter of those taxes to low income energy assistance.7/ As such, it made a very clear choice about social values and equity.

In a broader context, the Act may contain important lessons about equity/efficiency compromises -- an issue that is likely to be of considerable importance in the decade ahead. The type of commitment made in the Act was, in many respects, an intellectual, moral, and political quid pro quo for the decision to allow energy prices to rise sharply. That is, just about every major national research and policy institution maintained that, for efficiency reasons, it was necessary to let energy prices rise. And, just about every major research institution insisted that equity concerns demanded social responses outside of the marketplace.8/

Majorities of two-thirds or larger in both Houses of Congress endorsed this efficiency/equity arrangement. Insofar as this was the largest efficiency/equity deal of the 1970s and insofar as there are likely to be many loud calls for similar deals in the 1980s (as part of the economic revitalization or reindustrialization movement), the Crude Oil Windfall Profit Tax Act is an instructive backdrop for many of the social, economic, and equity debates of the 1980s.

Public Opinion About Energy

This understanding of the vital role that energy

plays in daily life-maintaining activities and the
potential threat that rising energy prices pose to the
survival of lower income households is not limited to
the halls of Congress. Surveys of public opinion
suggest that this is a widely held notion among the
public.9/ Two recent surveys can be used to highlight
the basic points made above.

One survey, entitled <u>Electricity Pricing: Choices
for the 1980's</u>,10/ conducted for the Union Carbide
Corporation, points out the widespread public support
for efforts to alleviate the burden placed on lower
income households by rising energy prices. The survey
reveals that 60 percent of the Americans polled feel
that the poor are entitled to a "certain basic amount of
electricity," even if government must "help the poorer
people pay." Support for this statement is maintained
across all income categories and sociodemographic
groups.

A second survey, conducted for the South Jersey Gas
Company, may shed considerable light on why there is
such strong recognition that rising energy prices place
a heavy burden on lower income households.11/ Asked
whether rising energy prices would force sacrifices, 39
percent of the respondents said they would be forced to
make many sacrifices. Unfortunately the study includes
no lower income respondents, as we have defined them,
but a close association between income and the expected
level of sacrifice was still evident.

Of those with annual incomes of $12,000 to $18,000,
55 percent said they would have to make many sacrifices.
Of those with annual incomes of $18,000 to $30,000, 42
percent said they would have to make many sacrifices.
Of those in the highest income bracket ($30,000 or
more), only 25 percent said they would have to make many
sacrifices.

The specific nature of the expected sacrifices is
also noteworthy. In the aggregate, the first sacrifice
expected was a reduction in energy consumption (43 percent). The second most frequently expected sacrifice
was in food prepared at home (18 percent).

The expected sacrifices by households in various
income categories underscore the burden that rising
energy prices are likely to place on low and lower
middle income families. Families with incomes in the
$12,000 to $18,000 per year range were half as likely to
project cutbacks in luxuries -- entertainment, travel,
dining out, frills -- as the higher income groups
(perhaps because they enjoy so few). They were more
than twice as likely, however, to project sacrifices in
the necessities -- food, housing, and medical expenditures. They were also two to three times as likely to
project being forced to spend less overall and to hunt
for bargains. Households with incomes between $18,000

and $30,000 projected cutbacks in the necessities twice
as frequently as upper income groups (incomes above
$30,000). Only the high income respondents projected
more cutbacks in luxuries than necessities.

Even without responses from truly low income households, it is clear that energy prices impose severe
burdens on the low and lower middle income population.
A similar survey conducted for the Pennsylvania Public
Service Commission yields similar results.12/

General survey evidence shows a strong belief that
rising energy prices impose a significant and inequita-
ble burden on middle and lower income households. The
evidence is both general and specific. It is general in
the sense that when people are asked to conceptualize
the impact of rising energy prices, they say it is
burdensome for all, but especially burdensome for lower
income households.13/ It is specific in the sense that
when individuals are asked to assess how they have been
affected by rising prices, lower income households
report greater and more serious effects.14/

Energy industry officials have come to recognize the
critical social problem that rising energy prices pose.
In a 1982 Op-Ed piece in The Washington Post, Donald J.
Heim, the President and Chief Executive Officer of
Washington Gas Light Company, argued forcefully for
active programs to alleviate the burden of rising energy
prices on the lower income population:

> While enjoying summer, it is all too tempting
> to forget the snow, ice and frigid temperatures
> that affected the entire area as recently as Janu-
> ary of this year.
> But low-income families that are still trying
> to cope with heating bills from last winter can't
> forget. Neither can the rest of us if we are to
> avoid a repeat performance of the same problems
> next winter.
> The poor and those living on low fixed incomes
> have been hit hard from all sides during the past
> year. They have borne the brunt of rising unem-
> ployment rates resulting from the national economic
> recession. They have suffered from inflation,
> which continues to erode incomes although at a much
> lower rate than in recent years. And an ever-in-
> creasing share of their limited resources is re-
> quired for the increased energy costs that in vary-
> ing degrees have affected us all. . .
> Most people would probably agree that helping
> the poor to pay for fundamental energy needs is an
> obligation of our society as a whole, just as So-
> cial Security payments, welfare for the needy, food
> stamps and other such programs are responsibilities
> shared by all Americans to help those less able to

pay their own way.

That obligation goes beyond merely parceling out available energy assistance funds. Governments must cooperate in a new effort to make sure aid to defray the energy costs of the poor is applied in the most efficient way.15/

In a similar vein, a recent paper on the impact of rising energy prices on the poor by Robert Hemphill, former Director of Energy Conservation and Rates of the Tennessee Valley Authority, and Robert L. Owens, an economist at TVA, acknowledges the fundamentally burdensome nature of increasing electric utility rates:

Increasing electric rates are regressive in nature because such increases will require a larger portion of the total income of low-income families than for high income families.16/

The difficulty that the poor have in cutting back their consumption was also recognized:

Unfortunately, while it is the low- and fixed-income persons who are hurt the most from the rapid increases in electricity rates, it is often these same people who seem to be either unwilling or unable to undertake measures to alleviate the problem.17/

The authors recognize the reality that confronts utilities as a result of these factors:

Any public utility faced with these facts has two basic courses of action: It can create conservation programs specifically targeted toward assisting this group of customers, and/or it can redesign its rates (or have them redesigned for it by the Public Utility Commission) to try to assist this group. TVA has certainly embarked on the former, and has also redesigned rates, although with a goal of general equity rather than intraclass subsidy.18/

The authors and most utility officials insist that decisions about social issues and equity should be made by social agencies, such as governments (through their power to tax and spend) and public utility commissions (through their power to set rates), rather than by utilities. Still, they acknowledge that utilities must act as socially responsible and accountable vehicles for programs to alleviate the burden on lower income households. In the process of doing so, they identify five different conservation programs and three different redistributive schemes -- one involving rates and two involving taxes -- which have been considered and endorsed by TVA.

Above all, they recognize that these decisions must be made and programs must be put in place quickly to alleviate the heavy burden that has been placed on lower income households. The central purpose of Part 2 of this study is to assess the burden by examining its most obvious impact, the impact of rising energy prices on household expenditures.

ANALYTIC FRAMEWORK

We believe that one analytic framework can be utilized to analyze each aspect of how low and lower middle income groups lose out as a result of an energy price shock -- impacts on home energy consumption, local public services, and the rental housing market. Without overstressing the precision of fit of the framework in each of the areas of analysis, we believe that they share a set of characteristics and constraints that make them sufficiently similar to fit under one framework.

The framework assumes that the ultimate impact of rising energy prices will be determined by the interplay of three elements -- changes in expenditures, changes in income, and what we call "avenues of retreat."19/ Figure 2.1 graphs the path of energy expenditures as a percentage of total income after an energy price shock. This pattern would be true of household budgets, rental housing operating budgets, municipal budgets, or even the national income. Table 2.1 gives a few specific examples of each of the analytic elements for households, public housing authorities, local governments, and major components of the national economy.

The important point to note is that while energy prices continue to rise, the rate of increase of energy expenditures as a percentage of income declines, because rational economic actors try to reduce the impact of rising prices. As energy prices rise, individuals, local governments, etc., will respond by trying to reduce their consumption while maintaining their "living standard." How high energy expenditures will rise as a percentage of income and the extent to which they force changes in budgetary and economic patterns depends on the effectiveness of the response and the magnitude of the price increase.

The initial, unavoidable jolt of an energy price increase is to raise energy bills -- both in absolute terms and in relative terms (i.e., as a percentage of income or expenditures). After the jolt has been felt responses will be elicited.

The initial response is to engage in simple behavioral conservation. Easy, largely cost-free measures

FIGURE 2.1
Basic Conceptualization: The Time Pattern of Increasing Energy Expenditures as a Percent of Income

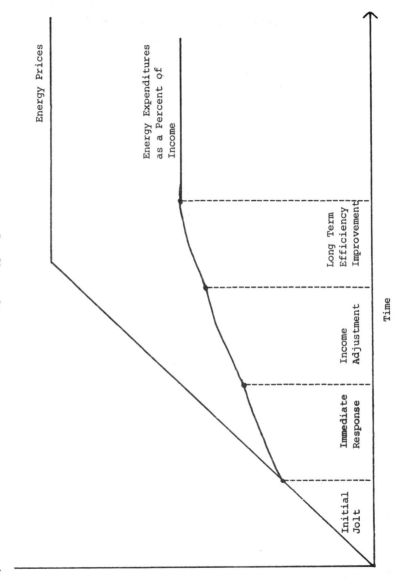

Energy Prices

Energy Expenditures as a Percent of Income

Initial Jolt | Immediate Response | Income Adjustment | Long Term Efficiency Improvement

Time

Energy Prices
or
Energy Expenditures as a Percent of Income

TABLE 2.1
A Framework for Analyzing the Impact of Rising Energy Prices on the Standard of Living of the Low Income Population

Analytic Categories	Household Budgets	Public Housing Authority Finances	Local Government Budgets	National Aggregates
Expenditures				
Energy	Home Fuels; Transportation Energy	Utilities	Utilities; Operating Expenses of Departments	Increase in Energy Cost Share of GNP
Other	Food, Clothing, etc.	Operating Expenses	General Operating Expenses; Capital Outlays	Aggregate Demand
Instantaneous Response	Behavioral Conservation; Reduced Saving	Behavioral Conservation; Drawdown Reserves	Behavioral Conservation; Deficits	Keynesian Recession; Behavioral Conservation; Reduced Demand
Income	Earned Income; General Transfers; Energy Transfers	Rent; Shift of Population Subsidy	Intergovernmental; Local Taxes; User Fees	Exchange Rate Alterations; Income Share Shifts
Avenues of Retreat				
Energy Management	Behavioral Conservation; Investment	Behavioral Conservation; Investment	Energy Use Management; Investment	Change in Driving Patterns, etc.; Shift in Energy Intensity of GNP
Debt	Indebtedness	Rechannel Capital and Reserves	Rechannel Capital Outlays	Increased Debt
Cutback	Direct Reduction of Living Standard	Neglect	Retrenchment	Reduction of Living Standard

will be taken to cut consumption. A classic example would be lowering the setting of thermostats in the winter.

These two initial impacts will follow closely one upon the other and we consider the initial behavioral response to be largely indistinguishable from the shock itself. If the shock is big enough, the reaction will be fairly instantaneous. This will be true of households, landlords, local governments, and national economic aggregates. For each of these cases the available data is not adequately refined to differentiate between the initial shock and the immediate behavioral response.

The second response is to adjust incomes. As soon as the opportunity presents itself, demands for increases in income will be made to offset the rise in energy prices. This will be true of households (who will seek pay increases), landlords (who will seek rent increases), local governments (which will seek to increase taxes and other sources of revenue), major economic aggregates (labor as a whole and capital as a whole), and specific industries (which will raise their relative prices). It is unlikely that these opportunities will be instantaneous or that success will be immediately achieved. Thus, the second response takes longer and is readily distinguishable from the first.

The third response we identify as avenues of retreat. On the positive side, permanent changes in energy consumption may be instituted, including more effective energy management and capital investments to reduce energy consumption. These require significant effort, both in terms of decision-making and in the allocation of resources. On the negative side, efforts may not be entirely successful in reducing energy consumption. That is, it may not be possible to reduce energy consumption dramatically. As a result, indebtedness may be increased in order to maintain consumption. Alternatively, cutbacks in consumption in nonenergy areas may be necessary.

Actual responses will include a combination of all of the above responses and the nature of the overall impact will be determined by the size of all of these factors. Further, each of the responses is ongoing, so that they overlap, even though they are likely to be initiated in sequence. The critical question is: How successful are low and lower middle income households in achieving favorable results or even holding their own as this process unfolds? Our research shows that they are not at all successful. As briefly described in Chapter 1 and discussed in greater detail in subsequent chapters, a combination of social, economic and political factors results in a disproportionate burden being placed on low and lower middle income households.

26

BASIC METHODOLOGICAL CHOICES

General Trends

The research agenda outlined in Chapter 1 is large
and the analytic task is complex. In the period on
which we are focusing, roughly the decade after the oil
embargo of October 1973, many factors in addition to
energy combined to place a great deal of pressure on the
living standard of lower income households. Determining
the precise part that energy played and demonstrating
the extent of the loss suffered by the lower income
population can be extremely difficult. In conducting an
analysis in which many factors must be considered, there
always comes a point at which one must choose between
placing the emphasis on a basic trend or placing the
emphasis on variations around the trend and/or on
mitigating factors. We have repeatedly chosen to
emphasize the trend. There are two primary reasons for
this.

First, we would like to balance the analytic record.
The "efficiency" decision to decontrol energy prices was
based on a simple assertion that the general effect or
trend would be an improvement in allocative efficien-
cy.20/ While the efficiency argument was being made, a
simple corollary assertion about the equity impact of
decontrol should have been made as well.21/ The
corollary is that the general effect or trend of
decontrol was certain to be a serious deterioration of
distributive equity. We believe the equity corollary
was a logical outgrowth of the price increase and
equally important and worthy of equal attention.

Second, and of utmost importance, we believe that
the risks associated with not emphasizing the basic
trends are much larger. If stress is placed on
variations around the trend and/or on mitigating
factors, thereby underestimating the seriousness of the
underlying trend, the mistaken conclusion is drawn that
the poorest and most vulnerable part of the population
is better off than it actually is. Policymakers then
design social responses that are inadequate and put that
part of the population at extreme risk of great deprivation. This has been the net effect of the first round
of policy analyses which emphasize efficiency at the
expense of equity.

If, on the other hand, stress is placed on the
trend, thereby overestimating its seriousness, society
may devote more resources to that part of the population
than is called for. The cost of doing so is spread
across the vast majority which, in spite of pressures on
its living standards, is in a much more secure position
and is much better equipped to absorb the cost of the
error.

The costs of underestimating the problem are, in our judgment, much greater than the costs of overestimating it. A humane society errs in the direction of protecting its weakest members, not in the direction of placing them at greater risk. It is important to recognize that such judgments cannot be avoided. Ultimately, even the most rigorous statistical analysis requires choices about which errors and threats to validity to minimize.22/ We state our choice at the outset to make it explicit. Wherever possible, we will provide the reader with the tools necessary to conduct the analysis with the emphasis reversed.

National Aggregate Data

This initial methodological choice has affected the type of data that is utilized in this study. Stressing basic trends, we have concentrated on national aggregate data. We recognize that averages and national aggregates hide a lot, but we believe that they also reveal a lot. Although no one is average, in social and economic analysis many people tend to be quite close to the average. Specific instances that contradict our basic conclusions can certainly be found, but arguing from cases is even more likely to be misleading than arguing from averages. In addition, we recognize that a great deal more detail could be added to the analysis. However, we do not expect that either case studies or additional levels of detail would alter the basic conclusions.

The data used for the analyses in this work are taken primarily from the Residential Energy Consumption Survey, conducted by the U.S. Department of Energy (DOE);23/ the Annual Housing Surveys, conducted by the U.S. Bureau of the Census for the U.S. Department of Housing and Urban Development (HUD);24/ the Consumer Expenditure Survey of 1972-73, conducted by the U.S. Bureau of Labor Statistics;25/ the survey of Five Thousand American Families, conducted by the University of Michigan;26/ the National Interim Energy Consumption Survey of 1978-79 (the predecessor to the Residential Energy Consumption Survey), conducted by the U.S. Department of Energy;27/ the 1977 Nationwide Personal Transportation Study, conducted by the U.S. Department of Transportation;28/ and City Government Finances, an annual survey conducted by the U.S. Bureau of the Census.29/

In several of these surveys, it is possible to analyze patterns and trends in different regions of the country. Regional differences have frequently played an important part in the energy debate because of the assumption that energy costs are very different in different parts of the country. Throughout the following analysis, we highlight different regions of the

country in order to gauge the impact of regional
differences on the burden that rising energy prices
place on the lower income population. The geographic
regions utilized are the standard Census regions --
Northeast, South, North Central, and West.30/
For the purpose of assessing the impact of climate
factors on the burden that rising energy prices place on
the lower income population, we contrast consumption and
expenditure patterns in various climate zones as defined
by the American Institute of Architects and the Department of Energy. These zones are described in Figure
2.2. As can be seen from Figure 2.2, Zone 1 has the
coldest climate and Zone 7 the warmest.

The Lower Income Population

Utilizing national averages and aggregates creates
certain difficulties in defining which groups fall into
the lower income category. In general, we focus on
those households which fall in the bottom third of the
income distribution scale. We call the bottom 13 percent, approximately, "low income." In 1972-73, this
included households with incomes below $3,000.31/ In
1979, it included households with incomes below
$5,000.32/ We call the next 20 percent, approximately,
"lower middle income." In 1972-73, this included households with incomes between $3,000 and $7,000. In 1979,
it included households with incomes between $5,000 and
$10,000. The major conceptual and empirical difficul-
ties in creating and reconciling these categories are
described in the Methodological Appendix, Section 1.
In large part, these definitions were a matter of
convenience. The available data can be aggregated quite
well using these cutting points. We are also quite
comfortable with these categories. The bottom third of
the population seems a reasonable approximation of
"lower" income. It would incorporate most of the
households society usually identifies as in need of
special social commitments -- in particular, the poor
and elderly.
This lower income population in 1979 can be
described briefly as follows. The lower income group
consisted of approximately 23 million households with a
total of approximately 50 million persons with incomes
below $10,000 per year (see Table 2.2). Approximately
32 million of those individuals were officially defined
as poor or near poor -- i.e., they had incomes at or
below 125 percent of the official Bureau of Labor
Statistics (BLS) poverty level. More than 90 percent of
all the households defined as poor or near poor by the
BLS would fall into the category of lower income
Americans as used in this study.

FIGURE 2.2
Climate Zones of the United States

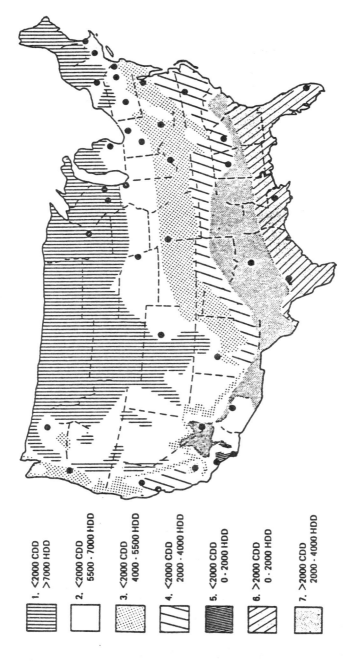

1. <2000 CDD
   >7000 HDD

2. <2000 CDD
   5500 - 7000 HDD

3. <2000 CDD
   4000 - 5500 HDD

4. <2000 CDD
   2000 - 4000 HDD

5. <2000 CDD
   0 - 2000 HDD

6. >2000 CDD
   0 - 2000 HDD

7. >2000 CDD
   2000 - 4000 HDD

Source: U.S. Department of Energy; American Institute of Architects.

TABLE 2.2
The Composition of the Lower Income Population, 1979
(Those With Incomes Less Than $10,000)

Category	Number of Persons (Millions)	Percent of Total
Poor or Near Poor (All Ages)	32	64
Elderly (65+ years of age) Not Poor or Near Poor	12	22
Near Elderly (55-65 Years of Age) on Fixed Incomes, Not Poor or Near Poor	2	4
Infirm or Unemployed Young	2	4

Source: See Methodological Appendix, Section 1.

        The second largest segment of the lower income group
would be the elderly. Approximately 12 million elderly,
who would not be officially characterized as poor or
near poor, are included in this group. An additional 2
million persons between the ages of 55 and 64, who are
not officially defined as poor or near poor, are retired
or disabled and fall in the lower income category.
        The final segment of the lower income group is those
individuals who are not poor or near poor, elderly or
near elderly. Approximately 2 million persons who fall
in this category are physically incapable of working or
unable to find work. Thus, the poor or near poor, the
elderly and near elderly, in all probability those on
fixed incomes (retirees), plus the young who are invol-
untarily unemployed, would constitute more than 90
percent of the group of persons we call lower income.
Clearly, the category we refer to as lower income
Americans is a vulnerable group, living on low and/or
fixed incomes.
        Throughout the analysis, we avoid referring to the
"poor" for a number of reasons. First, the seriously
disproportionate burden caused by rising energy prices
is not a problem only of the poverty population; it is a

problem of the lower income population. Second, the
definition of "poverty" is very ambiguous and subject to
manipulation and interpretation. Using the term
confuses the issue unnecessarily and charges it ideo-
logically. Third, almost no energy-related data is
collected with the categories of "poor" or "near poor"
in mind. Efforts to approximate the official categories
after the fact are doubtful at best.

Having chosen this approach and this type of data,
in many cases the analysis will depend on interpolation
and adjustment of existing survey evidence and estimation of various trends. In order to keep the analysis
fluid, we have placed the basic methodological and
statistical discussions in the Methodological Appendix
at the end of the work.

3
The Macroeconomic Background

The detailed empirical analysis in this study examines the impact of rising energy prices on specific aspects of the living standard of low and lower middle income Americans -- household energy costs, the rental housing market, and the delivery of local public services. No assessment of the burden of rising energy costs would be complete, however, without an analysis of the overall effect of rising energy prices on the economy and the indirect effects that a seriously weakened economy has on lower income Americans.

In part, such an analysis provides an anchor for the other three aspects. It was, after all, the pervasive economic impact of rising energy prices that ensured the severity of the adverse impact on low and lower middle income households. The relative incomes of lower income households could not adjust rapidly and easily in a depressed economy. Similarly, economic growth slowed so dramatically that, in a society geared to growth, there was extreme pressure generated by various claims for social resources. Amid these conflicting claims, the interests of the low and lower middle income population lost out.

To put this another way, rising energy prices played a very large part in creating the stagflation of the mid- and late-1970s. During periods of recession and inflation, it is those on low and fixed incomes who suffer most, because they are least able to maintain their incomes. This is true even after one takes into account the effects of income transfer and assistance programs -- assistance programs directly related to energy, as well as general income maintenance programs. Further, low and lower middle income households are unable to fend off cuts in the social programs and public services on which they rely.

The full extent of the blow that rising energy prices dealt to the economy during the 1970s is only now becoming clear. One recent estimate placed the loss of

output in the Western industrial economies, due to
rising energy prices, at $1.2 trillion.1/ If the
methodology used to arrive at this estimate is applied
to the United States alone, the American loss would be
$565 billion.2/ Using a somewhat more sophisticated
econometric technique, the Department of Energy
estimates that the United States alone lost between $300
and $400 billion in the eight years between January 1973
and December 1980.3/

With such huge sums at stake, a very careful review
of the empirical record and a clear understanding of the
dynamic forces underlying these awesome economic losses
is called for. Certainly, a discussion of the economic
losses provides a necessary background for the detailed
analysis of the impacts on households conducted in this
work. Although the subsequent discussion is by no means
exhaustive, it captures the main points necessary for an
understanding of the impact of rising energy prices on
the economy. First, we present a general conceptual
discussion and then we review the empirical record.

ENERGY AND THE ECONOMY: A GENERAL CONCEPTUALIZATION

The negative or recessionary impact of rising energy
prices occurs in two interconnected ways. To use
current terminology, these can be called the demand-side
effect and the supply-side effect. It is important to
remember, however, that the economy is a whole. While
the effort to distinguish the two sides may be helpful
in organizing the analysis of the economy, it is
nonetheless largely a cosmetic device and should not,
therefore, be taken too seriously as a basis for
policymaking.

The Demand Side

Rising energy prices have a tendency to reduce
aggregate demand and, therefore, to reduce economic
activity. This is particularly true in the short run
because it is difficult to find substitutes for energy
in many economic activities (i.e., energy is price
inelastic).4/

When prices rise, a larger share of income must be
devoted to energy because consumption cannot be reduced
in the short run. The increase in income devoted to
energy may appear in two ways. First, as argued in the
previous chapter, the income spent directly for energy
(e.g., household heating fuels) will rise. Second, the
energy costs required for producing all goods and
services will rise. If the producers of these goods and
services are able to pass through the increase in energy
costs to consumers, there will be a general increase in
the price level of those goods. If they are not able to

pass through the increase, there will be a reduction in
profits in non-energy sectors.

Given the general tendency of prices in our economy
to increase when costs increase, the response to a rise
in energy prices tends to be an increase in the general
price level. That is, rising energy costs will be
passed through. If the money supply does not expand to
accommodate the price increase and wages do not rise as
fast as prices increase, the price increase will reduce
real income (i.e., the same number of dollars will purchase fewer goods and services).5/ Reduced real income
leads to lower consumption outlays and lower real GNP.

This effect can be compounded by an increase in
interest rates.6/ Rising prices lead to an increased
demand for credit to finance higher levels of spending
or investment. Again, if monetary policy is not
accommodative, rising interest rates (due to increased
demand and tight money supply) increase the costs of
financing consumption and investment, and the level of
real spending declines.

In reality, the response of the economy to price
increases tends to be a mixture of these possibilities.
Most of the price increases are passed through (with a
lag) and wages are increased in an attempt to keep up
(with a longer lag). The general consensus is, however,
that in the short run there are unavoidable effects:
(1) an increase in prices, (2) a reduction in real
income, (3) a reduction in real output, and, as a
consequence, (4) an increase in unemployment. There is
also an emerging consensus that accommodative, rather
than tight, monetary and fiscal policy can reduce these
impacts, but not eliminate them, without being extremely
inflationary.

While there is a general consensus that short run
negative impacts occur when energy prices are increased,
there is no consensus about just how long the short run
is or how large the impacts will be.7/ Some argue that
the adjustment period can be quite long -- well over a
decade -- while others envision shorter periods of
adjustment -- up to a decade.

The Supply Side

On the supply side, there are two ways that rising
energy prices can have a negative impact on productivity.

First, the recessionary impact originating on the
demand side is translated into declines in productivity
because of the natural response of the supply side to a
recession. Two effects can be noted in this regard.

First, as economic activity declines, the utilization of labor and capital declines more slowly than the
decline of output. As a result, productivity declines.

Labor is "hoarded" and capital is not modified at a
sufficiently rapid pace to maintain productivity.8/
Second, as economic activity declines, the general rate
of investment declines. This slows productivity growth
in general.

The second major impact of rising energy prices on
productivity occurs because rising energy prices require
structural adjustments in the economy. These adjustments impose a cost in terms of productivity. As energy
prices rise, capital and labor are substituted for
energy in the production process. The result is less
output per unit of capital and labor input. Moreover,
since capital and labor are not perfect substitutes for
energy, there will be added losses of productivity due
to the inefficiency of the substitution. In addition,
the need to invest in energy efficiency delays the
investment in capital equipment designed to enhance
labor productivity. Similarly, it preempts research and
other activities intended to enhance the productivity of
capital with respect to other raw material resource
inputs.9/

The first set of effects -- the recessionary effects
-- are principally short term. The second set of
effects -- the structural adjustment effects -- tend to
be longer term in nature. Once again, there tends to be
general agreement that these effects will occur, but
there is rather wide disagreement about how large they
are or how long they last.

A BRIEF LOOK AT THE 1970s

The empirical specifications of these theoretical
arguments take the form of econometric models. Before
we launch into a review of econometric results, let us
first review some empirical data and relationships
presented in simple form. Frequently, the complexity of
econometric analyses obscures basic relationships that
are simple and intuitively clear.

Energy Prices

Figure 3.1 describes the pattern of energy price
increases over the 1972-81 period. It is readily
apparent that oil prices increased dramatically --
almost twelve-fold -- over the decade. The increase
took place in two giant leaps which were then followed
by periods of price stability. These two leaps (1973-75
and 1979-81) have come to be known as the oil price
shocks.10/ Note, however, that the price of natural gas
also surged ahead in close conjunction with the oil
price increases.11/ This was partly a result of policy
(these two primary energy sources were decontrolled

FIGURE 3.1
Crude Oil and Natural Gas Price Increases

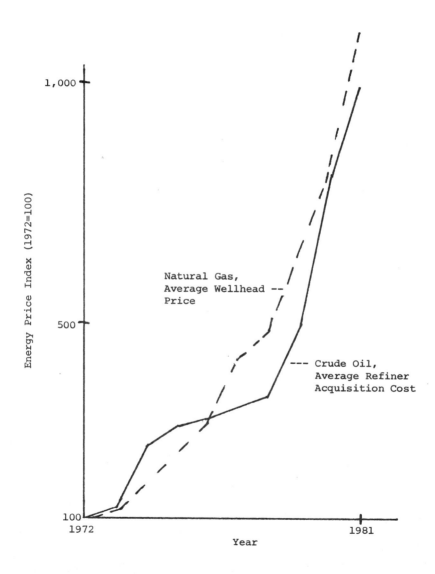

Source: U.S. Department of Energy, EIA, <u>Monthly Energy Review</u>
          (selected issues).

almost simultaneously in 1978-79) and partly due to the
fact that there is interfuel substitution and,
consequently, a tendency for energy prices to index
themselves to one another.

As made clear in the conceptualization, price
increases are meaningful only because they signal a
transfer of resources in the short term and the need to
adjust the mix of factors of production in the long
term. In most econometric analyses, it is the former
that is being modeled, rather than the latter. In the
social impact analysis, the aggregate resource transfer
is the central issue as well.

Table 3.1 shows an estimate of the total increase in
the energy bill over the years after the first energy
price shock. The increase is calculated by taking 1972
as the base year and estimating the increase (in current
dollars) over the price paid in 1972. All prices are
those paid by final consumers.

For purposes of later analysis, the estimate is made
by dividing energy use into two broad categories --
direct energy consumption and indirect energy
consumption. Direct energy consumption is defined as
energy consumed in the home and energy consumed for
private transportation (e.g., gasoline and diesel fuel
used by households). The term direct is applied since,
by and large, households pay directly for this energy.
Indirect energy consumption is defined as all energy
consumed by business, government, and industry. This is
energy consumed in the production of goods and services.
The energy is embodied in those goods and services and
households pay for the energy in the price they pay for
the goods and services.

The estimate of the total increase in the energy
bill is about $1.3 trillion. The methodology used to
derive the estimate is discussed in the Methodological
Appendix, Section 2. Of that $1.3 trillion, about $550
billion was paid for direct energy consumption and $750
billion was paid for indirect energy consumption.
Further, $400 billion was paid for oil and $900 billion
for other forms of energy. Finally, a rough estimate
shows that about $350 billion of the increase went to
foreign energy suppliers while $950 billion went to
domestic suppliers.

Whether domestic or foreign, this clearly was an
awesome quantity of resources -- approximately 5 percent
of GNP -- to transfer from consumers to producers in
such a short period of time. Theory and common sense
suggest that such upheavals in resource flows cause
major disruptions in the economy and impose severe costs
on it.

TABLE 3.1
Increase in the National Energy Bill, 1973 to 1981
(Trillion Current Dollars)

Direct Energy Consumption

Residential Energy
    Fuel Oil   .04
    Natural Gas   .06
    Electricity   .12
       Total   .25

Household Gasoline - Total   .30

    Subtotal Direct Consumption   .55

Indirect Energy Consumption

Commercial
    Petroleum   .03
    Natural Gas   .03
    Electricity   .10
       Total   .17

Industrial
    Petroleum   .13
    Natural Gas   .10
    Electricity   .10
       Total   .37

Transportation
    Motor Gasoline   .08
    Other Petroleum Products   .12
    Natural Gas   .01
       Total   .21

    Subtotal Indirect Consumption   .75

GRAND TOTAL   1.30

Note: Numbers may not add due to rounding and omission of minor components.

Source: See Methodological Appendix, Section 2 for a complete discussion of how these numbers were derived.

Energy Prices and the Economy

Figures 3.2 and 3.3, which show real energy price
increases in the 1962-81 period compared to changes in
economic activity (as measured by real GNP and changes
in the rate of unemployment), demonstrate the close
correlation between the large increases in energy prices
and the declines in economic activity. It is readily
apparent that energy prices had a massive impact on
economic activity. Note the dramatic coincidence of the
peaks of energy price increases and the valleys of
economic activity. The recessionary impact of rising
energy prices can hardly be doubted. Changes in the
unemployment rate appear to lag behind energy price
increases slightly as the recessionary impact works its
way through to layoffs, but there is no doubt about
their impact on unemployment as well.12/
Figure 3.4 shows the relationship between energy
prices and another significant economic indicator, the
rate of inflation. The coincidence of peaks and valleys
is, again, evident. Moreover, note that an index of all
commodities, less energy, also exhibits a close relationship to energy prices. This is due to the general
effect that rising energy prices have on the cost of
production of all goods and services.13/

ECONOMETRIC ESTIMATES OF THE IMPACT

Having seen the very clear relationship between
energy prices and major economic indicators, we turn to
econometric analysis to assess the strength of those
relationships. We need to know not only whether rising
energy prices depress economic activity, but also by how
much. The estimate of the magnitude should be made by
econometric methods.
There are a host of econometric models for analyzing
the general behavior of the economy which have been used
to estimate the impact of rising energy prices on
economic activity. These vary in size from small 10
equation models to the DRI mammoth which utilizes almost
1000 equations. The models differ in approach as well,
with some emphasizing Keynesian, demand-side processes
and others stressing supply-side (capital accumulation)
processes.14/ Moreover, the models differ in the way
they handle variables other than energy prices and most
do not consider policy changes that might be closely
linked to energy price behaviors.15/ The latter
shortcoming means that they oversimplify reality.
However, careful analysis of the results reveals
that the models reach very similar conclusions about the
impact of rising prices on the economy.16/ Table 3.2
presents estimates of the impact of the energy price
shocks on economic activity over the decade of the

FIGURE 3.2
Energy Price Changes and Changes in the Gross National Product

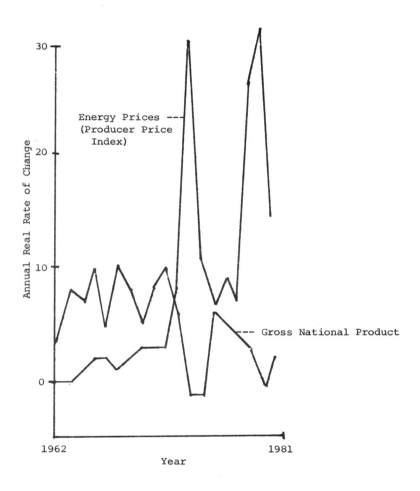

Source: U.S. Department of Labor, Bureau of Labor Statistics;
          U.S. Department of Commerce, Bureau of Economic Analysis.

42

FIGURE 3.3
Energy Price Changes and Changes in Unemployment

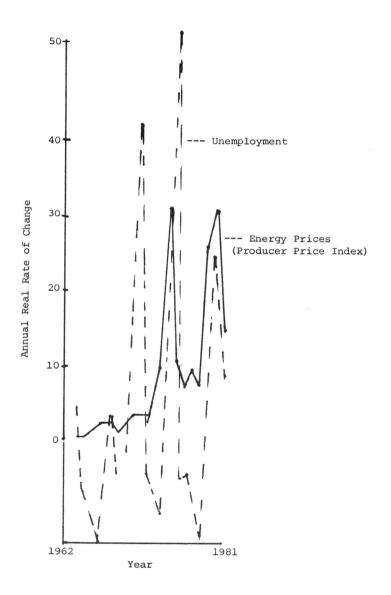

Source: U.S. Department of Labor, Bureau of Labor Statistics.

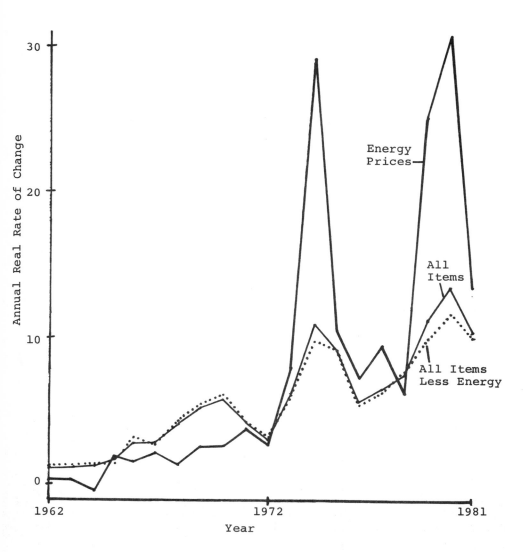

FIGURE 3.4
Changes in the Consumer Price Index and the Energy and
Non-Energy Components

Source: U.S. Department of Labor, Bureau of Labor Statistics.

TABLE 3.2
Analysis of the Economic Impacts of the Oil Price Shocks of the 1970s

Model	Length of Simulation	Average Annual Percent Changes			
		GNP Deflator	CPI	GNP	Unemployment
1972-75 Oil Price Shock					
Perry (FRB)	4.25	1.08		2.75	1.49
Perry (Michigan)	4.25	1.33		3.73	1.34
Dohner	3.78				1.51
Eckstein (DRI)	3.00	1.37	1.60	3.07	.83
1978-81 Oil Price Shock					
Mork/Hall	3.00	1.06		3.10	.83
Eckstein (DRI)	7.00	1.00	1.11	2.67	.77
Thurman/Berner (MPS)	4.50	1.16	2.43	2.93	.82
1972-1978 DOE (DRI and Wharton)	8.00	1.5-2.0	1.9-2.6	3.0-3.6	.9-2.1

	Average Annual Percent Changes per One Percent of GNP Resource Transfer			
	GNP Deflator	CPI	GNP	Unemployment
1972-75 Oil Price Shock				
Perry (FRB)	.43[a]		1.08	.60
Perry (Michigan)	.53[a]		1.08	.60
Eckstein (DRI)	.55[a]	.64	1.22	.33

1978-81 Oil Price Shock

Mork/Hall	.50[b]		1.48	.40
Eckstein (DRI)	.48[b]	.53	1.27	.37
Thurman/Berner (MPS)	.35[c]	.74	.89	.25
1972-1978 DOE (DRI and Wharton)	.28-.37	.36-.49	.57-.68	.17-.39
AVERAGE	.47	.64	1.21	.43
STANDARD DEVIATION	.07	.09	.21	.14

a Based on a resource transfer equal to 2.5 percent of GNP.
b Based on a resource transfer equal to 2.1 percent of GNP.
c Based on a resource transfer of 3.3 percent.

Sources: George Perry, "The United States," in Edward R. Friede and Charles C. Schultze (eds.), Higher Oil Prices and the World Economy: The Adjustment Problem (Washington, D.C.: The Brookings Institution, 1975), p. 96. The first quarter 1975 numbers have been utilized.

Robert S. Dohner, "Energy Prices, Economic Activity, and Inflation: A Survey of Issues and Results," in Knut Anton Mork (ed.), Energy Prices, Inflation, and Economic Activity (Cambridge, Mass.: Ballinger, 1981), pp. 34-36. Average of first three years.

Otto Eckstein, "Shock Inflation, Core Inflation, and Energy Disturbances in the DRI Model," in Mork, Energy Prices..., p. 76.

Knut Anton Mork and Robert E. Hall, "Macroeconomic Analysis of Energy Price Shocks and Offsetting Policies: An Integrated Approach," in Mork, Energy Prices..., p. 51.

Stephan Thurman and Richard Berner, "Analysis of Oil Price Shocks in the MPS Model," in Mork, Energy Prices.... Based on the sum of the June, 1979 scenario and the additional OPEC increase scenario. (Tables 5.3 and 5.5).

U.S. Department of Energy, The Interrelationships of Energy and the Economy (Washington, D.C.: July 1981), Chapter 2.

1970s, as measured by average annual changes in
inflation, GNP, and unemployment. Eight different
analyses have been included covering slightly different
time frames. Six different econometric models are
included in the group.17/
     The models all estimate impacts in the direction
that theory would predict -- increases in inflation and
unemployment, decreases in GNP. Although they appear at
first glance to be estimating quite different magnitudes
of impacts, if their results are standardized to reflect
the fact that each simulation is based on different sets
of price increases, they prove to be in rather close
agreement. The lower half of Table 3.2 expresses the
predicted economic impact for energy price increases
equal to one percent of GNP. The estimates are very
similar in each of the models.
     For each price increase equal to one percent of GNP,
the mean increase in inflation as measured by the GNP
deflator is estimated at .47 percentage points with a
standard deviation of .07 percentage points. The mean
estimated increase in the CPI is .64 percentage points,
with a standard deviation of .09 percentage points. The
mean estimated decrease in GNP is 1.2 percentage points,
with a standard deviation of .21 percentage points. The
mean estimated increase in unemployment is .43
percentage points with a standard deviation of .14
percentage points. The standard deviations are small
with respect to the means, suggesting a very small range
of variation in the results.
     Other econometric analyses of the oil price shocks
(especially the early shock) are available. They
produce similar, although not identical, results. The
Hudson/Jorgenson Dynamic General Equilibrium Model,
which is quite different in structure from these
standard econometric models, estimated similar GNP
impacts, but smaller unemployment impacts.18/ Pierce
and Enzler's analysis of the 1973-75 shock with the MPS
model estimated similar inflationary impacts, but
smaller GNP impacts -- but it used a different base
year.19/ On the other hand, the Federal Energy
Administration's analyses, using the DRI and the
Department of Commerce models, estimated much larger
impacts.20/ However, the analysis covered a shorter
time period and, therefore, did not reflect any
reequilibration of economic activity that tends to begin
in the third year after the shock.
     Specific year-to-year analyses of the impact of
energy price shocks also conform to the theory as
described above. First, impacts persist over the long
term. The headlines devoted to rising energy prices may
pass quickly once the shock is over, but the negative
economic impacts of those prices will keep working their
way through the economy. Most of the models project a

cumulative negative impact that lasts 5 to 10 years.
There then ensues a period in which part of the economic
losses may be recovered. In the long run, there remains
an appreciable loss in total GNP.

The behavior of specific elements of the economy
also conforms to the predictions of macroeconomic theory
(as described above). For example, in 1979 and 1980,
investment suffered a major setback as a result of the
oil price shock -- a reduction of as much as 12
percent.21/ Productivity was reduced, as well, by as
much as 3 percent.22/ Some estimates show that as much
as one-third to one-half of the slowdown in productivity
growth may have been due to energy price increases.23/
Expenditures on consumer durables were also particularly
hard hit.24/ Investment in residential housing structures may have been reduced by as much as 15-20 percent,
while sales of American automobiles may have been reduced by as much as 40 percent because of the explosion
in energy prices.25/

ASSESSING THE IMPACT

Judging the actual significance of the negative
economic impacts can be a matter of perspective. It has
become common among those inclined to downplay the
importance of energy to focus on the entire period after
the OPEC oil embargo (1973) in order to place the
1979-80 oil price shock in the context of a generally
bad economic period. Table 3.3 shows that the economy
took a decided turn for the worse between 1973 and 1980,
compared to the previous eight years. The rate of
growth of real GNP, real disposable income, investment
and productivity slowed dramatically, while inflation
and unemployment increased. Part of the downturn -- at
least one-third and probably one-half -- can definitely
be attributed to the energy price shock.

Some analysts focus on that part of the downturn
which energy prices did not cause and look for a bigger
"picture," thereby downplaying the importance of energy
price increases.26/ We are inclined to take the
opposite view.

We are struck by the fact that so much of the downturn can be attributed to this one factor. Energy is
obviously a very major influence on economic activity.
One will look in vain to find any other single factor
that is as important. Moreover, there are even ways in
which these analyses underestimate the impact that
rising energy prices can have.

First, when the econometric analyses are conducted,
only energy prices are changed in order to simulate what
would have happened in the economy without a change in
prices. This overlooks the fact that, as energy prices
rise, many policy decisions are made in response to

TABLE 3.3
The Importance of Rising Energy Prices in Determining Economic Performance

	1965-72 (1)	Actual 1973-80 (2)	Change: 1965-72 Compared to 1973-80 (3)	Hypothetical 1973-80, Assuming no Energy Price Increase (4)	Change Attributable to Energy Prices (5=2-4)	Percent of Change Attributable to Energy Prices (6=5/3)
Real Growth of GNP (Percent Per Year)	3.5	2.4	-1.1	2.8	-.4	36
Real Disposable Income (Percent Per Year)	4.0	2.4	-1.6	3.3	-.9	56
Growth of Real Fixed Investment	4.0	.4	-3.6	2.0	-1.6	44
Rate of Change in CPI (Percentage Points)	+4.1	+9.2	+5.1	+6.9	+2.3	45
Rate of Growth of Productivity (Percent Change Per Year of Output Per Person Hour)	2.0	.2	-1.8	1.6	-1.4	78
Unemployment Rate (Average Annual)	4.5	6.6	+2.1	5.4	+1.2	57

Source: U.S. Department of Energy, The Interrelationships of Energy and the Economy (Washington, D.C.: July 1981), Chapter 2.

those rising prices. Is it really possible to separate
energy price increases from the policy decisions which
they directly prompted?

The most important such policies are fiscal and
monetary. As rising energy prices increase the rate of
inflation, policymakers respond by tightening the money
supply and reducing fiscal deficits in an effort to slow
down inflation.27/ Of course, these policies have
recessionary impacts of their own, which reinforce the
impact of rising energy prices. Most analyses show that
the restrictive monetary and fiscal responses to rising
energy prices doubled the recessionary impact.28/ In
this sense, energy prices caused about one-third of the
economic problem directly and another one-third of the
problem indirectly through the impact of energy price
increases on monetary and fiscal policy. Thus, if one
assumes a different path of energy prices, one should
probably assume different fiscal and monetary policies
as well.29/

A second way in which the econometric analyses
underestimate the impact of rising energy prices is not
easily quantifiable, but it is nonetheless real. Rising
energy prices had a major impact on the mood of the
public and on policymakers. The econometric analyses
show that in the absence of rising energy prices, there
would have been almost no recession in 1974-75 and no
recession in 1980.30/ There would have been no "double
digit inflation" at any time in the decade.31/ In this
regard, energy pushed the economy past several major
psychological thresholds (i.e., into a recession and
over the double digit mark in inflation).

In 1980 alone, had energy prices not increased so
rapidly, as many as three million fewer people would
have been unemployed.32/ As many as two million more
American automobiles would have been sold and an
additional 250,000 housing starts would have been
undertaken.33/ Here, too, critical psychological
thresholds would have been avoided, especially rates of
unemployment that rivaled those of the Great Depression
in two of America's largest industries.

In short, the entire economic environment would have
been different.34/ The public mood would have been much
less pessimistic, and certainly could have led to
different consumption and savings patterns. Policymakers would not have been thrashing about in search of
economic quick fixes. The economy would have remained
much closer to its historical path of relatively rapid
and relatively stable expansion.

In this sense, energy may have been more than two-
thirds of the problem -- one-third due to the direct
impact of rising prices, one-third due to the indirect
impact through monetary and fiscal policy, and an
additional, unmeasurable, amount due to the qualitative

impact of having the economy appear to be in a state of utter chaos and on the brink of collapse. It is important to recognize that in the 1970s and especially the period after 1979, the economy was not collapsing -- rather, to a very considerable degree, it was being crushed by energy prices. Had this been recognized, very different economic and energy policy decisions might have been made.

Part 2

Household Impacts

4
Energy Consumption
in the Home

The central concern of policymakers and households has been the impact of rising energy prices on energy expenditures paid directly by households. Although the previous chapter suggests that the general impact of rising energy prices deserves equal attention, there is no denying the fact that the most visible and painful burden has taken the form of rising household energy bills.

If we are to assess properly the impact of rising energy prices on lower income households, we must examine a number of questions: Do low and lower middle income households spend a disproportionate share of their income on home energy? Does that share grow disproportionately as energy prices rise? If so, is this burden caused by the fact that home energy is a vital necessity? Have efforts to alleviate the burden been successful?

Only if low and lower middle income households actually do devote a disproportionate share of their income to energy expenditures and only if the cause of that burden is the morally compelling reason that energy is a vital necessity for basic health, safety, and well-being is the argument for a special social commitment itself compelling. Only if current efforts and existing mechanisms for alleviating the burden are inadequate is the threat that rising energy prices pose to lower income households a primary social issue.

Part 2 of our study establishes the basic facts that (1) low and lower middle income households do spend a disproportionate share of their income on home energy, (2) the burden grows disproportionately as energy prices rise, and (3) existing social responses are inadequate.

THE CONSUMPTION AND EXPENDITURE
PATTERN OF A VITAL NECESSITY

The morally compelling concern about energy

consumption stems from the fact that it is a vital
necessity. Therefore, at the outset, we should have a
very clear conception of what the pattern of energy
consumption and expenditures across income groups will
look like and why.

Because energy is a vital necessity it is difficult
to reduce its consumption beyond a certain point. As
income declines, so does consumption. There comes a
point, however, where energy consumption ceases to
decline since further reductions pose a threat to health
and safety. Stated this way, one would say that there
is a floor below which energy consumption cannot fall.

In reality, however, we are not likely to observe a
specific level of energy consumption below which no
household falls. Rather, we are likely to observe that,
as income falls, so does consumption, but consumption
falls more slowly because it becomes harder and harder
to find the next unit of energy to save. Stated in this
way, one would say that consumption approaches a floor
or minimum level.

On the other hand, as income rises, we would expect
to find that the consumption of energy would rise more
slowly than income. With discretionary income (to
spare), households might consume more energy than the
minimum. They would choose to use some of their discretionary income to consume more energy. We can assume
that households buy more energy in accordance with the
additional pleasure or satisfaction (utility) that they
extract from each additional unit of energy consumed.
We would expect to find that, as energy consumption
increases, the utility of consuming additional units
(its marginal utility) declines. That is, as more
energy is consumed, the value of additional units
declines and fewer are desired. Therefore, consumption
approaches some maximum level as income increases.

Figure 4.1 depicts this description of the relationship between income and energy consumption. At low
levels of income, energy consumption declines slowly,
approaching some minimum level of consumption. At high
levels of income, it rises slowly, approaching some
maximum level.

Having established the basic pattern of energy
consumption, we next turn to a discussion of the pattern
of expenditures. If we measure energy expenditures as a
percentage of income, we will find that, because consumption becomes ever more difficult to reduce as income
falls, energy expenditures constitute an ever larger
share of income. That is, more and more of the remain-
ing income is devoted to energy.

Similarly, as income increases, we would expect to
observe that the share of income devoted to energy
expenditures declines. Less and less of each additional
dollar of income is devoted to energy as income rises.

FIGURE 4.1
Energy Consumption at Increasing Levels of Income

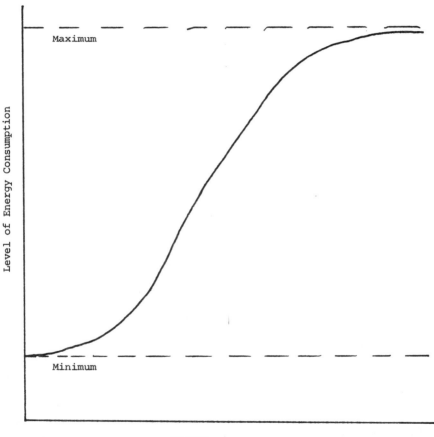

Figure 4.2 depicts this relationship. At low levels of income, energy accounts for larger proportions of income. At increasing levels of income, energy expenditures as a percentage of income decline. (Figure 4.2 depicts the actual 1979 estimate derived in this chapter.)

FIGURE 4.2
Home Energy Expenditures as a Percent of Income:
Basic Conceptualization

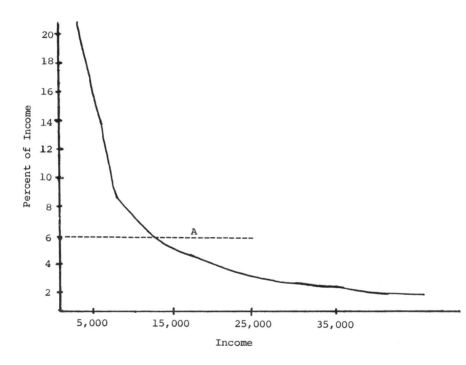

It is really the left side of the curve in which we are interested. If, for example, we find the average level of expenditure on energy, designated in Figure 4.2 as point A, then all points on the curve to the left of point A represent households which spend more than the average percentage of income on energy. That is, they spend a disproportionate share of their income on energy. The lower income population, as defined in this study, is actually far to the left of the mean. Their

disproportionate burden is quite large. These are
certainly the households with which Congress was
concerned when it passed the Crude Oil Windfall Profit
Tax Act, in the sense that it identified low and lower
middle income households as bearing a disproportionate
burden.

This basic conception can also be used to make
comparisons between the expenditure patterns for
different forms of energy or between expenditures for
the same form of energy at different points in time.
Following the arguments presented above, we would expect
that those forms of energy that are more vital (i.e.,
less discretionary) would have higher percentages of
income devoted to them at any given level of income.
The more vital a fuel is, the less a household can
reduce its consumption of that fuel at lower levels of
income. Similarly, if the price of a vital commodity
increased over time relative to other goods, we would
expect to observe increasing shares of income devoted to
it, since consumption cannot be easily reduced.

Figure 4.3 presents this concept graphically. The
curve on the left (P) is the basic curve showing the
percentage of income spent on energy at various income
levels. The curve on the right (P') shows the percentage of income that the same households would devote to a
more vital commodity or to the same commodity as in
curve P should the price of that commodity increase.
The expenditure levels for two hypothetical households
are depicted on the curves. The first household has an
annual income of $5,000. This household devotes
approximately 5 percent of its income to the commodity
depicted by curve P. The percentage of income it
devotes to the commodity depicted in curve P' is about
13 percent. The percentages of income the second
household (annual income of about $19,000) devotes to
the two commodities are 2 and about 4 percent,
respectively.

We see that while both households devote a greater
percentage of their income to the second commodity, the
percentage increase for the lower income household is
much greater than that of the higher income household.
There are two reasons for this. If, for example, the
curve P' depicts a price increase for the commodity in
P, the first reason is that the lower income household
has already reduced its consumption of the commodity to
such a low level that further reductions are almost
impossible. The household must pay the increased price.
Second, because this household's income is so much
lower, any dollar increase in price will take three
times the percentage of income that it would take for
the higher income household.1/

This then is our basic twofold premise: (1) that
even though lower income households consume less energy

58

FIGURE 4.3
Home Energy Expenditures as a Percent of Income: Patterns of
Expenditures for Different Commodities or Changes in Price Over
Time

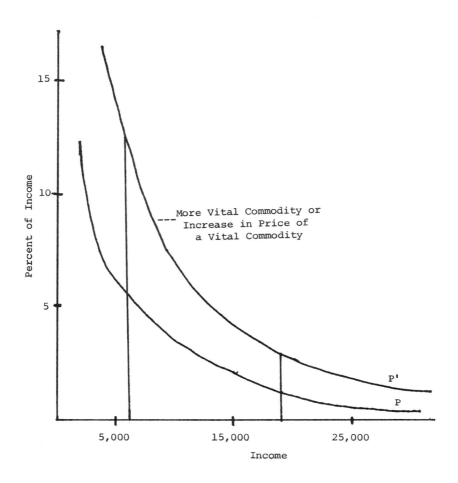

than higher income households, energy prices still take a much higher percentage of their income, and (2) that rising energy prices increase the burden on lower income households more than on higher income households.

ENERGY CONSUMPTION

Levels of Consumption

The evidence available from the Residential Energy Consumption Survey shows quite clearly that this conception fits the data. In each of the three surveys (1978, 1979, and 1980) low and lower middle income households consumed less energy than non-lower income households (see Figure 4.4). This was also true in each geographic region and climate zone (as defined earlier). In 1978, low income households consumed about 25 percent less energy than non-lower income households while lower middle income households consumed about 15 percent less. Between 1978 and 1980, low income households reduced their energy consumption by about 10 percent and lower middle income households reduced theirs by about 19 percent. In contrast, non-lower income households reduced their consumption by about 24 percent. Thus, in 1980, low income households were consuming about 18 percent less energy than non-lower income households and lower middle income households were consuming about 13 percent less.2/ This pattern is consistent with the energy-as-vital-necessity argument; low income households have more difficulty conserving energy because they have fewer "luxury" or discretionary uses on which to cut back. In addition, they lack the resources that are needed to invest in conservation.

A second aspect of the data that reaffirms this conception of energy consumption is the general tendency for low and lower middle income households to consume more energy relative to non-lower income households in the colder climate zones. One can argue that the rigors of the colder climates require the consumption of more home energy for survival. Therefore, lower income households consume more energy relative to non-lower income households in those regions. More discretion in the consumption of energy can be exercised in the warmer climate zones.

These conclusions that the pattern of energy consumption fit the energy-as-vital-necessity argument can be substantiated by other data in the surveys.

The Constituent Components of Consumption

Figure 4.5 demonstrates the relative inability of lower income households to cut back on consumption by

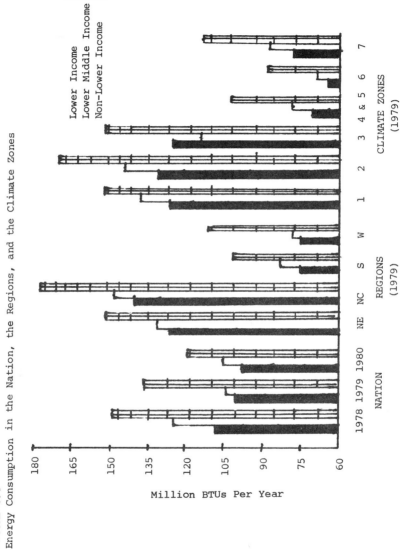

FIGURE 4.4
Energy Consumption in the Nation, the Regions, and the Climate Zones

Sources: U.S. Department of Energy, Residential Energy Consumption Survey: Consumption and Expenditures, April 1978 through March 1979 (Washington, D.C.: July 1980), Table 1.

U.S. Department of Energy, Residential Energy Consumption Survey: 1979–1980 Consumption and Expenditures, Part I: National Data (Washington, D.C.: April 1981), Table 1.

U.S. Department of Energy, Residential Energy Consumption Survey: 1978–1980 Consumption and Expenditures, Part II: Regional Data (Washington, D.C.: May 1981), Tables 1, 9.

U.S. Department of Energy, Residential Energy Consumption Survey: 1979–1980, Data tape.

U.S. Department of Energy, Residential Energy Consumption Survey: Consumption and Expenditures, April 1980 through March 1981 (Washington, D.C.: September 1982), Table 1.

62

FIGURE 4.5
Appliance Ownership

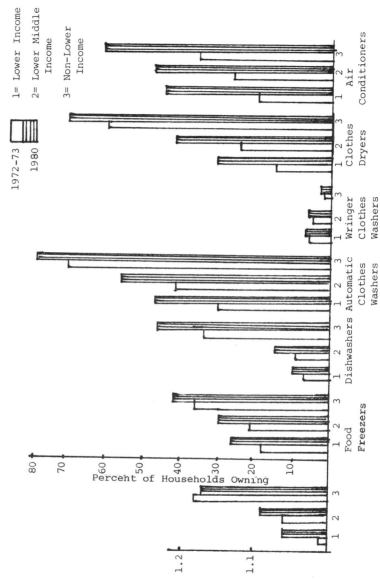

Sources: U.S. Bureau of Labor Statistics, *Consumer Expenditure Survey: Interview Survey, 1972-73 Inventories of Vehicles and Selected Household Equipment, 1973* (Washington, D.C.: 1978), Table 5.

U.S. Department of Energy, *Residential Energy Consumption Survey: Housing Characteristics, 1980* (Washington, D.C.: June 1982), Table 39.

substantiating the fact that they use energy for fewer discretionary purposes. The data show that the ownership of the most necessary appliances is roughly equal across all income groups but lower income groups own fewer luxury appliances. Thus, lower income households owned about the same number of refrigerators per household in 1980 as non-lower income households. However, the rate of ownership of other appliances was much higher among non-lower income households -- 4.7 times as high for dishwashers; 2.3 times as high for clothes dryers; 1.6 times as high for freezers and clothes washers; and 1.4 times as high for air conditioners.

These difference in the ownership of major appliances remained after a decade in which low and lower middle income households had done some "catching-up" in the ownership of appliances. As Figure 4.5 shows, low and lower middle income household ownership of all appliances (except dishwashers) had increased relative to non-lower income households.

A second factor that leads to lower energy consumption by the low and lower middle income population is consumption of less energy for heating purposes.

Survey evidence suggests that lower income households set their thermostats lower in the winter than non-lower income households.3/

Unfortunately, the most direct evidence of energy consumption for heating purposes -- actual energy usage for heating purposes only -- is not plentiful. Most heating fuels are also used for other purposes. Therefore, when data is collected, it is virtually impossible to separate out which part of the energy was used for heating and which for other purposes. Only actual monitoring on a case-by-case basis would provide the answers, but such approaches are too costly for national surveys and, to our knowledge, have not been done.

An alternative approach is to try to identify specific subsets of respondents from the existing surveys who use energy for various combinations of heating and non-heating purposes -- e.g., heating plus cooking, heating plus hot water, cooking plus hot water but no heating. One can then estimate the average usage for each purpose by subtracting the average consumption of one group from another, e.g., heating plus hot water minus hot water only equals heating. There are severe limitations in this approach as well. Any estimates of consumption based on this approach must be done with great care and be considered only rough order-of-magnitude estimates.

Table 4.1 shows estimates of energy consumption for heating purposes in various income categories for the major heating fuels used in each region. Focusing on major heating fuels within regions reduces some of the

65

TABLE 4.1
Energy Consumption for Heating Purposes Only (Million BTUs)

Income Category	NORTHEAST		NORTH CENTRAL	SOUTH		WEST
	Fuel Oil	Gas	Gas	Electricity	Gas	Gas
Low Income (Less than $5,000)	115	89	13	10	32	29
Lower Middle Income ($5,000 to $9,999)	128	100	94	16	33	33
Non-Lower Income ($10,000 or more)	147	116	115	23	55	42
Ratios						
Low/Non-Lower	.78	.77	.11	.43	.58	.69
LowerMiddle/Non-Lower	.87	.86	.82	.70	.60	.79

Source: U.S. Department of Energy, Residential Energy Consumption Survey: 1978-1980 Consumption and Expenditures, Part II: Regional Data (Washington, D.C.: May 1981), Tables 2, 3, 6.

problems with this approach, but not all.

In general, the results are consistent with the argument made throughout this chapter, that lower income households consume less energy. The data does show some erratic behavior. However, it is clear that heating energy consumption rises as income rises. Further, the data also supports our hypothesis that the rigors of climate dictate energy consumption more closely in colder climate zones. Note that the heating energy consumption of low and lower middle income households in the Northeast and North Central regions is larger relative to non-lower income consumption than it is in the South or the West.

More sophisticated statistical approaches to estimating heating energy consumption have been used.4/ These involve regression techniques which identify various uses and attribute specific quantities of energy to each use (via the inclusion of dummy variables in the regression equation). These analyses show that even after all of the major determinants of energy consumption are taken into account -- e.g., climate, family size, ownership of major appliances -- income still is a significant and strong determinant of energy consumption.

Table 4.2, which shows a cross-tabulation of energy consumption by climate, size of residence, and income, gives an indication of the strength of the relationship between income and consumption. Note that controlling for climate zone and size of residence (i.e., focusing on the energy consumption within each combination of climate zone and housing size), we still observe a strong tendency for lower income households to consume less energy.

Thus, the available evidence on heating energy use is quite consistent with the general conception of energy as a vital necessity.

The final important element in the burden that rising energy prices place on lower income households is their inability to cut back consumption by investing in conservation. They do not have the resources to invest in more energy-efficient equipment -- improvements in the thermal efficiency of their homes and appliances.5/

The available survey evidence to document these facts leaves much to be desired, but whatever evidence is available supports this interpretation of the plight of the lower income household. A comparison of the insulation and conservation equipment of the residences of lower income households with that of wealthier households draws out the striking disadvantage that the lower income households have in fighting high energy prices.

Lower income households inhabited less efficient residences in 1978 than non-lower income households, as

TABLE 4.2
Annual Energy Consumption in Relation to Climate and Household Size

Household Income	All Households	Less than 4,000 Heating Degree Days Size of Residence (square feet)			4,000 to 5,499 Heating Degree Days Size of Residence (square feet)			5,500 or more Heating Degree Days Size of Residence (square feet)		
		Less than 1,000	1,000 to 1,999	2,000 or more	Less than 1,000	1,000 to 1,999	2,000 or more	Less than 1,000	1,000 to 1,999	2,000 or more
Less than $5,000	98	64	90	114	68	103	162	106	145	205
$5,000 to $9,999	104	66	87	114	75	100	139	115	138	157
$10,000 to $14,999	102	61	91	102	82	113	123	106	130	135
$15,000 to $19,999	112	75	94	103	85	109	137	103	126	166
$20,000 to $24,999	126	71	91	131	95	125	154	110	149	168
$25,000 to $34,999	123	62	101	119	74	114	129	109	140	161
$35,000 or more	143	68	97	144	77	118	163	103	160	188

Source: U.S. Department of Energy, Residential Energy Consumption Survey, Consumption and Expenditures, April 1980 through March 1981 (Washington, D.C.: September 1982), Table 14.

measured by the level of insulation and glazing. They implemented fewer conservation measures between 1978 and 1980. Moreover, the more expensive the conservation measure, the larger the gap between lower and non-lower income households in implementing the measure.

The fact that the lower income population resides in less energy-efficient housing means that its effective heating is even lower than it appears compared to the national average. That is, for every BTU consumed by the lower income population, less heat is enjoyed, because it escapes more quickly. The burden of less energy-efficient housing is substantial. A rough estimate based on 1978 data shows that if the energy efficiency of the homes in the lowest income category could be raised to the level of the highest income category, the occupants would enjoy at least 10 <u>percent</u> more effective heat for the same dollar expenditure on energy.6/ Since 1978, matters have not improved.7/ Thus, the dramatic differences in consumption of energy between lower income Americans and the remainder of the population demonstrated throughout this chapter would be even greater if we could measure energy as the effective heat delivered to the living space, rather than simply the number of BTUs purchased.

Inhabiting less efficient housing and constrained in their ability to improve its efficiency, lower income households are forced to take extreme measures to cut their energy consumption, which leads to considerable hardship. Aside from setting thermostats at lower levels, survey evidence shows that they are forced to close off a greater amount of their living space during the winter. Not only do they have less living space to begin with, but they lose the use of more of it because it is unheated or because they cannot afford to heat it sufficiently.

In the Department of Energy survey, about 30 percent of the respondents in each income category said that they had closed off rooms in the winter of 1978-79. Because lower income households have much smaller residences, they lost the use of a much larger percentage of their space. The DOE data, unfortunately, does not permit a precise estimation of lost space as a percent of total space. However, a rough estimate would be that low and lower middle income households lost about 50 percent more space than upper income households.

For example, if the respondents who said they closed off rooms actually closed off only one room, the lower income households would have lost about 7 percent of their space. Non-lower income households closed off about 5 percent of their space.

The HUD 1978 data shows even more dramatic differences between low and non-lower income households (see Table 4.3). (Note that the income categories available

TABLE 4.3
Percentage of Households Reporting an Uncomfortably Cold Residence for 24 Hours or More

Income Group	Nation	South	Northeast	North Central	West
Low Income (Less than $3,000)	4.0	7.8	.5	.9	2.4
Lower Middle Income ($3,000 to $9,999)	2.0	4.7	.4	.4	1.0
Non-Lower Income ($10,000 or more)	.5	1.3	.2	.1	.4
Percentage of Low Income Households lacking Specified Heating Equipment	19.3	38.0	1.1	2.1	9.7

Source: U.S. Department of Housing and Urban Development, Annual Housing Survey: 1979, Part F: Energy-Related Housing Characteristics, (Washington, D.C.: March 1982), Tables A-2, B-2, C-2, D-2, E-2.

in the HUD data are different from those in the DOE
data.) Almost 11 percent of low and 7 percent of lower
middle income households closed off rooms, compared to
only 3 percent of non-lower income households. This
trend holds nationwide and also for the regions,
although there is wide variance in the actual percentages across the regions. For example, 15 percent of low
income households in the South closed off one or more
rooms, while only 5 percent in the West did.

The suggestion made above that the rigors of climate
dictate closely the behavior of lower income households
with respect to home energy use is borne out by these
regional numbers. In the colder climates -- the
Northeast, North Central, and much of the West region --
it would simply be intolerable to let the residence get
too cold. In the South, where winters are, on average,
milder, lower income households will forego heat and
suffer the greater discomfort due to the cold. The
implication of this pattern is that those in colder
climates will be forced to spend a much larger portion
of their income on home energy in order to avert the
cold. Their burden will be experienced as lost income.
In contrast, those in the warmer climates bear the
burden by enduring uncomfortably cold residences.

In this regard, it is interesting to look at one of
the questions asked in the 1979 HUD survey. The
question of whether the entire residence was uncomfortably cold for a 24 hour period was asked of households
lacking specified heating equipment (e.g., warm air or
steam furnaces, built-in electric units, room heaters
with flue). The purpose of the question was to find out
whether households suffered as a result of not having
this equipment. What is most revealing in Table 4.3 is
the significantly greater percentage of lower income
households in the South who suffered from uncomfortably
cold conditions for 24 hours or more. This is due, in
large measure, to the greater number of households in
the South whose residences lack the specified heating
equipment. Yet, that so many households in the South
live in such housing is an indication of the choice that
they must make between affordable housing and sufficient
heat. This explicit choice is equivalent to the choice
being made in colder climates by lower income
households. That is, because of the severity of the
climate, in general, one must have better heating
equipment, but, because of the cost of energy, families
are forced to choose between heat and other necessities.

A different question in the HUD data can lead to an
estimate of the unheated space in the residences of
households in the various income groups. Unheated space
-- defined as space lacking radiators, heat registers,
ducts, or portable heaters -- is not the same as rooms
closed off to reduce heating costs, but there is certain

to be a strong correlation between the two.

Table 4.4 shows the percentage of respondents with unheated rooms as well as the number of rooms lacking heat. We have calculated the average number of unheated rooms per household in each income group and the average percentage of unheated space per household in each income group (using the median number of rooms as the estimate of rooms per household). It is clear that households at the lower range of the income scale, whether they are owners or renters, have considerably more unheated space. Those in the lowest income group (annual incomes below $3,000) who own their own homes lost between three and five times as much space as those with incomes above $35,000 who own their own homes. Those with incomes below $3,000 who rent had between two and five times as much unheated space as those with incomes above $35,000 who rent.

TABLE 4.4
Percentage of Respondents Reporting Unheated Rooms

Income Category	Number of Unheated Rooms			Average Number of Unheated Rooms[a]	Median Number of Rooms	Average Percent of Space Unheated
	1	2	3			
Low	6.2	7.1	9.1	.477	4.8	9.9
Lower Middle	6.4	7.2	9.1	.481	4.5	10.7
Non-Lower	5.3	4.2	6.2	.323	5.6	5.8

[a] Calculated as meaning that respondents who reported three or more rooms closed, closed only three rooms.

Sources: U.S. Department of Housing and Urban Development, Annual Housing Survey: 1979, Part F: Energy-Related Housing Characteristics (Washington, D.C.: March 1982), Table A-2, Part C: Financial Characteristics of the Housing Inventory (Washington, D.C.: March 1981), Table A-1.

72

When rising energy prices lead to the loss of usable living space, such prices are undermining the quality of one of the most basic of human necessities -- shelter. For the lower income population, which inhabits much smaller residences than the national average, this is a particularly cruel form of deprivation.

Weather, Population Change, and the Misinterpretation of Conservation Data

In light of these observations on the relative efficiency of lower and non-lower income residences and the patterns of the loss of usable space, any interpretation of the data which suggests that conservation efforts are flowing along smoothly is especially misleading with regard to the lower income population. Nothing could be farther from the truth. What is equally troubling is that even the apparent energy conservation gains among non-lower income households do not stand up under careful scrutiny.

Table 4.5 shows the two critical factors -- weather and household size -- that have actually accounted for a large part of the apparent decline in average household energy consumption. The year 1978-79 (April to March) which provides the baseline in the DOE data was a very atypical year in terms of the severity of the winter. It was 8 percent colder, measured on the basis of national average heating degree days, than the norm. The following two years were much closer to the norm. Thus, 1978-79 was about 6 percent colder than the next two years. This accounted for a large part of the drop in consumption between 1978-79 and the next two years.

The impact of the severity of summers on energy consumption is less clear. The year 1978-79 was very close to the norm, while 1979-80 was 10 percent cooler than the norm and 1980-81 was 7 percent hotter than the norm. The very large drop in consumption in 1979-80 compared to 1978-79 is certainly related to weather since both the winter and the summer were milder.

In 1980-81, we might have expected an increase in consumption compared to 1979-80, due to the severity of the summer. However, two factors suggest otherwise. First, cooling energy uses generally have a much smaller impact on consumption than heating uses. Second, note the very large jump (5 percent) in the number of households reported. In the previous year (1978-79 to 1979-80) the increase in the number of households was only 1 percent. This increase in households certainly played a part in lowering the average consumption per household.

There has, in fact, been an increase in the number of households and a decrease in household size in recent years. However, the large jump between 1979-80 and

73

TABLE 4.5
Factors Affecting Average Residential Energy Consumption

| | Weather Data [a] | | DOE Data [b] | | | EIA Data [c] |
Year	Heating Degree Days	Cooling Degree Days	Total Consumption (Quad BTUs)	Number of Households (millions)	Household Consumption (Million BTUs)	Per Capita Energy Consumption (Million BTUs)
1978–79	5008	1192	10.6	76.6	138	73
1979–80	4721	1078	9.7	77.5	126	70
1980–81	4745	1285	9.3	81.6	114	67
Norm	4649	1199	N.A.	--	--	--

Sources: [a]U.S. Department of Energy, Residential Energy Consumption Survey: Consumption and Expenditures, April 1980 through March 1981, Part 1: National Data (Washington, D.C.: September 1982), Figure 9.

[b]U.S. Department of Energy, Residential Energy Consumption Survey: Consumption and Expenditures, April 1978 through March 1979 (Washington, D.C.: July 1980), Table 1; 1979–1980 Consumption and Expenditures, Part I: National Data (Washington, D.C.: April 1981), Table 1; Consumption and Expenditures, April 1980 through March 1981, Part 1: National Data (Washington, D.C.: September 1982), Table 1.

[c]U.S. Department of Energy, State Energy Data Report (Washington, D.C.: various issues), Per Capita Energy Consumption tables.

1980-81 is too large to reflect an increase in the
number of households. In reality, it reflects a statistical adjustment. This actually leads to an overestimate of energy conservation. For example, had the
number of households increased at the same rate between
1979-80 and 1980-81 as it had in the previous year, the
decline in consumption would have been only half as
large (from 126 million BTUs to 119 rather than 114).
Data from the Energy Information Administration on state
by state consumption corroborates this. The data shows
only a 4 percent decline in per capita residential
energy consumption between 1979 and 1980. This is more
consistent with an estimate of 119 million BTUs per
household.
    It is difficult to estimate these effects with
precision. However, we can reach some conclusions with
considerable confidence. It would seem that the apparent reduction in energy consumption among lower income
households is due to the unusual nature of the base
year. Little actual reduction in consumption was possible for these households and little occurred. Lower
middle income households achieved some energy conservation in the first year of the record energy price shock,
but having reached roughly the same level of consumption
as lower income households, they could conserve no more
in the second year. Non-lower income households
achieved conservation gains in both years, but when
stated as average household consumption in this data,
the gains are probably overstated by a factor of two.
    The central conclusion must be that the conservation
response has been extremely disappointing, especially
for the lower income population. Moreover, if the
actual conservation is only half as large as it appears
in the data, the price responsiveness of demand in the
residential sector is extremely low.

ENERGY EXPENDITURES

    Having shown that national and regional trends of
household energy consumption for lower income households
fit our understanding of energy consumption as a vital
commodity, we come to the central question: Do patterns
of energy expenditures as a percentage of income behave
as predicted by the energy-as-vital-necessity argument?
That is, are low income households forced to devote a
much larger share of their income to energy expenditures? Moreover, does the percentage of income they
devote to energy expenditures increase over time as
prices rise because they cannot reduce their consumption? This is the critical factor in the squeeze on
their household budgets and their living standard.

Levels of Expenditure

Energy Prices. Energy consumption is only one of
the determinants of energy expenditures. Energy prices
are the second determinant. A number of factors in the
energy delivery system have combined to make the price
that lower income households pay for each form of energy
higher than the national average. Therefore, the difference in the amount they spend for energy is less than
one would expect, given the difference in the amount of
energy they consume.

Inverted rate structures, with declining charges for
larger quantities of energy consumed on a regular basis,
disadvantage lower income households, which consume less
energy. This inverted rate structure appears to apply
to both regulated and unregulated sources of energy.
Over the period since the first energy price shock there
have been forces tending to counter these pricing practices, but as Table 4.6 shows, lower income households
paid more for each type of fuel than non-lower income
households in 1980. If anything, the situation had
become worse between 1978 and 1980. It may be that the
pattern observed in 1978-80 represents slippage after a
period of improvement, but a full time series on energy
prices paid by households in each income group is not
available.

It should also be noted that lower income households
had a lower aggregate cost of energy per BTU than
non-lower income households because they consumed less
electricity, which is by far the most expensive source
of energy and also has the most discretionary uses.
However, note that they suffered a deterioration of
their advantage between 1978 and 1980 and that only a
small part of the deterioration would appear to be due
to an increase in consumption of electricity. Thus, the
increase in price of energy relative to non-lower income
households contributed somewhat to the absolutely larger
burden placed on lower income households in the period.

Expenditures. Table 4.7 shows the energy bills for
low, lower middle, and non-lower income households for
the years 1972-73, 1978-79, 1979-80, and 1980-81. All
figures are in current dollars and the 1978-79 and
1980-81 figures have been adjusted so that the income
groups are comparable to the 1979-80 figures.

Table 4.7 shows that the total increase in the home
energy bills over the period for low income households
was $569. For lower middle income households it was
$558 and for non-lower income households it was $610.
The overall increase in the bills for low and lower
middle income households was only 6 percent lower than
for non-lower income households.

Note, however, the remarkable shift in the burden of

TABLE 4.6
Prices Paid for Fuels

Price	1978-79					1980-81				
	All Fuels	Natural Gas	Electricity	Fuel Oil	LPG	All Fuels	Natural Gas	Electricity	Fuel Oil	LPG
National Average	5.25	2.69	11.85	3.93	5.05	8.03	3.90	16.32	8.04	7.92
Low Income	4.86	2.73	11.86	3.88	5.43	7.68	4.01	16.64	8.08	8.00
Lower Middle Income	5.04	2.64	12.02	3.92	5.08	7.75	3.94	16.36	8.02	7.99
Prices Paid as a Percent of National Average Price										
Low Income	93	101	100	99	108	96	103	102	100	101
Lower Middle	96	98	101	100	100	97	101	100	100	101

Sources: U.S. Department of Energy, Residential Energy Consumption Survey: Consumption and Expenditures, April 1978 through March 1979 (Washington, D.C.: July 1980), Table 1.

U.S. Department of Energy, Residential Energy Consumption Survey: Consumption and Expenditures, April 1980 through March 1981, Part I: National Data (Washington, D.C.: September 1982), Table 1.

TABLE 4.7
Expenditures for Home Energy

Income Group	Home Energy Bills (dollars)				Increase in Home Energy Bills (dollars)			
	1972-73	1978-79	1979-80	1980-81	1972-73 to 1980-81	1972-73 to 1978-79	1978-79 to 1979-80	1979-80 to 1980-81
Low	190	515	609	759	569	325	94	150
Lower Middle	255	616	657	813	558	361	41	156
Non-Lower	402	810	911	1012	610	408	101	101

Sources: U.S. Bureau of Labor Statistics, Consumer Expenditure Survey: Interview Survey, 1972-73 Average Annual Income and Expenditures for Commodity and Service Groups Classified by Family Characteristics, Report 455-4 (Washington, D.C.: 1977), Table 1.

U.S. Department of Energy, Residential Energy Consumption Survey: Consumption and Expenditures, April 1978 through March 1979 (Washington, D.C.: July 1980), Table 1.

U.S. Department of Energy, Residential Energy Consumption Survey: 1979-1980 Consumption and Expenditures, Part I: National Data (Washington, D.C.: April 1981), Table 1.

U.S. Department of Energy, Residential Energy Consumption Survey: Consumption and Expenditures, April 1980 through March 1981, Part I: National Data (Washington, D.C.: September 1982), Table 1.

rising energy prices that took place over the decade. In the period between 1972-73 and 1978-79, lower income households suffered an increase of $329 compared to $355 for lower middle income households and $408 for non-lower income households. In this earlier period, the increase for non-lower income households was close to 20 percent higher.

With the onset of the second energy price shock, the trend was reversed. In the period between 1978-79 and 1980-81, the bills for both low and lower middle income households increased more rapidly than those for non-lower income households -- 20 percent in the case of the former, 10 percent in the case of the latter. The brunt of the burden came in the second year of the second price shock (1979-80/1980-81) with low and lower middle income households suffering increases in home energy bills that were $50 per year (50 percent) more than non-lower income households. The ability to continue to conserve, both behaviorally and through investments in improved efficiency, shielded the non-lower income households from a major part of the second energy price shock.

Energy Expenditures as a Percent of Income

National Patterns. Given the fact that the absolute increase in the energy bills of low and lower middle income households were only slightly lower than those of non-lower income households over the entire decade and were actually larger in the final years of the decade, we can expect to find a dramatic increase in the burden that rising energy price placed on lower income households relative to non-lower income groups. Figure 4.6 shows energy expenditures as a percent of income for households at various income levels at various points in time. Data from four different national surveys are included. Data from several points in the early 1970s and the late 1970s are also included.[8]/

The results are strikingly clear. The shape of the curves relating energy expenditures to income is consistent with the energy-as-vital-necessity argument. Lower income households devote a much larger share of their income to energy expenditures and that share has grown dramatically over the decade. For example, based on the survey data from the early 1970s (1971-73), a family with an income of $3,000 per year devoted about 7.5 percent of its income to household energy expenditures. By the late 1970s, a family with an annual income of $3,000 was devoting about 20 percent of its income to energy expenditures.[9]/ Thus, an additional 12.5 percentage points of income were devoted to energy expenditures.

In contrast, a middle income family with an income,

FIGURE 4.6
National Average Home Energy Expenditures as a Percent
Income in Current Dollars

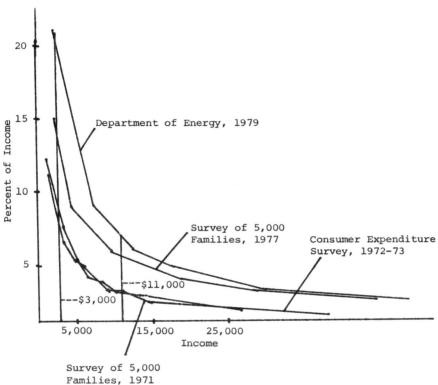

Sources: Richard D. Coe, "A Comparison of Utility Payments and
Burdens Between 1971 and 1979," in James N. Morgan and
Greg S. Duncan, eds., Five Thousand American Families:
Patterns of Economic Progress, Vol. VIII. (Ann Arbor:
Institute for Policy Research, 1980), pp. 339-380.

U.S. Department of Labor, Bureau of Labor Statistics,
Consumer Expenditure Survey: Interview Survey, 1972-73,
Average Annual Income and Expenditures for Commodity and
and Service Groups Classified by Family Characteristics
(Report 455-4, 1977), Table 1.

U.S. Department of Energy, Residential Energy Consumption
Survey, 1979-80, Consumption and Expenditures, Part I:
National Data (Washington, D.C.: April 1981), Table 1.

for example, of $11,000 per year in the early 1970s devoted about 3.2 percent of its income to energy expenditures. By 1979, this percentage had grown to about 7 percent.

Both families had experienced a more than doubling of energy expenditures as a percent of income, but the low income family had lost a much larger share of its income to rising energy prices. Compared to the middle income family, which had lost only 4 percentage points, the additional burden on the low income family was extreme.

The above comparison, based on income expressed in current dollars, may overstate the case somewhat. A family with $3,000 in income in 1979 was much poorer than a family with $3,000 in income in 1972-73, due to the impact of inflation. That is, $3,000 bought much more in 1972-73 than it did in 1979. Since the family with only $3,000 in income in 1979 was poorer, one would expect it to spend a larger share of its income on energy expenditures.10/ Therefore, in the above comparisons, the burden of rising energy prices is overstated to the extent that families at different effective levels of income are being compared.

To correct for this overstatement, we can compare the energy expenditures of families with the same real incomes. In Figure 4.7, the relationship between energy expenditures (as a percent of income) and income is depicted, with income stated in constant dollars.11/ A family with an income of $3,000 in 1972 would have devoted about 7.5 percent of its income to energy. In 1979, a family with a real income (in 1972 dollars) of $3,000 would have devoted about 15 percent of its income to energy expenditures. Thus, an additional 7.5 percentage points of income would be devoted to energy expenditures. In contrast, the family with $11,000 of real income in 1972 and its equivalent in 1979 would have devoted about 3.2 percent of income to energy in 1972 and 4.5 percent in 1979. It would have lost an additional 1.3 percentage points of it income to rising energy prices.

Expressing income in real terms and making comparisons between households with constant real incomes reduces the estimate of the magnitude of the loss of income due to rising energy prices by one-half to one-third. At the same time, however, it accentuates the relative burden placed on the low income household. The increase in the percentage of income that low income households devote to energy was six times greater than for the middle income household.12/

Having examined the movement of energy expenditures as a percentage of income for specific households, we next examine how the entire income groups have fared. In this case the 1980-81 figures are adjusted to be

FIGURE 4.7
National Average Home Energy Expenditures as a Percent of Income: Income
in Constant Dollars

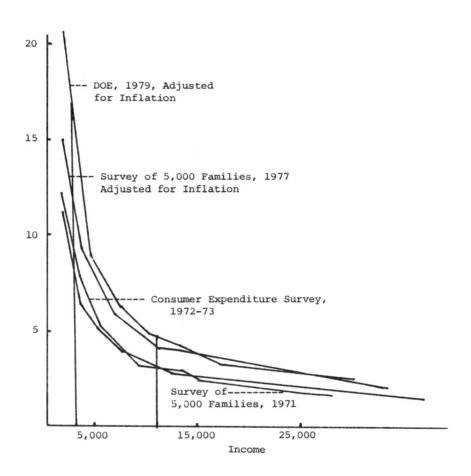

Sources: See notes to Figure 4.6 for data sources.   The personal
consumption deflators used to convert current to constant
dollars are taken from Council of Economic Advisors, Annual
Report (February 1982), Table B3.

82

compatible with the 1979-80 figures. Moreover, the
1979-80 groups were defined to be roughly compatible
with those in the 1972-73 data.
    As Table 4.8 shows, the lower income population lost
a much larger share of its income to rising home energy
costs. The low income population saw its expenditures
rise from 11.0 percent of income to 23.2 percent. The
lower middle income households saw their expenditures
rise from 5.2 percent to 9.7 percent. The non-lower
income households saw their expenditures increase from
2.5 percent to 3.5 percent. The lower income group lost
12 percentage points of their income to rising home
energy costs and the lower middle income group lost 4.5
percentage points, compared to only a 1 percentage point
loss suffered by the non-lower income group.

TABLE 4.8
Home Energy Expenditures as a Percent of Income

Income Category	1972-73	1979-80	1980-81
Low Income	11.0	21.1	23.2
Lower Middle Income	5.2	8.9	9.7
Non-Lower Income	2.5	3.5	3.5

Sources: U.S. Bureau of Labor Statistics, Consumer
          Expenditure Survey: Interview Survey, 1972-73
          Average Annual Income and Expenditures for
          Commodity and Service Groups Classified by
          Family Characteristics, Report 455-4
          (Washington, D.C.: 1977), Table 1.

          U.S. Department of Energy, Residential Energy
          Consumption Survey, 1979-80: Consumption and
          Expenditures, Part I: National Data
          (Washington, D.C.: April 1981), Table 1.

          U.S. Department of Energy, Residential Energy
          Consumption Survey, Consumption and Expendi-
          tures, April 1980 through March 1981, Part 1:
          National Data (Washington, D.C.: September
          1982), Table 1.

The relatively heavier burden placed on the low income household is very marked and a loss of income in absolute terms of at least 5 percent is quite serious. Of course, the impact of rising energy prices on specific households will reflect the interaction of a number of factors -- most importantly, the actual energy consumption patterns of the household, the actual prices they pay, and the ability of the household to maintain its income. Nevertheless, given the general evidence on the movement of national average incomes and expenditures, it seems clear that rising energy prices have placed a heavy, disproportionate burden on the low income population.

Regional Patterns

Figure 4.8 depicts the percentage of income spent on energy by households in the nation and in the Northeast, South, North Central, and West in 1972-73 and 1979. The data are taken from the Consumer Expenditure Survey for 1972-73 and the Residential Energy Consumption Survey for 1979. While the percentage of income spent on energy varies among the regions, the trend is clearly the same as at the national level.

In the four regions, the lowest income households spent from 10.3 to 12.2 percent of their income on energy in 1972-73, closely centered around the national average of 11.1 percent. This percentage declined across the income categories. Households in the highest income category spent from 1.2 to 1.8 percent of their income on energy, very close to the national average of 1.5 percent.

In all but one of the regions, these numbers had increased greatly by 1979. The lowest income households in the Northeast spent 28 percent of their income on energy, while those in the highest income category spent less than 3 percent of their income on household energy. In the North Central region, the ratios were 23 percent and 2.5 percent, respectively. The percentages in the South parallel the national average at a slightly lower level; the lowest income households spent about 19 percent of their income on energy while the highest income households spent less than 3 percent. In the West, the trend across income categories was the same although the percentages were smaller at all income levels. The lowest income households spent 13.4 percent of their income on energy while those in the highest income category spent only 1.3 percent.

Examination of the data in each climate zone reveals this same trend. In fact, there is less difference between climate zones than between geographic regions. In Zone 1, which is the coldest region of the nation, close to 24.6 percent of the income of the households in

84

FIGURE 4.8
Home Energy Expenditures as a Percent of Income: National Averages
and South, Northeast, North Central, and West Regions

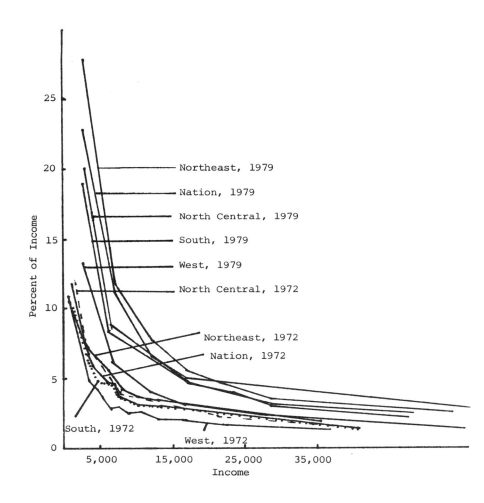

Sources: See Figure 4.6 for basic data sources. The South, North-
         east, North Central, and West Regions are identified as
         subsets of each major report in regional volumes.

the lowest income category was spent on energy. By
contrast, a scant 2.5 percent of the income of those
households earning $35,000 or more was spent for energy.
In Zone 7, the warmest region of the nation, the lowest
income households spent 16.5 percent of their income for
energy. Households earning $35,000 or more, on the
other hand, spent less than 2 percent of their income
for energy.

These patterns of energy expenditures are significant to the extent that a large number of variables --
predominant type of fuel consumed, fuel prices, and
average incomes -- are reflected in the energy expenditure figures. Despite all of these variables, consumers
in the same income categories in all regions of the
country experienced a similar impact from rising energy
prices. The greater variance in the percentage of
income spent on energy by low income households reflects
their inability to reduce energy consumption further.
They are at the minimum level of consumption feasible.
In colder climates, greater consumption of energy for
home use is essential. Higher income households appear
to have stabilized their energy consumption at a much
less onerous level. The fact that there is so little
variation in the percentage of income spent on household
energy by non-lower income households across the country
suggests that these households are probably at their
maximum consumption of energy.

Whatever unexpected variation there is can be
explained by the predominant type of fuel consumed in
each region. Electricity, the most expensive energy
source on a BTU-for-BTU basis, is more predominant in
the South than in any other region. Fuel oil, the
second most expensive energy source, is most prevalent
in the Northeast. Natural gas, the least expensive
fuel, is most predominant in the West and North Central
regions. In part, this accounts for the fact that the
burden of energy prices is higher in the Northeast and
South and lower in the North Central and West regions
than might be expected on the basis of climate factors
alone. That is, if low income households in the
Northeast paid the same price per BTU as those in the
North Central region, they would spend about the same
percentage of their income for energy used in the home.
Similarly, if low income households in the South paid
the same price per BTU as those in the West, they would
pay about the same percentage of their income for energy
used in the home.

The combination of three factors -- climate, energy
prices, and the fact that home energy, especially
heating energy, is a necessity -- is strikingly clear in
Figure 4.8. There was very little difference between
regions in expenditures as a percentage of income in
1972-73. By 1979, for the low income population, the

rigors of climate, as we have put it, had driven expenditures as a percentage of income in the Northeast and North Central regions far above the South and West. At the same time, price differences between the dominant home heating source had driven expenditures in the Northeast far above those in the North Central region.

Thus, we see that it is not only the length and severity of the heating or cooling season that determines the impact of rising energy prices on household budgets, but also factors which are associated with regions and are beyond the control of individual households. Having noted these important regional and climate differences in the consumption and expenditures for home energy, we will show in the next chapter that when gasoline consumption is taken into account a large part of the difference between regions is erased.

5
Gasoline Consumption
and Expenditures

Of all the issues in the energy policy debate, none
has been as hotly debated as gasoline consumption. In
the international community, gasoline consumption is the
symbol of America's profligate energy waste. In domestic politics, gasoline lines -- variously attributed to
the foreign oil cartel and/or the ineptitude of government regulation and/or the machinations of a domestic
energy oligopoly -- are the symbol of American frustra-
tion and impotence. In the economy, the collapse of the
domestic automobile industry -- caused, in large
measure, by a flood of fuel-efficient imports -- is a
symbol of severe economic decay. With considerable
justification, some analysts define the heart of the
energy crisis as a liquid fuel problem. As such, it is
a gasoline problem.

In many social impact analyses, gasoline is treated
as a pure luxury, whose consumption is completely
discretionary.1/ The burden of rising gasoline prices
enters these analyses as an afterthought, if at all. We
believe that such a view is incorrect when applied to
the lower income population. The quantities that the
lower income households consume and the purposes for
which they use gasoline suggest that, for them, gasoline
is more appropriately considered a necessity than a
luxury.2/

For those lower income households that own an
automobile, it is not primarily a vehicle for weekend
jaunts and frivolous recreation. It is a means of
transportation to undertake basic daily activities --
frequently the only available means of transportation.
The absence of alternatives suggests that, in the short
and middle term, the rising price of gasoline must be
paid if the household is to continue to function.
Insofar as the provision of alternatives, such as mass
transit, is a social decision, the middle term may prove
to be quite long. Moreover, the cost of improving the
efficiency of private transportation is very high

because it requires the purchase of new vehicles. Lower income households lack the resources for such purchases and therefore are forced to pay a very high price at the pump.

This chapter briefly analyzes gasoline consumption by lower income households. It demonstrates that consumption of and expenditure patterns for gasoline are consistent with the characterization of gasoline as a necessity for those lower income households that use it.

Having laid the basis for including gasoline in calculating the burden that rising energy prices place on lower income households, this chapter concludes with an overall summary of the analyses of household expenditures contained in Part 2.

AUTOMOBILE OWNERSHIP AND USE IN VARIOUS INCOME GROUPS

Our argument can be summarized as follows: Those lower income households that own automobiles do so because they are a necessity; they use them sparingly for basic transportation to conduct the vital activities of daily life. The evidence clearly supports this interpretation.

In order to demonstrate this point, the discussion which follows examines first the use of <u>all</u> modes of transportation; then we explore the use of automobiles for all purposes; then all transportation for home-to-work trips, because these are perhaps the most vital of all daily routine trips; and, finally, the use of automobiles for home-to-work trips.

Lower income households are much less likely than non-lower income households to own automobiles. According to the U.S. Department of Transportation <u>1977 Nationwide Personal Transportation Study</u> about 50 percent of the lowest income households (annual incomes of less than $5,000) own one or more vehicles.<u>3</u>/ In contrast, over 95 percent of those households with annual incomes of $15,000 or more own one or more vehicles. Moreover, those low income households that do own vehicles own only one-third as many vehicles as non-lower income households.

Low income households are much more likely than non-lower income households to use mass transit or to walk. Whereas 85 percent of all trips taken by non-lower income households are taken by car, only 66 percent of all trips taken by low income households are by car. Furthermore, if we examine the pattern of ridership in cars, we observe that non-lower income households are much more likely to be drivers than passengers. This suggests a tendency toward using the car for single passenger trips. In fact, much of this difference is the result of single passenger work-related trips (i.e., driving alone to work).<u>4</u>/ This pattern of

general transportation use would support the conclusion
that low income households economize on automobile usage
where possible.

When we examine the usage pattern of automobiles,
this conclusion seems reaffirmed. If we examine the
number of automobile trips taken per day for all
purposes by households in various income categories, we
find dramatic differences. Those in the lowest income
category (incomes less than $5,000) took far fewer trips
(between one-third and one-quarter as many) than those
with incomes above $10,000. Their trips were between 15
and 20 percent shorter, as well. Thus, non-lower income
households drove between 3 and 5 times as many miles as
low income households. The lower middle income group
(incomes between $5,000 and $10,000) falls half way
between the lowest income group and the non-lower income
group in its use of vehicles.

When we examine the purposes for which vehicles were
used, the differences remain striking. As Table 5.1
shows, households in the lowest income category took
between one-quarter and one-sixth as many trips related
to earning a living as those with incomes above $10,000.
Their usage, in fact, was lower for all activities.
They took one-third as many family and personal business
trips or civic/education/religious trips and one-half as
many social and recreational trips. In fact, households
with incomes above $10,000 took about three times as
many social and recreational trips per day as lower
incomes households took work-related trips.

Even when the number of trips is calculated on the
basis of only those households that own vehicles, the
differences in vehicle use are apparent, although
somewhat less pronounced. For example, in households
which own vehicles, those with incomes above $10,000
still took more than twice as many recreational and
social trips as those with incomes below $5,000 took
work-related trips. Clearly, vehicles represent very
different commodities for lower income households than
they do for non-lower income households.

When we zero in on all modes of transportation for
home-to-work trips, we find that the patterns are
repeated. Low income households are much more likely to
use public and other non-private vehicle means of transportation to get to work (20.4 percent) than households
with incomes above $10,000 (6-10 percent). They are
much less likely to be vehicle drivers (55 percent
compared to 72.2 percent or more).

Having established the fact that low income households use their cars less, even for work trips, we next
examine the reasons why they use them even though they
are very costly. Is it the fact that low income households do not have alternatives available for basic daily
activities that pushes them to the extremely burdensome

TABLE 5.1
Trips per Household per Day: All Households – Owners and Non-owners

Trip Purpose	Annual Household Income						
	Less than $5,000	$5,000 to $9,999	$10,000 to $14,999	$15,000 to $24,999	$25,000 to $34,999	$35,000 to $49,999	$50,000 or More
Earning a Living							
Home-to-Work	.27	.77	1.22	1.64	1.74	1.76	1.47
Work-Related	.07	.13	.20	.28	.39	.39	.43
TOTAL	.34	.80	1.44	1.92	2.13	2.15	1.90
Family/Personal Business							
Shopping	.28	.52	.69	.89	1.12	1.12	.94
Medical/Dental	.02	.04	.05	.07	.07	.12	.05
Other	.24	.47	.56	.73	.87	.89	.81
TOTAL	.54	1.03	1.30	1.69	2.06	2.13	1.80
Civic/Education/Religious	.13	.02	.25	.34	.43	.48	.35
Social/Recreational							
Visiting Friends & Relatives	.18	.31	.35	.41	.43	.43	.38
Pleasure Driving	.01	.02	.01	.02	.02	.02	.05
Vacations	0	0	.01	0	.01	.01	.01
Other	.15	.30	.44	.54	.63	.82	.79
TOTAL	.34	.63	.81	.97	1.09	1.28	1.23

Sources: U.S. Department of Transportation, Purposes of Vehicle Trips and Travel: Report No. 3, 1977 Nation-wide Personal Transportation Study (Washington, D.C.: December 1980), Tables 1, 9, 10, 11, 12.
U.S. Department of Transportation, Household Vehicle Ownership: Report No. 2, 1977 Nationwide Personal Transportation Study (Washington, D.C.: December 1980), Table 3.

expense of owning and operating an automobile?

Data from the survey of <u>Five Thousand American Families</u> can be used to show the very large differences in driving patterns of lower versus non-lower income households, especially with respect to the discretionary use of automobiles for purposes of commuting to work. In 1972, households in the top fifth of the income distribution scale were almost four times more likely to drive to work than households in the bottom fifth (67 percent compared to 17.5 percent). Of greater importance is the fact that only one out of every twenty five heads of lower income households chose to drive to work when alternative transportation was available, compared to one out of every five in the non-lower income group.5/

Thus, an analysis of the modes of transportation which are used to get to work is consistent with our assertion that low income households only use automobiles when they have to (i.e., they use alternatives whenever possible).

GASOLINE EXPENDITURES AS A PERCENT OF INCOME

National Patterns

The most important test of whether gasoline should be considered a necessity for low income households is the relative expenditure patterns for gasoline. In Chapter 4, we distinguished the consumption and expenditure patterns of vital necessities according to the premise that, at low levels of income, it would be difficult to reduce consumption. Therefore, expenditures for necessities would take a much larger share of the income of the lower income household.

Figure 5.1 compares 1972-73 household gasoline expenditures as a percentage of income to those in 1980, using a base of all households. It shows that gasoline expenditure increased sharply in all income categories. In the lowest income category, expenditures rose from 6 percent to about 13 percent. In the highest income category, expenditures rose from about 1.5 percent to 3 percent. Figure 5.2 shows similar curves with the percentage of income spent on gasoline estimated only for households that own automobiles. In the lowest income category, the percent of income spent on gasoline by households which own a vehicle is about 17 percent for 1979, up from 10 percent in 1972-73; in the upper income category, the percentage is 3.5, up from 1.6 percent in 1972-73.

Regardless of whether the figures are adjusted for ownership, lower income households lost a disproportionate share of their income to rising energy prices. Their loss was between 1.5 and 2 times as large as that of the highest income group.

92

FIGURE 5.1
Gasoline Expenditures as a Percent of Income

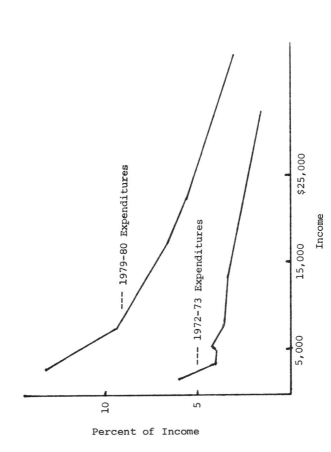

Sources: U.S. Bureau of Labor Statistics, Consumer Expenditure Survey: Interview Survey, 1972-73 Average Annual Income and Expenditures, Report No. 455-4 (Washington, D.C.: 1977).

U.S. Department of Energy, Residential Energy Consumption Survey: Consumption Patterns of Household Vehicles, June 1979 to December 1980 (Washington, D.C.: April 1982), Tables 17 and 18.

FIGURE 5.2

Gasoline Expenditures as a Percent of Income, Adjusted for Incidence of Ownership and Income

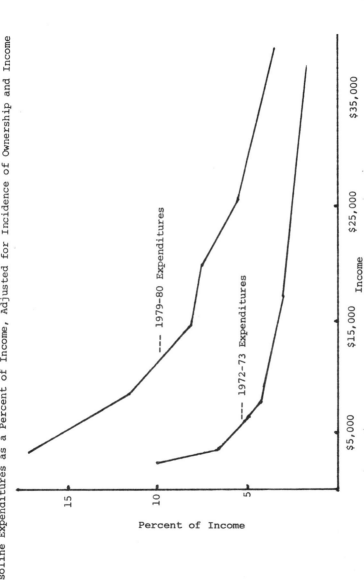

Sources: U.S. Bureau of Labor Statistics, Consumer Expenditure Survey: Interview Survey, 1972-73 Average Annual Income and Expenditures, Report No. 455-4 (Washington, D.C.: 1977).

U.S. Department of Energy, Residential Energy Consumption Survey: Consumption Patterns of House-Hold Vehicles, June 1979 to December 1980 (Washington, D.C.: April 1982), Tables 17 and 18.

Obviously, neither the absolute level of the burden placed on lower income households nor the relatively larger increase in the burden due to rising gasoline expenditures was as heavy as it was for home fuels. Nevertheless, the burden is greater on the lower income population and it has increased more rapidly for them than for other income groups. When added to the much larger burden of home fuels, rising gasoline prices make an already difficult situation considerably worse.

Regional Patterns

Gasoline consumption and expenditures exhibit a uniquely regional pattern that is of special importance in analyzing the burden on the lower income population (see Table 5.2). In 1972-73, the lowest income group in the West spent 9.5 percent of its income on gasoline -- a much larger percentage of its income than the national average. The lowest income group in the Northeast spent 4 percent -- much less than the national average. For the lower middle income group, the pattern is similar, although less pronounced.

The underlying cause of this pattern appears to be, primarily, the rate of ownership of vehicles rather than the amount of driving done by specific households. Fifty-three percent of the lowest income households in the West reported gasoline expenditures for non-vacation purposes. The national average was only 45 percent. In the Northeast, the percentage was only 32. In the lower middle income category, a similar pattern is in evidence, although less pronounced.

These differences across regions and income categories can be explained by the greater distances to be traversed in the West, in particular, and the resulting relative lack of mass transit facilities. In contrast, the Northeast is much more densely populated and has a relatively greater availability of mass transit. Thus, the percentage of households reporting mass transit expenditures in the Northeast is much higher than elsewhere. The percentage reporting inadequate public transportation is lower there as well. Although the lower income population is generally more dependent on mass transit, we observe a high incidence of vehicle ownership in the West because mass transit is in shorter supply and, therefore, the incidence of expenditures for public transportation by households is less as well.

An arithmetic exercise, based on Table 5.2, can be used to show the relative importance of the incidence of ownership and driving patterns. If low income households in the West had an ownership rate (incidence) of only 32 percent (the incidence in the Northeast), gasoline expenditures would have been only 5.7 percent of income, assuming constant driving habits. Therefore,

TABLE 5.2
Gasoline Expenditures and Public Transportation Availability, 1972-73

Income Category	Northeast	North Central	South	West
LOW INCOME ($3,000 or less)				
Gasoline Expenditure as a Percent of Income	4.0	6.3	6.6	9.5
Percent of Households Reporting Nonvacation Gasoline Expenditures	32	45	46	53.1
Percent of Households Reporting Public Transportation Expenditures	33	24	21.1	23.1
LOWER MIDDLE INCOME ($3,000 to $6,999)				
Gasoline Expenditure as a Percent of Income	3.1	4.1	4.8	5.1
Percent of Households Reporting Nonvacation Gasoline Expenditures	57	72	76	79
Percent of Households Reporting Public Transportation Expenditures	33	23	20	24
NON-LOWER INCOME ($7,000 or more)				
Gasoline Expenditure as a Percent of Income	2.6	3.1	3.0	2.9
Percent of Households Reporting Nonvacation Gasoline Expenditures	90	96	97	97
Percent of Households Reporting Public Transportation Expenditures	30	18	14	17

Source: U.S. Bureau of Labor Statistics, Consumer Expenditure Survey: Interview Survey, 1972-73 Average Annual Income and Expenditures for Commodity and Service Groups Classified by Family Characteristics, Report 455-4 (Washington, D.C.: 1977), Table 1.

more than two-thirds of the difference between the West
and the Northeast (3.8 ÷ 5.5 = .69) is due to the
difference in ownership. The remainder is due to
differences in driving patterns (probably distance). In
the other regions, ownership accounts for about three-
fourths of the difference. A similar pattern is
exhibited in the lower middle income groups.

A similar set of data broken down by region and
income group for more recent years is not readily
available. However, the available data suggests that
the pattern has not changed much since 1972-73. The
average household consumption of gasoline, the ownership
of vehicles, and the perceived inadequacy of public
transportation is still higher outside of the Northeast
and the differences between regions have remained about
the same, with increases in the inadequacy of public
transportation outside of the Northeast. Given this
evidence, we assume that the expenditure patterns
relative to the national average observed for 1972-73
held in 1979-80 as well.

These patterns of expenditures for gasoline balance
the pattern of home energy expenditures observed in
Chapter 4. Very high home energy expenditures in the
Northeast by lower income households are offset by low
expenditures on gasoline. Low expenditures in the West
on home energy are offset by higher gasoline expenditures. The result, as we show in the next section, is
to create a more even pattern of energy expenditures
across regions than an analysis of either gasoline or
home energy expenditures alone would suggest.

SUMMARY AND CONCLUSION TO PART 2: DIRECT
EXPENDITURES FOR ENERGY AS A PERCENT OF INCOME

The previous analyses have given a detailed picture
of the dramatic increase in the burden that rising
energy prices place on lower income households (see
Table 5.3). For households in the lowest income group,
direct energy expenditures constituted 17 percent of
income in 1972-73 and increased to about 36 percent of
income in 1980. For lower middle income households,
they increased from 9.4 percent to 19.2 percent. For
non-lower income households, they increased from 5.2
percent to 8 percent. Low income households lost 19
percentage points of income, while lower middle income
households lost 10 percentage points, and non-lower
income households lost only 3 percentage points.

In the case of low income households, three-fourths
of the loss was due to home energy expenditures and
one-fourth to gasoline. In the case of lower middle
income households, two-thirds of the loss was due to
home energy and one-third to gasoline. In the case of
non-lower income households, only two-fifths of the loss

TABLE 5.3
Direct Energy Expenditures as a Percent of Income: 1972-73, 1979-80, and 1980-81

Income Category	1972-73 Home Energy	1972-73 Gasoline	1972-73 Total Direct Energy	1979-80 Home Energy	1979-80 Gasoline	1979-80 Total Direct Energy	1980-81 Home Energy	1980-81 Gasoline	1980-81 Total Direct Energy
NATION									
Low	11.0	6.3	17.3	21.1	9.8	30.9	23.2	13.4	36.6
Lower Middle	5.2	4.2	9.4	8.9	6.3	15.2	9.7	9.5	19.2
Non-Lower	2.5	2.7	5.2	3.5	4.3	7.8	3.5	4.5	8.0
NORTHEAST									
Low	11.2	4.0	15.2	28.2	6.2	34.4	---	---	---
Lower Middle	6.1	3.1	9.2	11.6	4.7	16.3	---	---	---
Non-Lower	2.8	2.6	5.4	5.0	4.1	9.1	---	---	---
NORTH CENTRAL									
Low	12.2	6.3	18.5	23.0	9.8	32.8	---	---	---
Lower Middle	5.6	4.1	9.7	10.5	6.2	16.7	---	---	---
Non-Lower	2.6	3.1	5.7	4.5	4.9	9.4	---	---	---
SOUTH									
Low	10.9	6.9	17.8	19.2	10.2	29.4	---	---	---
Lower Middle	5.0	4.8	9.8	8.2	7.2	15.4	---	---	---
Non-Lower	2.4	3.0	5.4	4.1	4.8	8.9	---	---	---

TABLE 5.3 (cont'd)

Income Category	1972-73			1979-80			1980-81		
	Home Energy	Gasoline	Total Direct Energy	Home Energy	Gasoline	Total Direct Energy	Home Energy	Gasoline	Total Direct Energy
WEST									
Low	11.3	9.5	20.8	13.4	14.8	28.2	--	--	--
Lower Middle	3.8	5.1	8.9	5.9	7.7	13.6	--	--	--
Non-Lower	1.8	2.9	4.7	2.6	4.6	7.2	--	--	--

Sources: U.S. Bureau of Labor Statistics, Consumer Expenditure Survey: Interview Survey, 1972-73 Average Annual Income and Expenditures for Commodity and Service Groups Classified by Family Characteristics, Report 455-4 (Washington, D.C.: 1977), Table 1.

U.S. Department of Energy, Residential Energy Consumption Survey: Consumption Patterns of Household Vehicles, June 1979 to December 1980 (Washington, D.C.: April 1982); the 1980 consumption data is used to interpolate missing data points for 1979.

U.S. Department of Energy, Residential Energy Consumption Survey, 1979-1980 Consumption and Expenditures, Part I: National Data (Washington, D.C.: April 1981), Table 1.

U.S. Department of Energy, Residential Energy Consumption Survey, 1978-1980 Consumption and Expenditures, Part II: Regional Data (Washington, D.C.: May 1981), Table 1.

U.S. Department of Energy, Residential Energy Consumption Survey, Consumption and Expenditures, April 1980 through March 1981, Part I: National Data (Washington, D.C.: September 1982), Table 1.

was due to home energy, while three-fifths was due to gasoline.

The impact of rising energy prices varied considerably across regions, although less than one might expect. In the Northeast, where the burden was heaviest and where it increased the most, direct energy expenditures as a percentage of income for low income households rose from 15.2 percent in 1972-73 to 34.4 percent in 1979-80. In the West, where the energy cost burden is lightest, it increased from 20.8 percent to 28.2 percent. The other regions fall between these two extremes, with the North Central (32.8 percent in 1979-80) closer to the Northeast and the South (29.4 percent) closer to the West.

How one assesses these numbers is a matter of perspective. Some analyses stress regional differences, usually without taking gasoline into account.6/ Other analyses go behind the averages to dwell on the fact that those households which do not heat or drive, or which have access to inexpensive fuel (natural gas), will spend a much smaller percentage of their income on direct energy consumption.

As stated in Chapter 2, we take a different view. These averages do not materialize from thin air. The typical lower income household does heat and does operate a vehicle, which it uses for basic daily activities. The averages indicate that a large number of lower income households are paying a very hefty portion of their income for direct energy consumption.

We are struck by the fact that even in the West, low income households were forced to devote almost 30 percent of their income to direct energy expenditures in 1979-80. We would prefer to stress this fact rather than the fact that those in the Northeast devoted almost 35 percent of their income to direct energy expenditures. It is important not to let the dramatic increase in the burden in the Northeast obscure the fact that the West, as well, bore a very heavy burden.

Moreover, it is important not to overlook the fact that lower middle income households devote almost twice as much of their income to energy as non-lower income households. Indeed, after a decade of rising energy prices, the lower middle class has been placed in the position that low income households were in before the energy price spiral began. In 1979, they were forced to devote almost as large a share of their income to direct energy expenditures as low income households did in 1972-73. In this sense, the lower middle class has been truly impoverished by rising energy prices.

6
The Loss of Purchasing Power
Suffered by Lower Income Households

As noted in Chapter 3, there was a massive transfer of wealth -- as much as $1.3 trillion -- underlying the large negative economic impacts from rising energy prices. With respect to the macroeconomic impacts, the gross size of the transfer is critical since it triggers economic losses. With respect to social impacts, the specific burden borne by various groups is of paramount importance. The analysis in Chapters 4 and 5 of the percent of income spent on energy really reflects two factors -- changing energy expenditures and changing income. From those analyses we know that low and lower middle income households suffered greatly. We know that they were on the losing end of the massive transfer of resources. Moreover, we can also estimate the aggregate loss of purchasing power suffered by the entire group of low and lower middle income households and compare that loss to offsetting transfer payments and energy assistance payments.

In this analysis, we focus on direct energy consumption expenditures because these are the least discretionary uses of energy. As we discussed earlier, direct energy consists of home energy and gasoline, which are specific commodities vital for maintaining health, safety, well-being, and daily activities. The low income household has cut back as far as possible on the direct consumption of energy for basic household uses and transportation, for which there are few substitutes. In contrast, indirect energy expenditures are spread across a wide range of goods and services. There is much more discretion in consumption and latitude for substitution -- i.e., there are greater possibilities for spreading the burden of increased prices.1/ Of course, insofar as energy price increases drive up the general rate of inflation, they impose a serious burden. It is direct energy expenditures, however, that constitute the major burden placed on lower income households. Moreover, the evidence

suggests that, if anything, indirect energy expenditures
compound the disproportionate burden on lower income
households.

ENERGY CONSUMPTION OF LOWER INCOME
GROUPS AS A PERCENTAGE OF THE TOTAL

Home energy consumption was analyzed in detail in
Chapter 4. Here we need only estimate the portion of
the total home energy bill paid by the low and lower
middle income population. Low income households
accounted for about 7.5 percent of all expenditures for
home energy in 1972-73. Their expenditures for electricity were much lower relative to the non-lower income
population than for the other sources of energy. By
1979-80, low income households accounted for a somewhat
larger percentage of all expenditures for home energy,
although still less, relative to the size of the group,
than any other income group. Again, their expenditures
for electricity were the lowest relative to the other
income groups, but they had increased significantly.2/
Lower middle income households accounted for about 15
percent of total home energy expenditures in 1972-73 and
1979-80.

As shown in Chapter 5, the distribution of private
transportation energy is quite different from the
distribution of home energy. The lower income group
accounted for about 3.9 percent of all gasoline
expenditures by households in 1972-73 and about 4.4
percent in 1979-80. As argued earlier, we believe that
the evidence strongly supports the notion that the
little gasoline they do consume is a necessity. The
lower middle income groups accounted for about 11.7
percent of all expenditures for gasoline in 1972-73.
There would appear to be a slight downward trend in
their expenditures as a share of the total from 1972-73
to 1979-80.

Before we make the estimates of lost purchasing
power, a note on indirect energy expenditures will be
helpful. We have seen in great detail that direct
energy consumption places a disproportionate burden on
lower income households. But what about indirect energy
consumption? The part of the total energy supply which
is not consumed directly by households is consumed
indirectly. It is used to produce goods and services
and, in essence, is consumed when those goods and
services are consumed. It is paid for in the price of
the goods and services. Because upper income households
consume so much more goods and services in general, and
therefore so much more indirect energy, the case is
frequently made that the consumption of indirect energy
is a factor that balances out the relative burden placed
on various income groups by rising energy prices.

Estimates of the indirect energy consumption of
households are extremely scarce. Such estimates require
a precise specification of the goods and services
consumed by individual households and a careful
estimation of the amount of energy embodied in each good
or service. Clearly, any effort to estimate these
quantities will lead only to rough estimates of indirect
energy consumption.

The available estimates are based on the 1972-73
Consumer Expenditure Survey. They show that indirect
energy expenditures are at best proportionate and might
even be slightly regressive. That is, expressed as a
percentage of income, indirect energy expenditures
probably place a slightly higher burden on lower income
households.3/

AGGREGATE LOSSES OF PURCHASING POWER

In order to estimate the loss of purchasing power
suffered by low and lower middle income households, we
must combine the above shares of total energy expenditures with an estimate of the total loss of purchasing
power by consumers. For the purposes of this analysis,
we have calculated the total loss of purchasing power
with respect to the base year of 1972. We measure lost
purchasing power as well as offsetting transfer payments, energy assistance funds, and changes in income in
current dollars, primarily because, as we show later,
the standard deflators used to estimate constant dollars
(the Consumer Price Index) can be misleading.4/

Table 6.1 shows the calculation of lost purchasing
power for the low income population, while Table 6.2
shows the calculation for the lower middle income group.
From 1973 to 1979, households in the low income category
lost approximately $17 billion due to rising energy
prices. Of this, about $11 billion was due to home
energy prices and $6 billion due to gasoline. In the
lower middle income category, the loss was $36 billion
total: $19 billion for home energy and $17 billion for
gasoline.

Tables 6.1 and 6.2 also show the losses of purchasing power for 1980 and 1981. These estimates are
based on the assumption that the trends in the share of
consumption of the low and lower middle income households continued. The losses escalated dramatically in
1980-81, totalling $17 billion for low income households
and $30 billion for lower middle income households. In
each case slightly more than half of the loss in purchasing power was due to home energy price increases.

OFFSETTING TRANSFER PAYMENTS

As discussed in Chapter 2, rising energy prices have

TABLE 6.1
Loss of Purchasing Power by the Low Income Population (Billions of Dollars)

	1972	1973	1974	1975	1976	1977	1978	1979	1980	1981
Gasoline										
Low Income Expenditures as a Percent of Total Expenditures[a]	4.0	4.0	4.0	4.1	4.1	4.2	4.3	4.4	4.4	4.4
Loss of Purchasing Power[b]	—	.18	.62	.77	.88	1.65	1.15	1.97	3.73	3.39
Home Energy										
Natural Gas										
Low Income Expenditures as a Percent of Total Expenditures[a]	8	8.6	9.1	9.7	10.2	10.8	11.3	11.9	12.5	13.1
Loss of Purchasing Power[b]	—	-.04	.04	.18	.35	.57	.80	1.21	1.66	2.68
Electricity										
Low Income Expenditures as a Percent of Total Expenditures[a]	3.9	4.5	5.2	5.8	6.4	7.0	7.7	8.3	8.9	9.5
Loss of Purchasing Power[b]	—	.07	.26	.43	.57	.80	1.06	1.35	1.98	2.71
Fuel Oil										
Low Income Expenditures as a Percent of Total Expenditures[a]	8.3	8.6	9.0	9.3	9.7	10.0	10.3	10.7	11.1	11.4
Loss of Purchasing Power[b]	—	.14	.27	.32	.41	.52	.59	.68	.91	1.25
TOTAL LOST PURCHASING POWER	—	.35	1.49	1.52	2.21	2.94	3.60	5.21	7.58	9.44

a 1972 percentages from U.S. Bureau of Labor Statistics, Consumer Expenditure Survey: Interview Survey, 1972-73 Average Annual Income and Expenditures for Commodity and Service Groups Classified by Family Characteristics, Report 455-4 (Washington, D.C.: 1977), Table 1. 1973 to 1978 percentages are interpolated. 1979 and 1980 percentages from U.S. Department of Energy, Residential Energy Consumption Survey: 1979-1980 Consumption and Expenditures, Part 1: National Data (Washington, D.C.: April 1981), Table 1; Consumption Patterns of Household Vehicles, June 1979 to December 1980 (Washington, D.C.: April 1982), Tables 17, 18. 1981 percentages are linear extrapolations.

b See Methodological Appendix, Section 2.

TABLE 6.2
Loss of Purchasing Power by the Lower Middle Income Population (Billions of Dollars)

	1972	1973	1974	1975	1976	1977	1978	1979	1980	1981
Gasoline										
Lower Middle Income Expenditures as a Percent of Total Expenditures[a]	11.7	11.5	11.3	11.1	11.0	10.8	10.6	10.4	10.2	10.0
Lost Purchasing Power[b]	-	.53	1.75	2.08	2.35	2.71	2.82	4.65	7.01	7.72
Home Energy										
Natural Gas										
Lower Middle Income Expenditures as a Percent of Total Expenditures[a]	16.9	16.8	16.7	16.6	16.5	16.4	16.4	16.3	16.2	16.1
Lost Purchasing Power[b]	-	.08	.07	.30	.56	.86	1.16	1.66	2.15	2.56
Electricity										
Lower Middle Income Expenditures as a Percent of Total Expenditures[a]	14.6	14.5	14.4	14.3	14.2	14.1	14.0	13.8	13.7	13.6
Lost Purchasing Power[b]	-	.24	.71	1.05	1.27	1.63	1.93	2.24	3.06	3.89
Fuel Oil										
Lower Middle Income Expenditures as a Percent of Total Expenditures[a]	16.0	16.0	16.1	16.1	16.2	16.2	16.3	16.3	16.3	16.4
Lost Purchasing Power[b]	-	.30	.54	.64	.81	.98	1.06	1.27	1.76	2.16
TOTAL LOST PURCHASING POWER	-	1.15	3.07	4.07	4.99	6.18	6.97	9.82	13.98	16.33

a 1972 percentages from U.S. Bureau of Labor Statistics, Consumer Expenditure Survey: Interview Survey, 1972-73 Average Annual Income and Expenditures for Commodity and Service Groups Classified by Family Characteristics, Report 455-4 (Washington, D.C.: 1977), Table 1. 1973 to 1978 percentages are interpolated. 1979 and 1980 percentages from U.S. Department of Energy, Residential Energy Consumption Survey: 1979-1980 Consumption and Expenditures, Part 1: National Data (Washington, D.C.: April 1981), Table 1; Consumption Patterns of Household Vehicles, June 1979 to December 1980 (Washington, D.C.: April 1982), Tables 17, 18. 1981 percentages are linear extrapolations.

b See Methodological Appendix, Section 2.

been recognized as a major social problem. Some efforts have been made to offset the burden that they place on low and lower middle income households. This section examines the magnitude of those efforts relative to the loss of purchasing power.

The most explicit recognition of the burden that rising energy prices placed on lower income Americans came in the form of energy assistance. Such assistance takes two forms -- funds to defray the cost of heating and cooling energy and the provision of goods and services to provide more heat and comfort (i.e., weatherization of homes, space heaters, blankets, and warm clothing). Through the early part of the 1970s, assistance programs were small.5/ Between 1973 and 1976, a total of about $250 million was spent. In 1977 and 1978, about $300 million was spent in each year and in 1979 about $400 million was spent.

In 1980, spurred by funds from the Crude Oil Windfall Profit Tax Act and by the second oil price shock, assistance funds increased sharply. In 1980, about $1.8 billion was appropriated and in 1981 and 1982 about $2 billion was appropriated per year.

These programs have generally been operated in conjunction with other assistance programs, using similar income limitations. Thus, recipients of certain other public assistance benefits (e.g., Supplemental Social Insurance or Food Stamps) qualify automatically, while others who apply on a case-by-case basis can receive benefits if they meet the income guidelines (usually 125 percent of the OMB poverty level). In general, the assistance programs appear to have reached about half the eligible households, which is typical of most welfare programs. Payment levels vary widely from state to state, but they generally cover less than one-sixth of the annual home energy bills of the typical low income household. Weatherization services have been provided to less than 5 percent of the low income households (assuming that 125 percent of OMB poverty level income is the cutoff).

The general inadequacy of these payments and programs can be seen by comparing the aggregate appropriations with the loss of purchasing power. The aggregate loss of purchasing power by low and lower middle income households was about $100 billion, as shown in Tables 6.1 and 6.2, dwarfing the $7 billion in energy assistance. Even if we focus on the loss of purchasing power due to home energy expenditures, the inadequacy of transfers is striking. Against a loss of about $55 billion, these programs have delivered about $7 billion.

Energy assistance is not the only form of assistance that low and lower middle income households receive. It is frequently argued that any social accounting must factor in transfer payments (through general income

maintenance programs) which take place as a result of
rising energy prices. The argument is occasionally
carried so far as to suggest that general income
maintenance programs are adequate to offset the burden
of rising energy prices. However, using estimates of
the effect of rising energy prices on general income
transfer programs through the mechanism of inflation-
indexed payments, we will show that they have not come
close to alleviating the burden.

It is possible to make a fairly precise estimate of
the impact of rising energy prices on the magnitude of
inflation-indexed transfer payments. Using econometric
estimates of the effect on CPI of rising energy prices
(as discussed in Chapter 3), we can estimate the portion
of increased payments which is attributable to rising
energy prices. We can then estimate that part of the
energy-related increases which have been directed to low
and lower middle income households. These calculations
are summarized in Table 6.3.

The total inflation-indexed expenditure estimates
for the transfer payment programs are taken from an OMB
study of budget outlays.6/ The energy-induced inflation
figures are taken from a Department of Energy study on
the impact of rising energy prices on the economy.7/
The portion of each type of transfer payment going to
the low and lower middle income groups is taken from the
1972-73 Consumer Expenditure Survey.8/

Each set of estimates is subject to some uncer-
tainty. Even prior to formal indexing, some increase in
payments may have been induced by inflation. The estimate of inflation itself will vary somewhat from one
econometric model to another. Over the years since
1972-73, the share of transfer payments received by each
income group has probably changed somewhat. Nevertheless, for purposes of comparison with the estimate of
lost purchasing power, these estimates are more than
adequate. They certainly make it clear that losses of
purchasing power due to rising energy prices were 5 or 6
times greater than increases in income transfer payments
due to rising energy prices.

Between 1972 and 1979, the increase in inflation-
indexed transfer payments due to rising energy prices
totaled about $2.5 billion for the low income population
and about $4 billion for the lower middle income
population. These population groups experienced losses
of purchasing power of $17 billion and $36 billion,
respectively. In 1980 and 1981, transfer payment
increases due to rising energy prices for the low income
group were about $2 billion and those for the lower
middle income group were about $5 billion. These
transfers are compared to losses of purchasing power of
$16 billion and $30 billion, respectively.

TABLE 6.3
Inflation Indexed Transfer Payments (billions of dollars)

	SOCIAL SECURITY				GOVERNMENT RETIREMENT				WELFARE			
Year	Total	Total due to Energy	Paid to Low Income	Paid to Lower Middle Income	Total	Total due to Energy	Paid to Low Income	Paid to Lower Middle Income	Total	Total due to Energy	Paid to Low Income	Paid to Lower Middle Income
1973	-	-	-	-	9.9	.025	.001	.005	3.6	.009	.003	.004
1974	-	-	-	-	11.7	.374	.017	.066	4.4	.141	.044	.068
1975	70.8	1.70	.304	.658	14.2	.341	.011	.063	6.6	.158	.056	.076
1976	80.6	1.61	.289	.623	16.5	.330	.015	.061	8.0	.160	.056	.077
1977	92.3	1.29	.231	.499	18.7	.262	.012	.049	8.5	.119	.038	.057
1978	101.0	.61	.109	.236	21.0	.126	.006	.023	8.7	.053	.017	.026
1979	122.3	2.45	.432	.948	28.8	.576	.026	.107	10.7	.214	.067	.103
1980	128.2	5.90	1.060	2.280	30.2	1.389	.063	.258	13.3	.612	.193	.296
1981	150.9	3.47	.621	1.340	35.2	.810	.036	.151	15.1	.347	.110	.168

Source: See text.

AN AGGREGATE ACCOUNTING

It is obvious from the previous two sections that transfer payments linked directly and indirectly to rising energy prices have fallen far short of compensating for losses in purchasing power. With, at most, $21 billion in transfer payments -- general and energy assistance -- and $100 billion in lost purchasing power suffered by low and lower middle income households, the net loss is roughly $80 billion.

It goes without saying that this figure represents a major loss of purchasing power. Yet, remarkably, the notion still seems to persist that low and lower middle income households have somehow done better than non-lower income households, due to the fact that part of their income is indexed to inflation. Is it possible that when one moves away from a strict concern with energy, as reflected in the above calculations, and looks at all elements of income and all elements of the cost of living, that lower income households somehow came out better than non-lower income households? The answer is decidedly negative.

In fact, only a small part of the income of the low and lower middle income groups is indexed. That part of their income which is indexed to inflation has not kept up with their true cost of living. Moreover, that part which is not indexed has lagged far behind. As a result, these income groups have suffered an erosion of real, aggregate purchasing power that has been much larger than the loss of purchasing power suffered by non-lower income groups.

In Table 6.4 we show the income and earnings for households that are recipients of Aid to Families with Dependent Children (AFDC), Social Security, and Supplementary Social Insurance, relative to the total income and earnings for non-recipient households. In every category except female-headed AFDC households, the recipient group lost ground compared to non-recipient households. The largest relative decline was for single person households receiving Social Security, where income for the average household declined from 82.2 percent of non-recipient income to only 65.3 percent.

In every category the critical factor was a loss of ground in earnings. If earnings had kept up, almost no ground would have been lost, except in the category of multi-person Social Security households. We would attribute the failure of earnings to keep pace to the weakness in the economy resulting from the energy price-induced recession discussed in Chapter 3.

A study prepared by the Bureau of Labor Statistics can be used to show the expenditure side difficulties.9/ As we discussed in Chapter 4, energy consumes a much larger part of the income of low and lower middle income

TABLE 6.4
Income and Earnings: Transfer Payment Recipients
Relative to all Non-Recipients

	Income		Earnings	
	1976	1980	1976	1980
Multi-person Households				
AFDC with Male Head	.577	.439	.408	.278
AFDC with Female Head	.303	.312	.120	.159
Supplemental Security Insurance	.595	.465	.369	.172
Social Security/RR Retirement	.724	.689	.263	.258
Single-person Households				
Supplemental Security Insurance	.382	.365	.222	.206
Social Security/RR Retirement	.822	.653	.472	.377

Source: U.S. Congressional Budget Office, _Indexing with the Consumer Price Index: Problems and Alternatives_ (Washington, D.C.: June 1981).

households than of non-lower income households. By 1979, energy was taking about three times as much out of the income of lower income households as the weight assigned to it in the CPI. A detailed analysis of the cost of living increase for retirees, who make up a large part of the lower income population, shows that between 1972 and 1980 (second quarter) their cost of living increased almost 6 percent more than the national average.10/ Rising energy prices were the single largest factor, accounting for about half of the increase above the national average. This estimate is based on the version of the index now generally considered the most accurate -- the rental equivalence approach soon to be implemented by the BLS.

Similarly, an analysis of increases in the cost of living for different income groups, as measured by the rental equivalence approach, shows that lower income groups had higher increases than upper income groups.

The cost of living for low and lower middle income
households increased about one percentage point more
than for non-lower income households, while the cost of
living for the elderly (as opposed to retirees)
increased by 4 percentage points more.

A study of the elderly which combines both inflation
factors and income factors shows that if earnings had
kept up, or the cost of living of the elderly had not
been higher than for the non-elderly, they would not
have lost ground.11/ The total real income of the
elderly increased relative to the non-elderly between
1970 and 1974 (see Table 6.5). It then declined
steadily, falling almost to the 1970 level by 1979. The
relative earnings of the elderly declined steadily over
the decade, while property income and transfer payments
rose between 1970 and 1974, then declined through 1977.

One way to summarize these effects is to examine
real purchasing power, taking energy expenditures,
inflation, and changes in income into account. How much
real purchasing power did households have left to spend

TABLE 6.5
Ratios of Income and Components of Income of the
Elderly to the Non-Elderly

(Adjusted for the Group Specific Increases in
the Cost of Living)

Year	Total Income	Earnings	Property Income	All Transfer Payments
1970	.491	.212	2.83	4.38
1974	.541	.192	2.93	4.41
1977	.539	.170	2.82	4.15
1979	.492	N.A.	N.A.	N.A.

Sources: Benjamin Bridges, Jr. and Michael D. Packard,
"Price and Income Changes for the Elderly,"
Social Security Bulletin, 44:1, January 1981,
for all years except 1979, which is calculated
from U.S. Bureau of the Census, Money Income
of Households in the United States: 1979
(Washington, D.C.: June 1981), Table 3.

after they paid their energy bills? As Table 6.6 indicates, a family at the mean of the low income category
in 1972-73 had almost 27 percent more purchasing power
after energy expenditures and inflation were taken into
account than a family at the mean of the low income
category in 1980. Increases in real energy costs
accounted for the entire loss in purchasing power.
Lower middle income households had lost about 20 percent
of their real purchasing power. About two-thirds of
this loss was due to rising energy prices. A family at
the mean of the non-lower income group had only 8 percent less purchasing power in 1980 compared to 1972-73
after inflation and energy expenditures were taken into
account. About two-thirds of the loss was due to rising
energy prices. The loss for the lower income households
has been much larger.12/

TABLE 6.6
Loss of Purchasing Power by Income Groups
(in 1972 Dollars)

Income Group	Real Purchasing Power after Energy Expenditures		Loss of Real Purchasing Power Due to Rising Energy Prices
	1972-73	1979-80	
Low Income	1,523	1,106	449
Lower Middle Income	4,659	3,713	605
Non-Lower Income	15,929	14,658	838

Source: See text.

Part 3

Rising Energy Prices and the
Lower Income Rental Housing Market

7
The Crisis in the Rental Housing Market and the Role of Energy Prices

In Part 2 we examined the direct effect of rising energy prices -- the huge bite that they have taken out of household budgets. Other social impact analyses have rarely looked beyond these impacts. We have chosen to go further and examine two indirect effects of rising energy prices on lower income households -- their impact on the rental housing market and on the delivery of local public services. These two areas have been chosen because they are of considerable importance to the lower income community and the impact of rising energy prices in these areas has created a disproportionately heavy burden on low and lower middle income households.

Part 3 examines the rental housing market. The lower income population is much more dependent on rental housing than the non-lower income population. For many lower income households, rising energy prices do not appear directly in energy bills, but rather in the form of rising rental costs, i.e., rising shelter costs. It is our hypothesis that rising energy prices have a dynamically negative impact on the rental housing inhabited by the low and lower middle income community. The ultimate cost of rising energy prices in deteriorating buildings and declining neighborhoods is larger than a simple increase in the energy bill.

In the past few years a lively debate has flared up among economists and policy analysts about the status of the rental housing market. Some argue that it is suffering through a major crisis in which rising costs are leading to a deterioration of the quality of the available housing stock.[1] Others argue that this is not the case at all.[2] Among those who see a crisis in the rental housing market, there are some who blame it on government intervention in the marketplace,[3] others who blame it on the failure of the government to intervene,[4] and still others who maintain that it simply reflects the natural workings of the marketplace and has little to do with government policies.[5]

117

We have undertaken to analyze the impact of rising energy prices on the rental housing market and, in the process, address several of the most important issues in the debate over the status of that market. We suggest that energy prices have played a critical role in the deterioration of the lower income rental housing market and we argue that prior analyses have not given adequate emphasis to this factor. In order to analyze the role of rising energy prices in the rental housing market and to contribute to the debate over conditions in the market, this chapter establishes the framework of our empirical analysis with a brief description of the "crisis" in the rental housing market, the different interpretations of its causes, and a specification of the role that we believe energy prices have played in creating the crisis.

THE CURRENT DEBATE OVER THE "CRISIS"
IN THE RENTAL HOUSING MARKET

The "crisis" of the rental housing market as defined in the current debate is depicted graphically in Figure 7.1. Rents have been rising faster than the income of renters, but slower than the operating costs of land-lords.6/ As a result, two forms of pressure on the rental housing market are created. First, the resources of tenants are squeezed -- as rents increase faster than incomes, they take a large share of the household budget, leaving households with fewer resources for the purchase of non-shelter goods and services. Second, the resources of landlords are squeezed -- as costs increase more rapidly than rents, profits decline, leading to a flight of capital out of the rental housing industry, which ends in a deterioration of the housing stock.

The Squeeze on Renters

There are two sets of disagreements about the above description of the rental housing market. First, some argue that it is partially incorrect.

To begin with, some analysts make the case that in a properly defined technical sense rents have not been inflating as fast as they seem to be.7/ If rising prices or inflation is defined as paying more for the same amount, or less, of a product, then it is possible to argue that rents have not inflated. If one looks at the quantity and quality of housing actually occupied, it can be argued that rent per unit of standard housing service is not increasing. In other words, some argue that the increase observed in average monthly gross rent is not caused by rent inflation, but rather by the fact that the average household is choosing to purchase more and better quality housing services. The average

FIGURE 7.1
Indices of Rent, Operating Costs, and
Tenant Income for Rental Housing

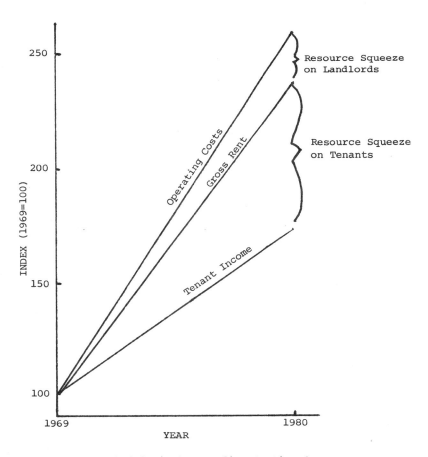

Source: See Methodological Appendix, Section 3.

household is living in a bigger unit with more
amenities. It is purchasing more and paying for it.
    Other analysts argue that, when carefully analyzed,
the income of the renter population is not lagging
behind rents by as much as it appears at first glance.8/
Instead, the composition of the renter population is
shifting. Over the past decade, the trend toward
smaller households (i.e., households with fewer
members), especially among renters, may mean that income
per household has lagged but income per person has not.
Moreover, the increase in home ownership over the past
decade may mean that, in the aggregate, the average
income of all renters has lagged because higher income
households have left the rental market. It does not
necessarily mean, however, that the income of any of the
households which continue to rent has failed to keep up.
That is, the households which continue to rent may have
gained ground, but the average income of all renters has
declined because the wealthiest renters have become
owners.
    Taken together, these two counter-arguments would
negate the first source of pressure on the rental
housing market. That is, the squeeze on tenant incomes
due to rising rents is reinterpreted to mean that a
different set of renters, i.e., those with lower (but
not declining) incomes, on average, are purchasing more
housing services.
    In the aggregate, there may be some merit to the
argument. Figure 7.2 shows an estimate of the change
between 1969 and 1980 in rent per room per person, and
the change in average income of the rental population,
estimated as if there had been no population shift.9/
It controls for the quantity of space consumed and for
the change in population. These modifications do
provide a significantly different picture. Instead of
rents increasing by 70 percentage points more than
incomes, they appear to increase by only 26 percentage
points more. The estimate of the apparent squeeze on
tenants is reduced by almost two-thirds of what it was
in Figure 7.1.

The Squeeze on Landlords

    The second dispute over the "crisis" in the rental
housing market deals with the second source of pressure,
i.e., the observation that operating costs have been
increasing faster than rents. No one disputes the fact
that operating costs have, indeed, been rising faster
than rents. The dispute is over the reason why rents
have failed to keep up with costs. The explanations
offered cover the full range of economic arguments
currently being discussed in policy analyses and they
have radically different implications for policy.

FIGURE 7.2
Indices of Rent per Room per Person and Tenant Income Standardized
for Population Shifts for Rental Housing

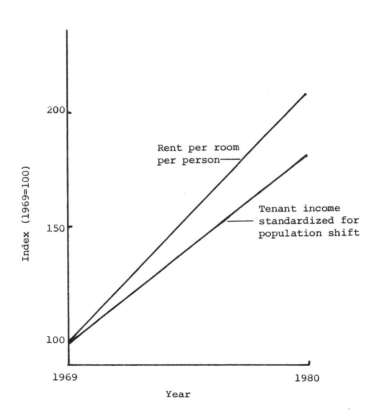

Source: See Methodological Appendix, Section 3.

For some analysts, government intervention in the marketplace is blamed -- including, but not limited to, rent control, zoning ordinances, and the perverse incentives created by welfare and public housing policies.10/ The obvious policy conclusion that results from this line of reasoning is for government to get out of the way and let the market work.

Other analysts believe that the market is working and that the pressure on profits is simply a function of excess supply (both in the aggregate and in specific regional markets). These have been created, in part, by the very attractive tax and capital gains advantages for home ownership as well as by shifts in the national economy.11/ For these analysts, the crisis is a painful, but inevitable, readjustment of supply and demand. From this perspective, the policy prescription is to do nothing. Or, if the outcome in the marketplace is deemed socially unacceptable, then the suggested policy response is to restore the general competitiveness of rental housing in capital markets by such measures as restoring the balance of tax treatment.

Still other analysts argue that the marketplace cannot work to provide adequate rental housing, especially for low income tenants. This argument can be made for either slack or tight market situations. In slack markets, the argument is that the limited availability of economic resources in the renter community and the geographic shift of economic activity (between center city and suburbs within regions and between frost-belt and sun-belt within the nation) have created large concentrations of deteriorating and vulnerable rental housing in deteriorating regions and cities.12/ Only specific government policies to support the rental housing market would make living conditions tolerable. In tight markets, the argument is that the response of the market to balance supply and demand is so slow and the market structure so imperfect that rent gouging will be inevitable.13/ Decent housing at a fair price is thus not available. In a sense, taken together, these two arguments suggest that there may be no circumstances, or very few, in which a sustained market equilibrium persists over a long period.

ENERGY AND THE PRIVATE RENTAL HOUSING MARKET

In the next chapter we demonstrate certain basic facts about conditions in the low income rental housing market and the role of rising energy prices in creating those conditions.14/ With respect to the first source of pressure on the rental housing market, we show that when the market is broken down into lower and non-lower income segments, the counter-arguments lose their force. In the next

123

chapter, we show that the lower income segment of the
market was, indeed, witnessing rent inflation that
cannot be explained as an increase in the quantity and
quality of housing services consumed. Further, we show
that the lag in incomes relative to rents cannot be
explained away by a shift in the low income rental
population. For the lower income population the gap is
large. It is not an illusion.

With respect to the second source of pressure on the
rental housing market, we document the impact that
rising energy prices have had on operating costs. We do
not explicitly address the issue of why rents have not
kept up.15/ However, it should be noted that the
earlier analyses in Chapters 3 and 6 have shown that
energy prices had an enormous, negative impact on the
economy as a whole and the incomes of the lower income
population, in particular. More than $100 billion in
lost purchasing power, with a greater than average loss
in colder climate zones, certainly imposed some
constraints on the ability of lower income households to
pay rent increases.

Moreover, we stress the fact that rising energy
prices had a dynamically negative effect on the lower
income rental housing market for three basic reasons. A
general constraint on economic resources in the tenant
community, the nature of landlord/tenant relations which
inhibits energy conservation investments, and the
response of landlords to rising energy prices all
compound the impact of energy price increases on the
rental market.

The Economic Constraint

If there is a general income constraint operating,
it can have an especially powerful effect on the lower
income rental market. The limited ability of a
community to meet the pressures of rent increases caused
by rapidly rising energy prices poses an overall threat
to the housing quality of the entire community.16/ For
example, the inability of a significant number of
tenants in a building to cope with rising costs can
ultimately affect the condition and value of the entire
building. Similarly, the deterioration of a number of
buildings in a neighborhood can ultimately affect the
condition and value of the entire neighborhood.

The critical factor is the general income constraint
shared by the members of the low and lower middle income
community or neighborhood. As rising energy prices, in
the form of rising rent, make housing unaffordable for
the general population of the community, landlords find
it more difficult to replace lost income. Uncollectables mount, but evictions lead to vacancies, not
replacement tenants, because those who can afford the

rent are hard to find. As individual units cease to
generate income, either because they are vacant or
because rents go uncollected, cutbacks in services may
occur. As a consequence, the value of all units -- not
just those which are actually in arrears -- is
reduced.17/

Landlord/Tenant Relations and
Energy Conservation Investment

This threatening economic condition is compounded by
the effect that landlord/tenant relations have on
conservation investments. It is less likely that the
pressure on the tenant community from rising energy
prices will be mitigated because conservation investments are less likely.18/
The difficulty of sharing the benefits of conservation between landlords and tenants may delay or forestall responses which would mitigate the impact of
energy price increases. On the one hand, capital
outlays to improve energy efficiency are not attractive
from the tenants' point of view, since tenants do not
own the building and are not likely to capture the full
stream of benefits. On the other hand, to the extent
that the full benefits of capital outlays are dependent
on tenant behaviors, landlords find such outlays less
compelling.
Thus, although landlords and tenants share an
interest in energy efficiency improvements, they may
have difficulty in negotiating an effective arrangement
which actually enables them to share the benefits and,
therefore, to proceed with the conservation investment.
This increases the pressure on resources available in
the tenant community by allowing valuable energy dollars
to fly out the window because practical and available
conservation measures are not employed.

Landlord Responses to Rising Energy Prices

As energy prices rise and place pressure on rental
markets, landlord responses may exacerbate the problem.
Two responses -- both rational from the landlord's point
of view but detrimental to the tenant community -- are
of special note.
First, the landlord has different, more
restricted options in responding to rising energy prices
than, for example, an owner-occupant. The owner-
occupant will spread the burden across different types
of consumption -- food, clothing, luxuries or housing.
The landlord must focus all of the response on
housing.19/ In a sense, the landlord will have to make
the building pay the full price of the rising energy
bill. If the price cannot be extracted from the

tenants, then the maintenance of the building will be made to pay the price. Faced with increasing vacancy rates or rising uncollectables, the landlord has little choice but to reduce operating costs. In this fashion the quality of the housing stock suffers.

Second, landlords probably apply different economic criteria to their decisions than the tenants or owner-occupants would. This is because the burden of rising energy costs does not weigh on them directly and their long range objectives will vary from those of tenants or owner-occupants.20/ In particular, given different opportunity costs of capital, landlords may maximize immediate cash flows by reducing operating costs. Similarly, they may minimize long-term risk by holding down capital outlays. As a consequence, properties will deteriorate faster. These responses may be entirely rational from the landlord's point of view. They would simply be maximizing different values than individual tenants would be likely to do.

Indeed, we stress the fact that the mounting financial pressure on the lower income rental market and the special problem that it creates for the tenant community is not determined by the good or bad intentions of landlords and tenants. Rather, it assumes only the presence of rational actors in a situation in which institutional arrangements and economic constraints combine to create and compound a social problem.

THE PUBLIC SECTOR RENTAL HOUSING MARKET

When analyzing the impact of rising energy prices on the lower income rental market, one must pay special attention to public housing. A significant part of the lower income population occupies public housing. Slightly more than 10 percent of those who are classified as poor participate in federal public housing programs. Moreover, those who participate in public housing tend to be in the lowest income categories. Among those with incomes below $7,000 in 1979, about one-fifth of all renters were in public housing programs. At higher levels of income, the participation rate declines sharply.

We will examine the impact of rising energy prices on the operating costs of public housing authorities (PHAs), which were dictated, in large part, by the financial structure of the PHAs.

Public housing authorities are local level independent entities which provide housing to lower income individuals with the aid of federal subsidies administered by the Department of Housing and Urban Development (HUD). Local tax dollars are generally not used in providing this housing. The PHAs, however, may

arrange to utilize such municipal public services as
police, fire, and sanitation, for which they pay a fixed
portion of the PHA rental income.21/
    The structure of public housing finances in the
1973-80 period should have limited the impact of rising
energy prices on individual PHA tenants. Beginning in
1970, the amount that PHA tenants could be charged for
housing, including utilities, was limited by federal law
to 25 percent of their income. When the cost of the
dwelling unit exceeded this 25 percent-of-income
ceiling, HUD was to make up the difference with an
operating subsidy to the PHA. This was in addition to
the capital subsidy HUD already provided to amortize the
property and physical plant.
    As long as HUD came through with the subsidies, PHAs
-- and therefore tenants -- were spared financial
difficulty.22/ However, the HUD subsidies grew rapidly
in the early 1970s, and, under pressure from Congress
and the Office of Management and Budget (OMB), HUD
developed a funding formula intended to hold down the
federal cost of public housing.

The Performance Funding System

    In 1975, HUD adopted a complex subsidy program
called the Performance Funding System (PFS). PFS was
intended to provide adequate subsidies to PHAs, but was
designed to offer incentives for prudent management.
That is, HUD -- or more precisely, OMB and Congress --
was not going to give PHAs a blank check for the
difference between rental income and operating
expenses.23/
    In essence, the PFS subsidy was designed to provide
funds at the level necessary for a "well-managed" PHA.
"Inefficient" PHAs were simply pressured to tighten
belts and improve management. The subsidy was adjusted
by an inflation factor each year and the subsidy base
was adjusted if a PHA's operating conditions changed.
    Thus, in its simplest form, PFS established an
allowable operating expense level for each year for each
PHA. A PHA would cover as much of the PFS allowable
expense level as it could through rental income. HUD
would then make up the difference with an operating
subsidy. The allowable operating expenses would be
projected in advance by the PHA under HUD guidelines and
the PHA would receive an advance subsidy based on such
projections.
    In theory, the HUD subsidies should be adequate to
prevent fiscal stress on PHAs, since they are intended
to cover any deficit between rental income and total
operating expenditures. But there are two reasons why
the subsidies may fail to prevent fiscal stress. First,
due to budget pressures, the estimated "allowable

expense levels" in the PFS subsidy program may simply be
too low. That is, even if HUD obtains the appropriations necessary to cover 100 percent of the PFS funding
needs of PHAs, the PFS estimates may systematically
understate certain costs for some PHAs. Second, very
rapid increases in operating costs can create cash flow
problems, which, if chronic, may have the same effect as
budget retrenchment. Because PFS is a forward funding
system involving cost projections (which are strictly
limited by HUD), repeated underprojections of costs can
accumulate into large deficits.

The Impact of Utility Cost Increases

The PFS guidelines treat utility and non-utility
costs separately. Until 1982, utility costs in public
housing were treated essentially as pass-throughs. HUD
adopted a historical utility consumption base for each
PHA and allowed the PHA to budget this base level of
consumption for the coming year at the prevailing
utility rates. If energy prices went up, HUD would
automatically cover any deficits caused by higher rates,
provided that consumption levels were within the base.
If the PHA used more (or less) energy than the base, HUD
and the PHA shared the added cost (or benefit).24/
Although PFS allowed an adjustment for increased
utility costs, payments for the utility cost adjustments
did not arrive until the next year's funding cycle.
This created the potential for cash flow problems.
Nevertheless, utility costs were virtually a complete
pass-through to HUD.
The non-utility expenses in PFS (e.g., maintenance
and administrative costs) were calculated from a complex
equation of cost components which were adjusted for
inflation based on estimates of local housing expenses
and wage factors (provided by the Bureau of Labor
Statistics). Unlike the utility component, the non-
utility expenses were not simple pass-throughs, but
imposed discipline on PHA management to hold down costs,
bargain hard on wage demands, and aggressively collect
rents. If the non-utility costs of operating a PHA rose
significantly more than rental income or the HUD subsidy
level, there was no mechanism for PHAs to appeal to HUD,
and no forthcoming adjustments to close the deficit.
The dual cost structure within PFS obligated HUD to
pay any deficits resulting from rising energy prices.
Therefore, utility cost increases could easily drive up
the entire PFS subsidy paid nationally by HUD. This, in
turn, would systematically increase the level of
appropriations HUD requested from Congress through OMB.
To the extent that HUD was pressured to hold down
spending -- or Congress refused to appropriate the full
amount HUD requested -- the only effective strategy for

holding down costs in PFS was to moderate the non-utility component. Under the PFS structure, utility costs could not be restricted.

This basic structural characteristic of the HUD subsidy formula means that the impact of utility cost increases will probably be reflected in non-utility areas or in general finances. That is, as utility costs skyrocketed, pressure would be exerted to hold down subsidies, which would also skyrocket. Because HUD was obligated to pay utility costs, budget cuts would have to be made in non-utility expenses. PHAs would be forced to either spend less on non-utility operating costs or allow their overall financial condition to deteriorate. In either case, tenants would lose service or quality of housing. If PHAs encounter a serious fiscal crisis, tenants could be faced with a loss of available units as the deterioration of these units makes them uninhabitable or as PHAs shift toward higher income households in order to increase rental income.

Thus, the critical points in the process may be slightly different (e.g., the point at which rent collections become inadequate) and the sequences may be slightly different (e.g., whether tax subsidies are explicit and exist before the financial crisis or implicit and exist after the crisis), but the net effect will be much the same in the public and private sectors -- a severe crisis in the lower income rental housing market.

8

An Assessment of the Impact of Rising Energy Prices on the Low Income Rental Housing Market

This chapter analyzes the impact of rising energy prices on the costs and quality of rental housing. The chapter has two objectives. First, we show that the rapid escalation of costs in the private and public sectors are similar. Second, evidence regarding the condition of housing in the lower and non-lower income segments of the rental market, which is almost entirely confined to the private sector, is presented to show that there is a crisis in the lower income housing market.

THE PRIVATE SECTOR

Energy Costs, Operating Costs, and Rents

Data on energy prices and operating costs of private sector rental housing are not plentiful or systematic. The HUD Annual Housing Survey and the regular decennial Census are the best available sources.1/ Because the data was not explicitly designed for analyses of costs such as those presented below, there are a number of problems in arriving at estimates. These are discussed in detail in Section 3 of the Methodological Appendix. Between 1969 and 1980, operating costs increased by about 10.7 percent per year in the public sector and about 9.1 percent in the private sector as a whole (see Table 8.1).2/ The available evidence suggests that the increase in operating costs in the lower income segment of the private sector was higher than the average for the private sector as a whole. This was the case after the 1973-74 energy price shock in large part because energy constitutes a larger component of the costs of operating lower income rental housing.3/ Since public sector housing tends to be lower income housing, this would account for the somewhat more rapid increase in operating costs in the public sector. The greater increase in gross rent (rent plus utilities) in the

130

TABLE 8.1
Percentage Increase in Operating Costs and Rents

Time Span	Operating Costs		Gross Rent[c]		
	Public Sector[a]	Private Sector[b]	Lower Income	National Average	Non-lower Income
1969-80	10.7	9.1	9.0	7.7	6.6
1973-80	11.5	9.9	9.0	7.6	6.6

[a] See Figure 8.1 below.
[b] David Scott Lindsay and Ira S. Lowry, Rent Inflation in St. Joseph County, Indiana, 1974-78 (Santa Monica, Cal.: The Rand Corporation, November 1980).
[c] See Methodological Appendix, Section 3.

lower income rental market is also an indication of the relative changes in operating costs. In both the 1969-80 and the 1973-80 periods, gross rents for lower income rental units increased about 2.5 percentage points per year more rapidly than for non-lower income units.4/

In order to estimate the role of energy prices in the private sector rental market, we must make two important estimates of which the reader should be aware -- the choice of a formula for operating ratios to derive operating costs from contract rents, and the estimate of energy costs as a percent of operating costs. The derivation of the estimates, which are based on a Rand Corporation study, is discussed in the Methodological Appendix, Section 3. They are rough estimates, but, as discussed in the Appendix, they are entirely consistent with the available various sources of data.

As Table 8.2 shows, almost $50 out of the $133 increase in average gross rent between 1969 and 1980 can be attributed to energy costs. Similarly, of the $108 increase in average gross rent between 1973 and 1980, we attribute about $49 to energy costs. This means that energy costs accounted for approximately 37 percent of the increase in gross rent between 1969 and 1973 and 46 percent in the period after the first energy price shock (1973-80). Similarly, we estimate that energy price increases accounted for about 39 percent of the increase

TABLE 8.2
Energy Costs in the Rental Housing Market
(in dollars unless otherwise specified)

Year	Gross Rent[a] (1)	Contract Rent[a] (2)	Operating Ratio[b] (3)	Operating Cost (4=2x3)	The Energy Proportion of Operating Costs[c] (5)	Landlord Energy Cost (6=4x5)	Tenant Energy Cost (7)	Total Energy Cost (8)
1969	108	89	.436	39	.14	5.5	19	24.5
1973	133	116	.484	56	.14	7.7	17	24.7
1980	241	203	.577	117	.31	36.3	38	74.3
Change								
1969-80	141	114		78		30.8	19	49.8
1973-80	108	87		61		28.6	21	49.4

[a] U.S. Department of Housing and Urban Development, Annual Housing Survey, selected years.

[b] Lowry operating ratio as percent of rental revenue multiplied by .9 to adjust for vacancy rates and uncollectibles.

[c] See Methodological Appendix, Section 3.

[d] See Methodological Appendix, Section 3.

in operating costs between 1969 and 1980 and 46 percent
in the 1973-80 period.5/
    The estimates enable us to comment directly on the
squeeze on landlord resources discussed in Chapter 7.
With energy costs increasing so rapidly, the rate of
increase in operating costs was pushed well above the
rate of increase in rent. The rate of increase in rent
was falling short of the rate of increase in operating
costs by about 3 percentage points per year and falling
short of the rate of increase in the general rate of
inflation by 1 percentage point per year. The squeeze
on landlords was thus very real. A slow but steady
erosion of the viability of the rental housing market
was taking place. Furthermore, as we stated earlier,
the impact of rising energy prices on the operating cost
and gross rents of lower income rental units has been
generally one-third greater than the national average,
because energy is a larger component of the gross rents
and operating costs of these units.6/

The Quantity and Quality of Housing Services

    Having demonstrated the cost pressures placed on the
lower income rental housing market as a result of rising
energy prices -- i.e., the squeeze on landlord resources
-- we now must ask whether those pressures translated
into a deterioration in the quality of housing and
significant pressures placed on tenant resources. This
is the true measure of the crisis. We must also look
closely at the quality and quantity of the housing stock
and the composition of the renter population to be sure
that the national average figures at different points in
time are not giving a misleading picture.
    Is there a crisis in the rental housing market after
all factors are taken into account? The answer is
simple. It depends on where you look and how you look.
If you look at national averages, you can explain away a
large part of the crisis by noting changes in quality
and quantity of housing and in the make-up of the
population. However, if you distinguish between the
lower income and non-lower income segments of the
market, you quickly discover that the crisis is much
more real in the lower income segment than in the
non-lower income segment.
    We begin with the question of the quantity of rental
housing consumed. Unfortunately, there is no complete
data series available for the square footage of rental
units. Therefore, as a proxy, we use the number of
rooms per person as a measure of the space occupied by
households.
    Over the period from 1973 to 1980, the national
average number of rooms per person in rental units has
increased from 1.62 to 1.72 (see Table 8.3). More rooms

TABLE 8.3
Indicators of Rental Housing Quantity

	Number of Households	Number of Rooms[b]	Number of Persons[c]	Rooms per Unit	Rooms per Person	Persons per Household
TOTAL						
1973	24,685	98,608	61,046	3.99	1.62	2.47
1980	27,556	110,531	64,207	4.01	1.72	2.33
LOWER INCOME[a]						
1973	11,979	44,675	25,844	3.73	1.73	2.16
1980	13,089	49,737	28,027	3.80	1.77	2.14
NON-LOWER INCOME[a]						
1973	12,706	53,933	35,202	4.24	1.53	2.77
1980	14,467	60,794	36,203	4.20	1.68	2.50

a Lower income is incomes less than $7,000 in 1973 and less than $10,000 in 1980.

b Number of rooms is estimated by assuming that all categories of 6 or more rooms as reported in the survey equals 6. In the 1973 data, the smallest category is 2 rooms or less. Therefore, we established the percentage of lower income households who live in two room units, using 1969 and 1980 Census data. The percentages were 63 and 62 percent, respectively. It is obvious, therefore, that the percentages are essentially constant across time and can realistically be used to estimate the total number of rooms in 1973.

c Number of persons is estimated by assuming the category of 6 or more persons as reported in the survey equals 6.

Sources: U.S. Department of Housing and Urban Development, Annual Housing Survey: 1973, Part C: Financial Characteristics of the Housing Inventory (Washington, D.C.: April 1976), Table A-1.

U.S. Department of Housing and Urban Development, Annual Housing Survey: 1980, Part C: Financial Characteristics of the Housing Inventory (Washington, D.C.: November 1981), Table A-1.

are definitely being occupied. However, when the
population is divided between lower income and non-lower
income groups, we discover that there has been almost no
change in the number of rooms per person in the lower
income group (1.73 to 1.77). It is the non-lower income
group that has increased its consumption of space as
measured by rooms per person (from 1.53 to 1.68). For
lower income households, there was a slight decrease in
the number of rooms per unit and a slight decrease in
the number of persons per household, to keep the number
of rooms per person relatively constant. For non-lower
income households, a large decrease in the number of
persons per household led to a large increase in the
number of rooms per person.7/ Thus, an increase in the
quantity of space consumed by lower income households
(as measured by rooms per person) can explain very
little of the increase in rents paid by lower income
households.

The picture with respect to the quality of housing
services consumed is less clear (see Table 8.4). Lower
income households are apparently receiving more amenities for their rent. Fewer of them lacked plumbing,
complete private kitchens, or bathroom facilities in
1980 than in 1973. However, the rate of increase in the
provision of these amenities did slow considerably after
1973 compared to the 1959-73 period.8/ In the non-lower
income group, there was little change in the amenities
provided.

The situation with respect to the condition of
housing is quite different. Lower income renters
suffered a significant decline in the condition of their
housing.9/ Almost every indicator shows an increase in
the percent of households reporting deficient conditions. More lower income households are reporting
cracks in their walls, peeling paint, broken plaster,
and holes in their floors. For the non-lower income
group, two of the three indicators show improvement
rather than deterioration. The deterioration comes in
the category of peeling paint or cracked plaster, while
the improvement comes in the more serious conditions of
cracks or holes in walls, ceilings, and floors.

With respect to neighborhood quality, all of the
indicators show a deterioration for both the lower and
the non-lower income groups. Both income groups report
an increase in abandoned buildings on their streets,
litter in the streets, and streets in need of repair.
However, the deterioration suffered by the lower income
groups is much larger -- on average, about twice as
large.

The picture of the housing stock we get by distinguishing the lower from the non-lower income group
clearly suggests that the greater increase in rent paid
by the lower income population cannot easily be

TABLE 8.4
Indicators of Housing Quality (Percent of Households)

| | OWNERS | | | | RENTERS | | | | ALL | | | |
| | Lower Income | | Non-lower Income | | Lower Income | | Non-lower Income | | Lower Income | | Non-lower Income | |
	1973	1979-80	1973	1979-80	1973	1979-80	1973	1979-80	1973	1979-80	1973	1979-80
RESIDENTIAL AMENITIES												
Lacking Complete Private Bath	7.0	4.5	1.2	1.0	11.3	6.7	1.9	2.0	9.1	5.6	1.4	1.3
Lacking Complete Private Kitchen	3.0	2.0	.3	.5	6.6	4.7	1.4	1.7	4.7	3.4	1.6	.8
Lacking Complete Plumbing	6.3	4.0	.7	.7	10.1	6.0	1.8	1.4	8.1	5.0	1.0	.9
Percent in Housing 30 Years Old or Older[a]	48.9	48.9	29.3	31.2	55.9	56.2	44.7	43.3	52.1	52.5	34.2	34.4
RESIDENTIAL CONDITIONS												
Walls and Ceilings Cracks or Holes	4.9	4.4	2.4	2.3	13.6	13.8	9.1	8.2	9.0	9.3	4.3	3.9
Broken Plaster/ Peeling Paint	3.9	6.7	2.3	3.4	9.4	18.9	6.9	10.8	6.5	12.9	3.6	5.4
Holes in Floors	1.9	1.7	.6	.6	5.0	5.7	2.4	2.6	3.4	3.8	1.1	1.1
NEIGHBORHOOD CONDITIONS												
Abandoned Buildings	6.3	4.2	4.4	2.1	8.5	13.8	6.3	8.2	7.4	7.6	4.9	2.7
Litter	12.8	17.5	10.3	13.9	16.1	24.9	13.3	17.0	14.4	22.9	11.2	20.1
Streets need Repair	16.6	24.6	14.5	20.8	12.8	21.3	11.7	18.2	14.8	21.4	13.7	14.7

a In this category only, there is 1970 rather than 1973 data, as the latter is not available.

136

TABLE 8.4 (cont'd)

Sources: U.S. Department of Housing and Urban Development, Annual Housing Survey: 1973, Part C: Financial Characteristics of the Housing Inventory (Washington, D.C.: April 1976), Table A-1.

U.S. Department of Housing and Urban Development, Annual Housing Survey: 1973, Number 1: Financial Characteristics by Indicators of Housing and Neighborhood Quality (Washington, D.C.: March 1976), Tables 2, 4.

U.S. Bureau of the Census, Census of Housing: 1970, HC 7-4 (Washington, D.C.: 1973), Table A-1.

U.S. Department of Housing and Urban Development, Annual Housing Survey: 1979, Part B: Indicators of Housing and Neighborhood Quality by Financial Characteristics (Washington, D.C.: February 1982), Tables B-3, C-3, D-3, E-3.

U.S. Department of Housing and Urban Development, Annual Housing Survey: 1980, Part C: Financial Characteristics of the Housing Inventory (Washington, D.C.: November 1981), Tables B-1, C-1, D-1, E-1.

attributed to the increase in the quality and quantity
of housing services consumed. For the non-lower income
population, the quantity of housing services consumed
could be an important explanatory factor.

More importantly, perhaps, we see a striking picture
of the decaying residential environment of renters, in
general, and lower income renters, in particular.
Between 1973 and 1980, there was about a 10 percentage
point increase in the number of lower income renters
reporting broken plaster or peeling paint on the walls,
litter in the streets, and streets in need of repair.
In 1979-80, one out of every four or five lower income
renters was reporting these conditions. In addition,
one out of every seven lower income renters was
reporting cracks and holes in their walls and abandoned
buildings on their streets.

Non-lower income renters reported problems with the
conditions of their residences and their neighborhood
about one-third less frequently than lower income
renters. Owners reported far fewer problems with the
condition of their residences. They also reported far
fewer abandoned buildings and less litter, but did
report equal problems with streets in need of repair.
One can certainly conclude from this evidence that a
serious deterioration in the housing stock of lower
income rental households occurred in the period when
energy prices were driving up costs.

Examination of regional data only reinforces this
conclusion. The incidence of the problems in the
condition of housing, as well as the rate of deterioration over the period since the first energy price
shock, has been greatest in the colder climate zones of
the Northeast and North Central regions. Utility price
increases for renters have been highest in these regions
and increases in contract rents have been lowest. These
data certainly support our hypothesis that rising energy
prices simultaneously placed a squeeze on renters by
raising their bills and on landlords by putting a lid on
the increases in contract rents they could achieve,
although they do not rule out the possibility that other
factors contributed to this pattern as well.

Population Dynamics

The second set of factors used to explain away the
crisis in the rental housing market deals with the
make-up of the population. As noted in Chapter 7, rents
increased much more rapidly than the median income of
the rental household. Whereas rents increased by about
10 percent per year between 1973 and 1980, the median
income of renters increased only 5.7 percent per year.
This leads to the assertion that tenant incomes were
being squeezed. The counter-argument put forward is

that a shift in the make-up of the population (rather
than the failure of the incomes of individual households
to keep up) accounts for the apparent lag in the income
of renters. The shift in the make-up of the population
is attributed partly to the fact that wealthier households escaped the rental market in the 1970s and partly
to a change in the general make-up of all households.

If this counter-explanation holds, it would not
explain away the part of the rental housing crisis that
deals with landlords -- not as defined above. The
flight of wealthier families from the rental market
would mean, from the landlords' point of view, that the
rental housing market is less attractive. The economic
resources available in it would be declining and the
market would be deteriorating. This explanation would
be targeted at explaining away the apparent squeeze on
renters. The resources of the renters who remain in the
market are not more strained than they have been in the
past. Rather, the mix of renters has shifted so that
fewer of those who are less strained remain in the
market.

When we examine the make-up of the renter population, we discover that the changing composition of the
lower and non-lower income groups differs dramatically.

First, the lower income group has not increased its
rate of home ownership. Actually, the percentage of
renter-occupied households in the bottom third of the
income distribution increased from 48 percent in 1973 to
51.6 percent in 1979. In contrast, the percentage of
non-lower income households who rent decreased from 28.6
percent in 1973 to 26.4 percent in 1979. Thus, while
there would appear to be some basis to suppose that the
higher income households were escaping the rental
housing market, there is no basis for assuming the same
process was altering the make-up of the lower income
rental group.

Moreover, the number of persons per household
declined more for the non-lower income population than
for the lower income population. Table 8.3 shows that
the number of persons per household has declined much
more rapidly in the non-lower income group (from 2.77 to
2.50) than the lower income groups (from 2.16 to 2.14).
Since most survey data report income on a per household
basis, this means that the apparent decline in income in
most data is overstated. That is, household income is
being spread over fewer persons. The overstatement is
much larger for the non-lower income households than for
lower income households.

Finally, both the lower and the non-lower income
groups did undergo a change in composition. Among lower
income renters, the most notable change is a decline in
husband and wife multi-person households (HWMP) with the
head under 65 years of age and a rise in female-headed

multi-person households (FHMP) with the head under 65.
Insofar as the median income for the FHMP was half the
median income of the HWMP, this could constitute an
important change in the population.

Among the non-lower income rental households, the
most dramatic changes were a decline in HWMP with the
head under 65 years of age, a rise in single-person
households (SP) with the head under 65 and a rise in
FHMP with the head under 65. This, too, could
constitute a significant shift since the median incomes
of the latter two are half that of the former. The
shift in the composition of households is much larger,
however, for the non-lower income group.

Thus, a shift in the composition of the renter
population might be a factor that tends to make the
crisis of rental housing look worse than it is, but the
magnitude of these shifts probably cannot explain the
failure of incomes to keep up with rent -- especially in
the lower income market.

Estimates of the actual magnitude of the rent
increase relative to the change in incomes, adjusted for
the size and composition of households, are necessarily
very rough. Between 1973 and 1980, gross rent per room
per person appears to have increased by 8.8 percent per
year for the lower income renter population and 4.3
percent per year for the non-lower income renter popula-
tion.10/ Income per person appears to have increased
about 5.3 percent per year for the lower income renter
population compared to a national average for the renter
population of 6.6 percent.11/ Thus, the rent per unit
of space (measured by rooms) for lower income households
increased about 3.5 percentage points per year faster
than did income. For non-lower income households, rent
per unit of space increased about 2.3 percentage points
slower than income. If income per person is calculated
holding household type constant, it appears that the
income of lower income renter households increased 7.1
percent per year, whereas it increased for non-lower
income households by at least 7.5 percent per year.
Rent increases for lower income households still exceed
the increase in income by 1.7 percentage points per
year, while the rent increases for the non-lower income
households lagged the increase in income by 3.1
percentage points.

A more precise and more telling piece of evidence
with respect to the burden of shelter costs is a
calculation of the percentage of the population which is
devoting a large share of its income to shelter costs.
For example, a rent-to-income ceiling of 25 percent was
set by Congress for public housing, since this figure
frequently is assumed to represent a reasonably bearable
burden for shelter costs. Table 8.5 shows the percentage of households in the lower and non-lower income

140

groups whose gross rent was 35 percent or more of
income. For 1980 it also separates those whose rent was
more than 50 percent of income. It includes data on the
population within metropolitan areas, as well as the
entire population of the U.S.

TABLE 8.5
Percent of Households Paying 35 Percent or More
of Their Income for Rent

	All U.S.		Metropolitan Areas Only	
Year	Lower	Non-Lower	Lower	Non-Lower
1959	N/A	N/A	46.1	1.4
1973	50.0	2.0	53.3	2.2
1980	63.7	7.6	65.9	7.9
50 percent or more	51.0	1.4	43.2	1.6

Sources: U.S. Bureau of the Census, Census of Housing:
1960, HC 1-1: United States Summary
(Washington, D.C.).

U.S. Department of Housing and Urban Develop-
ment, Annual Housing Survey: 1973, Part C:
Financial Characteristics of the Housing
Inventory (Washington: D.C.: April 1976),
Table A-1.

U.S. Department of Housing and Urban Devel-
opment, Annual Housing Survey: 1980, Part C:
Financial Characteristics of the Housing
Inventory (Washington, D.C.: November 1981),
Table A-1.

The table shows a dramatic deterioration of the
income of lower income households relative to their
shelter costs, for the metropolitan population. In
1959, 46.1 percent of lower income households in
metropolitan areas spent 35 percent or more of their
income on rent. In 1973, 53.3 percent of the lower

income population in metropolitan areas spent 35 percent
or more of their income on shelter costs. Between 1973
and 1980, the percentage of families in metropolitan
areas devoting 35 percent or more of income to shelter
costs had jumped to 65.9. In 1980, 43.2 percent of the
lower income population was devoting 50 percent or more
of its income to shelter costs.12/

In contrast, only 7.9 percent of the non-lower
income metropolitan population was devoting more than 35
percent of its income to shelter costs in 1980. Only
1.6 percent was devoting more than 50 percent of its
income to shelter costs. The percentage of the lower
income rental population devoting 50 percent or more of
its income to shelter costs was more than 25 times as
large as the percentage of the non-lower income rental
population doing so.

The available estimates of the percentage of income
spent on shelter costs in all areas cover only the
1973-80 period. However, they are very close to those
for the metropolitan areas. It is clear that the jump
in shelter costs after 1973 was very large.

With gross rents taking such a huge part of the
income of the lower income group, there can be little
doubt that the economic resources of the lower income
community have been severely strained. The biggest jump
in the burden of gross rent came between 1973 and 1980
and, as we have seen, the single largest factor in the
increase in gross rents during that period was energy
price increases.

In short, the evidence is overwhelmingly clear.
There is a crisis in the rental housing market, but it
is concentrated in the lower income segment of the
market. The crisis became decidedly worse after the
1973 energy price shock. There is no doubt that energy
prices were a major factor contributing to the crisis
and to the deterioration of conditions in the market.
Whatever other factors may be playing a part, and there
may be many, energy prices must be seen as one of, if
not the, leading factor.

THE PUBLIC SECTOR

Comprehensive data on the finances of PHAs are
available for the period 1969-78 in a study conducted
for HUD by Abt Associates. Abt collected data on a
sample of 368 PHAs, selected to approximate the size
distribution of all PHAs, and weighted the sample
according to the number of rented units in each
authority. Unfortunately, this data set does not cover
the second oil price shock (1978-80). Although HUD
maintains a number of more recent national aggregate
data sets, none is a statistically sound sample entirely
adequate for this analysis.13/ In order to capture the

second oil price shock (1978-80) in the analysis, we
have estimated annual price escalators for later years
and used them to extrapolate data from the last year for
which sound statistics are available.14/

Expenditures

The three major operating costs of PHAs are utilities, maintenance, and general and administrative (G&A).
Using HUD cost inflators for 1979-81, we see that between 1969 and 1981 the average cost of providing public
housing per unit per month (PUM) tripled in nominal
terms (see Table 8.6) and increased 30 percent in constant 1969 dollars (see Figure 8.1). A simple breakdown
of expenditures makes it very clear that utility costs
are the driving force behind these increases.

TABLE 8.6
Expenditure Levels for Major Components of Total PHA
Operating Expenditures (Current Dollars PUM)

	1969[a]	1971[a]	1975[a]	1978[a]	1980[b]	Increase 1969-80
TOTAL	40.39	48.40	66.73	92.44	123.83	83.44
Administra- tion[c]	13.07	16.02	19.51	26.45	34.28	21.21
Utilities	12.31	14.70	23.87	34.43	46.72	34.41
Maintenance	12.10	14.50	18.94	24.83	35.14	23.04

Note: Numbers will not add due to minor omissions.

[a] Abt Associates, "Evaluation of the Performance
Funding System" (Cambridge, Mass.: May 1980), Table
2-8.
[b] See text.
[c] Including general expense.

Utility expenditures have increased by a factor of
nearly four, which is nearly double the rate of
non-utility costs. In constant dollars, non-utility

FIGURE 8.1
PHA Utility and Non-Utility Expenditures (constant 1969 dollars)

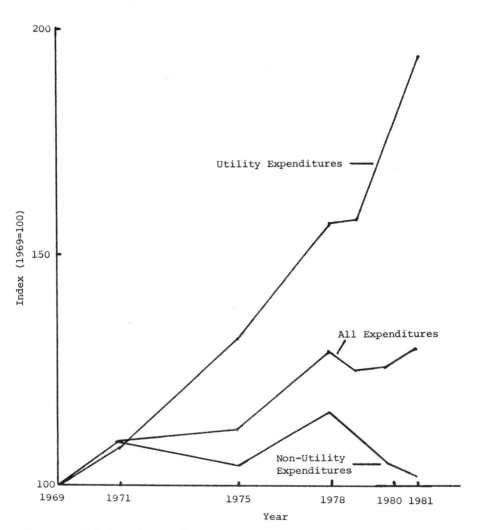

Source: Abt Associates, "Evaluation of the Performance Funding System,"
draft prepared for the U.S. Department of Housing and Urban
Development (Cambridge, MA: July 1981).

Cost escalators for the period 1978-81 provided by the U.S.
Department of Housing and Urban Development.

144

expenditures declined during two periods -- 1971-75 and
1978-81 -- when the major oil price shocks occurred.
    Unless one assumes that sudden bursts of efficiency
improvements to reduce non-utility costs -- without
reducing service -- just happened to take place at
exactly the moment that the oil shocks occurred, the
pattern suggests an erosion of service caused at least
indirectly by rising utility costs.
    Utility costs surpassed general and administrative
costs as the single largest expense in the wake of the
1973-75 oil price shock. In constant 1969 dollars,
utility costs were $12.31/PUM in 1969 (30 percent of
total expenditures), G&A was $13.07/PUM (32 percent of
expenditures), and maintenance was $12.10/PUM (30
percent of expenditure). By 1981, utility costs had
almost doubled in real terms to $23.96/PUM, or nearly 41
percent of total expenditures. G&A remained at
$13.05/PUM (25 percent of the total) and maintenance
held at $12.25/PUM (35 percent of the total). Thus, the
30 percent real increase in overall expenditures is
almost entirely due to utility increases, while non-
utility expenditures have held nearly constant. In
current dollar terms, about 45 percent of the total
increase in operating expenditures is due to rising
energy prices.
    It is important to note the close connection between
declines in non-utility expenditures and the two energy
price shocks. Between 1971 and 1975, G&A and maintenance expenditures declined 8 and 2 percent (real),
respectively. Likewise, between 1978 and 1981, G&A and
maintenance expenditures both fell approximately 12 percent in real terms. These were the periods of the most
intensive energy price increases.

Revenues

    PHA revenues have increased at roughly the same rate
as expenditures. That is, PHAs have not, in the
aggregate, run deficits. The most striking trend in the
1969-78 period is clearly the increased dependence of
PHAs on HUD subsidies. Figure 8.2 shows a major real
decline in locally-generated revenue, primarily rent,
which fell from $46.01 to $35.42/PUM during the period.
Part of this trend resulted from the introduction of HUD
operating subsidies in 1970. Until 1970 there was
virtually no HUD subsidy, so, to remain solvent, PHAs
had to collect almost 100 percent of their revenue from
local rental income. The imposition of a limit on
tenant rent payments would have caused a drop in
locally-generated revenue between 1969 and 1971. All
other things being equal, however, the local share
should have stabilized after the initial drop, albeit at
a lower percentage of total revenues.

FIGURE 8.2
PHA Operating Expenditures and Revenue (1969 dollars/PUM)

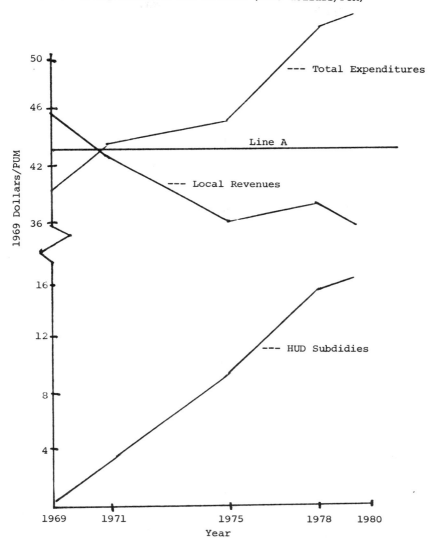

Source: Abt Associates, "Evaluation of the Performance Funding System," draft prepared for the U.S. Department of Housing and Urban Development (Cambridge, MA: July 1981).

This was not the case. The downward trend in locally-generated revenue continued virtually unchanged through 1975. This suggests that either the income of PHA tenants was declining relative to revenue needs (i.e., the 25 percent-of-income ceiling placed on rents meant that the total collections could not keep up with total expenses) or that PHA rent collection was deteriorating (i.e., they had large uncollectables). In addition, note that between 1975 and 1978 local revenues increased slightly. This was a period of relative energy price stability and economic recovery from the initial price shock. Our estimate shows that real local revenues again declined in 1979 (by about 5 percent). This is the beginning of the second energy price shock. We would suggest that uncollectables mount during such price shocks, partly because other prices increase so rapidly and partly because economic activity slows. As a result of these two factors, the lower income population suffers a severe loss of purchasing power and may become unable to meet rental costs.

As Figure 8.2 shows, local revenues first fell below total operating costs in 1971. The gap between locally-generated revenues and operating costs continued to grow through 1979. HUD subsidies, therefore, grew steadily to fill the deficit between local revenues and total expenditures. Since we have shown that non-utility expenditures were nearly constant over this period, it is clear that virtually the entire subsidy burden was created by utility cost increases, caused by rising energy costs.

This can be visualized by referring to Line A, which is the level at which PHA finances were perfectly balanced following the imposition of the 25 percent-of-income ceiling in 1970. The area below Line A and above the Local Revenue Line is the amount of HUD subsidy necessitated because of declining rent collection (if one could assume constant expenditures). The area above Line A and below the Total Expenditure Line is the amount of HUD subsidy necessitated by rising utility expenditures (because utility expenditure increases accounted for the entire increase in total expenditures). We can see that utility costs were a source of considerable fiscal strain on PHAs.

Energy price increases have left a clear mark on PHA finances in the 1969-81 period. The HUD subsidies appear in this aggregate analysis to have been successful in preventing PHAs from running ongoing deficits. However, it is not possible to determine, from a simple analysis of income and expenditures, what measures PHAs have taken to balance their books. In the last chapter we discussed two ways in which the structure of HUD subsidies may cause a PHA to become financially distressed. First, the Performance Funding System may not

provide an adequate measure of the cost of operating a
PHA. Second, rapid cost increases in utility bills, as
have occurred during the period, may create chronic cash
flow problems because of the lag created by the forward
funding system.

The most direct way to gauge the financial soundness
of PHAs is to examine operating reserves and year-end
surpluses. Under PFS, operating expenses and income are
projected so that the HUD subsidy may be provided in
advance. If the PHA runs out of funds, it can draw from
a cash reserve it maintains for major repairs and
improvements. If the PHA has funds in surplus, it can
build the reserve fund back up to a maximum level
stipulated by HUD.

The reserves are maintained as a matter of prudent
management. Their purpose is to ensure that adequate
working capital is available for basic operations and
minor capital improvements. HUD has set the maximum
level for reserve funds at 50 percent of annual routine
expenditures.15/ By law, HUD will not accept PHA
budgets which contain reserve levels below 40 percent of
the maximum allowable level unless the PHA can show
special circumstances. A 1979 HUD memo has suggested
that PHAs with reserves below 30 percent of the maximum
be allowed a one-time adjustment to bring the reserve
level up to 50 percent. HUD certainly indicates by
these policies that adequate reserves are an important
ingredient of fiscal good-standing for PHAs. A business
as large as a PHA has great difficulty operating without
such reserves.

The reserves of all PHAs were at 90 percent of the
maximum in 1969 (i.e., 45 percent of operating costs),
but had fallen to 66 percent by 1978 (33 percent of
operating costs). For extra-large PHAs (over 6,592
units), reserves declined from 65 percent to 41 percent
of allowable levels (barely 20 percent of operating
costs). These major declines clearly show that PHAs
have repeatedly dipped into reserves to make ends meet,
but have never received enough revenue to build them up
to previous levels. In the case of extra-large PHAs,
reserves have fallen to near critically low levels as
defined by HUD. This places the PHAs at significant
financial risk.

The extent to which cash flow patterns imposed by
rapid utility cost increases may have contributed to
these negative financial trends is indicated by the size
of year-end utility cost adjustments that PHAs receive.
Under the PFS, any over- or under-projection of utility
costs is corrected in a year-end adjustment. Rapid
increases in utility costs, as occurred during the
decade, could result in repeated under-projections of
utility costs. Under-projections would create cash flow
problems for PHAs, despite the fact that the PHA would

be reimbursed at the end of the year. The severity of the burden placed on PHA finances can be gauged by the size of the year-end utility cost adjustments.

Data on the year-end utility cost adjustments are only available for the years 1976-78, although a clear trend is evident. In 1976, 59 percent of all PHAs underestimated utility costs by an average of $3.22/PUM and 41 percent overestimated by an average $3.29/PUM. By 1978, the portion of PHAs underestimating utility costs had grown to 74 percent, averaging $4.13/PUM, while 26 percent overestimated by an average of $3.83/PUM. Since HUD regulations required PHAs to use current utility rates (or rate increases already granted for the coming year) in their projections, by 1978 it had clearly become the norm that PHAs could not budget the full cost of utilities and had to wait until the next year's funding cycle to receive their full utility subsidy.

Thus, we see that PHAs have been increasingly unable to project utility costs accurately, while reserve funds are drawn down significantly. In addition to these signs of financial stress, utility cost increases have clearly held down non-utility expenditures while creating heavy reliance on HUD for operating subsidies.

HUD Actions and Proposals

As our general argument suggests and the above evidence demonstrates, utility cost increases have placed significant pressure on the finances of PHAs and, in turn, on HUD's Performance Funding System. The mounting pressures have given rise to a wide-ranging series of HUD proposals to cut costs and increase revenues. In order to hold down the large increases in operating subsidies, HUD has taken a number of steps since 1978 which seek to limit PHA expenditures and increase the rental income generated locally. The overall effect of these policy changes and proposals is to increase the portion of income that PHA tenants must pay toward rent and utilities, to force very low income tenants out of public housing, and to further increase the financial pressure on PHAs.

In order to hold down utility expenditures, HUD has reduced the base level of utilities that PHAs are allowed to consume. This reduction is based on the private sector energy savings that took place in the 1976-81 period.16/ The capital to fund this improved energy efficiency would come from the Comprehensive Improvement Assistance Program (CIAP) which was established to fund basic physical improvements to PHA buildings. In 1981, only about 4 percent of these funds -- or $37 million -- was used for energy-related improvements because non-energy capital replacement already placed heavy demands on the funds.17/ It seems unreasonable to expect that PHAs, in a single year, using funds that are already heavily taxed for other essential purposes, could implement energy efficiency improvements equal to those made in the private sector over five years. HUD assumes that some of these energy efficiency improvements have already been made, although no systematic analysis has been done to demonstrate that they have.18/ There has never been an incentive for PHAs to make such improvements.

HUD has also proposed cutting utility costs by requiring that some tenants pay for utilities, regardless of their income.19/ Until now, PHA tenants who pay for utilities directly have had the cost of those utilities included in the housing cost subject to the 25 percent-of-income limitation. In some cases, utility costs are so high or incomes are so low that tenants actually pay no rent, and occasionally receive payments from the PHA to compensate for utility costs in excess of the income ceiling. In many PHAs, however, tenants are entitled only to a fixed allowance of utility consumption measured by individual meters. Any excess is paid directly by tenants.

The HUD proposal would establish utility costs as a "minimum rent" so that the PHA would never make payments for utilities. This would transfer the entire problem of energy price increases from HUD to the tenant. This policy would have the dual effect of reducing PHA utility expenditures and increasing PHA rental income, since the lowest income tenants would be forced to pay more or move out and be replaced by higher income tenants.

In a more straightforward policy change, HUD has begun to phase in an increase in the income ceiling from 25 percent to 30 percent. Since tenant incomes have failed to rise as quickly as the cost of public housing, this is clearly an effort to force some of the fiscal burden of rising costs onto tenants.

There have also been proposals to shift basic financial responsibility for public housing away from the federal government. The top public housing official at HUD has stated explicitly that the PHAs' problems are fundamentally local problems which should be shared with local governments by simply reducing federal outlays.20/ In its FY 1982 subsidy projections, HUD subtracted $40 million from the subsidies required by PHAs on the assumption that state and local governments would fill the funding gap.21/ It is important to point out, however, that there has been no such contribution in the past. The inclusion in budgeting projections of arbitrary, unlikely state and local contributions is an indication of HUD's attempt to shift the responsibility for public housing onto someone else.

In order to hold down utility subsidies to PHAs, HUD

has gone so far as to refuse to distribute any emergency supplemental appropriation for PHAs unless they waive their right to collect year-end utility adjustments.22/ Yet, the size of the supplemental appropriations was not based on covering utility adjustments as well as non-utility shortfalls. In fact, since the year-end utility adjustment is "subject to the availability of funds," PHAs are having difficulty obtaining it with or without the waiver. Several large authorities were unable to pay their utility costs during the first six months of 1982, and one PHA is being sued by the local utility company for failure to pay.23/

One can only surmise from this pattern of policy proposals and changes that HUD is no longer willing to shoulder the burden placed on public housing authorities by rising energy prices. The financial data make it clear that it was only HUD's willingness to accept utility cost pass-throughs in the 1969-78 period that kept PHAs above water. Even with HUD's full cooper- ation, PHA finances have deteriorated significantly. In the current search for ways to cut its subsidies, HUD has no choice but to target utility expenditures and tenant rent payments. Non-utility expenditures have already been held to a minimum under the Performance Funding System. The overriding indication is that without energy price increases, PHA operating costs would now be, in real terms, lower than they were when HUD instituted the subsidy program in 1970.

Part 4

Rising Energy Prices and the
Delivery of Public Services

9
Public Services and the Lower Income Population

In addition to the impact of rising energy prices on household budgets and housing rents, both of which are aspects of shelter, we believe there are other indirect effects of rising energy prices that are of considerable magnitude and importance. One area where the potential indirect impact is large is the delivery of local public services. The lower income population is much more dependent on local public services for the maintenance of their living standard than are non-lower income households. Local public services constitute a much larger part of the goods and services they consume. It is our hypothesis in Part 4 that rising energy prices place pressure on local level finances, resulting either in a reduction of services on which the lower income population depends or in an increase in offsetting revenues, which falls disproportionately on low and lower middle income households.

In this chapter we outline a framework for analyzing public service finance and delivery and the manner in which cutbacks in services or increases in revenues are likely to affect lower income households. First, we demonstrate that local public services play an important part in the overall consumption of low and lower middle income households. Second, we draw on an exhaustive literature review on the nature of public services in order to construct a general framework for analyzing responses to resource pressures placed on local governments by rising energy prices. The next chapter examines the available empirical evidence.

AN ESTIMATE OF THE IMPORTANCE OF LOCAL
PUBLIC SERVICES TO THE LIVING STANDARD OF
THE LOW AND LOWER MIDDLE INCOME POPULATION

At the outset, we must ascertain the relative importance of local public services to the low and lower middle income population. If we find that such services

154

constitute a disproportionately large share of the
consumption of this population, we establish the basis
for a concern that rising energy prices could adversely
affect their standard of living through reductions in
delivery of local public services or increased costs for
such services.

The logical basis for such a concern is straightforward. Local governments are the primary providers of
many basic services, such as transportation, health
care, and education. Low and lower middle income households are disproportionate consumers of many of these
services. Public services also constitute a larger
share of the total consumption of goods and services for
lower income groups than for middle and upper income
groups.1/ Consequently, if rising energy prices place
pressure on local resources, and local governments
respond in turn by cutting back services or increasing
charges or taxes for such services, the low and lower
middle income population could be made to bear a
seriously disproportionate burden as an indirect result.

Empirical evidence to support this simple, logical
explanation of the importance of local public services
to the low and lower middle income population is not
plentiful. However, by estimating the share of income
that local level services constitute for the low and
lower middle income population and the extent to which
subsidies for these services enable them to increase
their consumption of all goods and services, we can
evaluate the importance of local level services to this
population. This is the general approach used in the
energy/equity analyses noted in Chapter 2.2/

Unfortunately, estimating exactly how much local
level services contribute to the living standard of the
low and lower middle income population is a difficult
task. It is considerably more difficult than calculating household energy expenditures, the most
frequently used indicator of the impact of rising
prices. Nevertheless, rough estimates can be made.

Table 9.1 presents estimates of the percentage of
household income devoted to various forms of consumption
by households in various income groups. The estimates
are based on the 1972-73 Consumer Expenditure Survey.
This is the only detailed consumption survey currently
available. Although there will have been some changes
in consumption patterns over the decade since the survey
-- many of them due to rising energy prices -- the
changes are not likely to have been so large as to alter
our basic conclusion, which is that public services
constitute a larger percentage of the total consumption
of lower income households than of non-lower income
households. For the purpose of demonstrating a general
tendency (rather than a precise estimate), these data
are more than adequate.

TABLE 9.1
Household Expenditures and Local Subsidies as a Percent of Household Income, 1972-73

Income Category	Household Energy[a]	Water, Trash, and Sewerage Expenditures[a]	Water, Trash, and Sewerage Subsidy[b]	Transit Expenditures[a]	Transit Subsidy[b]	Local Level Public Assistance[a]	Total Local Income Transfer
Under $3,000	11.1	1.6	.69	2.2	1.2	1.3	3.2
$3,000 to $3,999	6.4	1.0	.42	1.2	.7	.9	2.0
$4,000 to $4,999	5.5	.8	.34	.9	.5	.5	1.3
$5,000 to $5,999	5.0	.8	.34	.8	.4	.3	1.0
$6,000 to $6,999	4.4	.7	.30	1.1	.6	.2	1.1
$7,000 to $7,999	4.0	.6	.26	.6	.3	.1	.7
$8,000 to $9,999	3.4	.6	.24	.5	.3	.04	.5
$10,000 to $11,999	3.2	.5	.23	.4	.3	.03	.4
$12,000 to $14,999	2.9	.5	.22	.3	.2	.02	.4
$15,000 to $19,999	2.5	.5	.21	.3	.2	.01	.4
$20,000 to $24,999	2.1	.4	.19	.3	.2	0	.3
Over $25,000	1.5	.3	.14	.3	.2	0	.3

[a] U.S. Bureau of Labor Statistics, Consumer Expenditure Survey: Interview Survey, 1972-73 Average Annual Income and Expenditures for Commodity and Service Groups Classified by Family Characteristics, Report 455-4 (Washington, D.C.: 1977), Table 1.

[b] U.S. Bureau of the Census. Subsidies based on the percentage of operating expenses covered by user fees as follows: transit = .44, water = .85, trash and sewerage = .37.

Table 9.1 combines 1972-73 <u>Consumer Expenditure</u>
<u>Survey</u> data with Census Bureau data for all local level
governments for 1972-73.<u>3</u>/ Two types of services are
readily identifiable in the consumption survey. One
category combines water, trash, and sewage, which are
all major local level services. The other category is
identified as non-recreational, non-private vehicle
transportation. We assume that this primarily constitutes intracity mass transit expenditures. Table 9.1
includes the percentage of income devoted to home energy
expenditures as a point of reference. Since home energy
expenditures motivated Congress to provide low income
energy assistance in the Crude Oil Windfall Profit Tax
Act, this presents a useful basis of comparison for
gauging other impacts.

In Table 9.1 we have estimated how much more households in each income category would have been forced to
pay, as a percentage of income, for these services had
the services not been subsidized. That is, if households had paid user fees to cover the full cost of
service and the level of consumption was not reduced,
then a significantly larger share of income would have
been spent on these services. For instance, households
in the lowest income category would have been forced to
devote an additional 1.2 percent of their income to
acquire mass transit services and .7 percent more of
their income for water/trash/sewage. These percentages
decline steadily as income increases. In the highest
income category, less than .2 percent of income would
have been needed to offset transit subsidies and only
.14 percent of income to offset water/trash/sewage
subsidies.

Table 9.1 also contains an estimate of the importance of local level public welfare, or assistance
payments, to the lower income population. This estimate
is based on the assumption that 8.5 percent of the total
resources devoted to welfare are provided from locally
generated revenues. This is the national average figure
for 1973.<u>4</u>/ Further, it is assumed that the local assistance funds are distributed among income groups in
the same proportion as the total assistance income reported in the <u>Consumer Expenditure Survey</u>. This
approach is somewhat simplistic, since it overlooks the
fact that many local level services are in-kind services, not cash transfers. Furthermore, it probably
underestimates the concentration of local public
assistance on lower income groups. Nevertheless, it
does yield a rough order of magnitude estimate.

As Table 9.1 makes clear, subsidies for these local
level services contribute significantly to the income of
low and lower middle income households. Subsidies for
water, trash, and sewerage equal about .7 percent of the
income of low income households and .3 to .4 percent of

the income of lower middle income households. This
percentage declines steadily to .1 percent in the
highest income group. Transit subsidies are equal to
about 1.2 percent of the low income household's income
and .5 to .7 percent of the income of the lower middle
income household. This declines to .2 percent of income
in the highest income groups. Local level public
assistance makes an even larger contribution to the
consumption of lower income households. In the two
lowest income categories, it accounts for 1.3 and .9
percent, respectively, of total income. The
contribution of public assistance to household income
declines rapidly as income rises and becomes virtually
nil by the middle of the income distribution.

Thus, these local level services -- mass transit,
water and sewerage, and public assistance -- constitute
a significant part of the overall consumption of low and
lower middle income households. Had the subsidies been
eliminated in 1972-73, those in the lowest income category (with incomes below $3,000 per year) would have had
their effective income reduced by more than 3 percent.
That is, the combination of increased costs for some
services (transit, sewerage, and water) and the
decreased income from local level public assistance
would have reduced their effective purchasing power by 3
percent (assuming no change in consumption patterns).

Of course, some part of that 3 percent could have
been made up in savings on local level taxes. General
revenue needed to subsidize specific services would have
been reduced and general taxes could have been reduced.
However, insofar as there is a fairly large net subsidy
for these services for low income households, there
would be a significant net loss of purchasing power if
these subsidies were eliminated.

For households with incomes between $3,000 and
$4,000, the effective loss in purchasing power would
have been 2 percent of income. For households with
incomes between $4,000 and $7,000, the effective loss in
purchasing power would have been over 1 percent. It
should be remembered that because more taxes are paid by
those at higher income levels, more of the decrease in
services could have been offset by a decrease in local
taxes (i.e., the net subsidy is smaller for these
groups).

Thus, we see that, as a percentage of income, the
subsidies for these services could have constituted a
share of income that was, in effect, about 25 percent as
large as the household expenditure for home energy.
Other local services, such as education and hospitals,
are difficult to estimate, but they would certainly
double or triple the impact of the few analyzed above.
Consequently, even though we cannot arrive at a precise
estimate, it seems clear that local public service

subsidies constitute an important component of lower
income household consumption. If rising energy prices
place pressure on the provision of local level services,
they would pose a major threat to the living standard of
low and lower middle income households, particularly if
those pressures lead to service cutbacks or increases in
fees or taxes. The analysis in Chapter 10 shows that
the basis for concern is very real. In order to conduct
that analysis, we establish a framework for discussing
the impact of rising energy prices on local public
services.

THE IMPACT OF CHANGES IN PUBLIC SERVICES
ON LOW AND LOWER MIDDLE INCOME HOUSEHOLDS

The impact of rising energy prices on the lower
income population, through its impact on local public
services, can be described as follows. Energy prices
contribute to increased fiscal stress. Fiscal stress
creates pressures to reduce services and raise
revenues.5/ As measures are taken to relieve this
stress, low and lower middle income households are more
deeply affected than other groups for two primary
reasons.

First, locally provided public goods and services
constitute a larger share of the total consumption of
goods and services for low and lower middle income
groups than they constitute for non-lower income groups.
Consequently, any service cutbacks will affect them more
than other groups.

Second, the actual cutbacks in services or increases
in revenues are not likely to be evenly distributed
across specific services or sources of revenue. Rather,
service cutbacks are likely to be concentrated in the
area of redistributive services, of which low and lower
middle income households are disproportionately large
consumers. Similarly, revenue increases are likely to
be concentrated in those sources of revenue (regressive
taxes and user fees) that fall most heavily on low and
lower middle income groups.

The first point should be obvious. Service cutbacks
are likely to result from declining real resources
available at the local level due to rising real energy
prices. If cutbacks occur, and even if they are evenly
distributed across services, low and lower middle income
households will be hurt most, simply because they are
more dependent on public services in general.

The second point is more subtle. Knowing that cutbacks or revenue increases will take place does not tell
us anything about patterns of change in expenditures and
revenues. It does not tell us which services will be
cut and why or which taxes will be raised and why. We
believe that the patterns will be such that the burden

placed on low and lower middle income households will be compounded.

Public Services: A Categorization and Hypothesis

Our argument is simply that during times of fiscal stress those services which are defined as less "public" in nature will be cut back more, or will have their subsidies reduced more by increases in user charges for the services. That is, those services which can be readily provided in the private sector, or which are not deemed "essential" functions of the public sector, will have their claim to public resources weakened. Those services whose users can be easily identified and whose costs can be readily calculated -- called "toll goods" -- will be put on a pay-as-you-go basis.

An extensive body of literature on the nature of public services has appeared in recent years. In Section 4 of the Methodological Appendix, a brief review of the literature is presented to demonstrate that there is broad agreement on the general categorization of services with respect to their public versus non-public nature. The important point is that a clear distinction is made between what have been called allocative and redistributive services (see Table 9.2).6/ Allocative services are public goods in the sense that, "in the absence of governmental intervention, too few resources would be devoted to the production of what have come to be called public goods."7/ The reason that too few resources would be devoted to them is that the costs and benefits of the goods are not amenable to calculation or allocation in private transactions. Since private provision of the goods is unlikely, but society will benefit if the services are provided, the public sector intervenes. Police and fire protection and public health programs are the classic examples of public goods.

Redistributive services are "actions that influence the incomes received by different persons."8/ Thus, rather than being provided in the public sector because they cannot be provided in the private sector, these goods are provided because their distribution in the private sector through market or private transactions is deemed unacceptable. Education, public housing, and the provision of welfare are examples of redistributive services.

Although this is an extreme simplification of a very complex topic, we believe that the basic distinction is conceptually sound, as described in the Methodological Appendix. The classification of services in Table 9.2 also proves to be a useful empirical tool for analyzing local government expenditures as discussed in the next chapter.

TABLE 9.2
Categorization of Services

Area-Wide Allocative Services
    Streets and Highways
    Sewerage and Sanitation
    Water Transport
    Airports

Local Allocative Services
    Fire
    Police
    Libraries
    Parks and Recreation
    Parking

Redistributive Services
    Education
    Hospitals
    Health
    Housing
    Welfare

Source: Richard Muth, Urban Economic Problems
          (New York: Harper and Row, 1975), passim.

        Implicit in the above distinction between allocative
and redistributive services is the idea that the community as a whole is the primary beneficiary of allocative
services (actually, property holders are the primary
beneficiaries), whereas those groups who are on the
receiving end of redistributive services are the primary
beneficiaries of such services. This is not a rigid
distinction, since the community as a whole will be
better off if the beneficiaries of redistributive
services are healthier, better housed, better educated,
etc. Nevertheless, the primary beneficiaries of each
type of service differ. To put this another way, the
distribution of the net benefits enjoyed by various
groups differs significantly between allocative and
redistributive services.
        In this sense, the distribution of resources among
various services will be part of a political process.9/
Groups will mobilize to defend their own interests --
defined as maintaining an adequate level of those services from which they benefit most. Insofar as lower

income households are underrepresented in the political
process, they will be less able to maintain funding for
the services upon which they rely most, i.e., redistributive services.

Local Government Revenues

Service cutbacks are only one possible response to
resource pressures created by rising energy prices. A
second major response is to increase income or revenues
to offset the increase in energy costs. The earlier
discussion in this chapter and the conceptual model
discussed in Chapter 2 lead directly to several predictions about how local government revenues will be
increased.

First, efforts will be made to get other levels of
government to pay for the price increase. This response
is limited by the ability to convince other levels to
increase their support.10/

Second, insofar as public services fall into the
toll goods category, there will be efforts to increase
user fees to offset the actual cost of providing the
services.

Third, general tax revenues will be increased.
Within the context of local government finance, a political process will again determine which of the general
taxes will be increased. Insofar as low and lower
middle income households are a minority or underrepresented in the process, they will be less able to forestall tax increases that affect them most.11/

There is a significant disagreement over which taxes
fall most heavily on low and lower middle income households. The general consensus is that sales taxes are
regressive while property taxes are proportional or
moderately progressive.12/ However, there can be
exceptions to these general rules. The exemption of
food, clothing, and other necessities from sales taxes
can make them progressive; assessment practices may make
property taxes regressive.13/ Nevertheless, the general
pattern, especially for national aggregate data, appears
to be as follows: sales taxes and user fees are the most
regressive, while property taxes are at least proportional, if not slightly progressive. Income taxes are
the most progressive.

In sum, we believe that the pattern of expenditure
changes and revenue increases brought on by the resource
shock of rising energy prices is likely to have imposed
a disproportionate burden on low and lower middle income
households in a manner that is readily explicable within
the framework of any of a number of research approaches
to local government services. In one sense, this impact
is simple arithmetic -- lower income households depend
more on these services. But, in another sense, the

162

impact stems from basic issues of policy and politics. Under fiscal stress, public opinion and political processes will focus fiscal pressures on those services upon which low and lower middle income households are most reliant.

10

The Impact of Rising Energy Prices on the Delivery of Public Services

In this chapter we analyze the actual expenditures for local services, such as those discussed above, as well as changes in local revenue sources. As our analysis shows, vital services on which low and lower middle income households rely for a significant part of their total consumption have suffered over a decade of declining real expenditures by local governments. We attribute the failure of these expenditures to keep up with inflation to the severe burden that rising energy prices have placed on the operating budgets of local governments.

DATA AND METHOD

First, we review budget line items in general expenditure categories. We call this the aggregate expenditure analysis. These figures are familiar to both local government officials and policy analysts in this field. Official budgets are written and discussed in the media in these terms.

However, for the purposes of examining the impact of rising energy prices on redistributive services, budget line items are not sufficiently precise, because they do not factor out "intergovernmental transfers" or user charges. That is, they do not reflect a careful deline-ation of the origin of resources used for each service. Therefore, from the second point of view, we examine expenditures net of intergovernmental transfers and user fees to identify local government general revenues devoted to each type of service. We call this the net expenditure analysis.

Throughout the analysis, we examine, where possible, all local governments as a whole -- i.e., cities, counties, towns, school districts, and other special districts -- and cities only, as a subset of all local governments. There are three reasons for this.

First, several key pieces of data are available for

cities only, but not for all local governments, while
other key pieces of data are available for all local
governments, but not for cities only. By examining each
separately, we fill as many gaps as possible.

Second, the fiscal year 1972-73, which would be the
most appropriate base year for the analysis, appears
quite erratic in the data for all local governments.
Therefore, we were forced to use 1971-72 as the base
year for all local governments. This was not the case
for the cities-only data. Examining cities separately
enables us to utilize the preferable base year for a
large subset of local governments.

Third, there are some differences between the impacts and responses for cities and other forms of local
governments.

GENERAL INDICATIONS OF THE IMPORTANCE
OF ENERGY TO LOCAL GOVERNMENT BUDGETS

The starting point for our analysis of local
government expenditures must be a demonstration that
rising energy prices are a sufficiently important factor
to cause local governments to alter their spending
patterns. That is, if the fiscal stress is not large,
we will not see the responses that we expect.

Local governments have had a great deal of
difficulty in quantifying the cost of the energy they
use. In the past, energy supply purchases have been
embodied in sub-program level budgets, making it
difficult even for department heads to know exactly how
much energy they purchased. Although local governments
are now beginning to account for energy expenditures,
data on municipal energy use is still scarce.

A 1979 survey of local government officials reveals
that for most cities and counties energy costs are the
second largest operating expense, next only to wages and
salaries.1/ A 1975 study of 20 Texas cities put direct
energy expenditures at between 7 and 11 percent of total
spending.2/ The city of Los Angeles put its 1980 energy
use at 5 percent of total spending, not including utility energy use.3/ Overall, energy expenditures seem to
range between 5 and 10 percent of total local government
expenditures.

When a single commodity that comprises even 5 percent of a total budget more than doubles in price in
less than 8 years, strain is certainly likely to devel-
op. For a city which is already under severe fiscal
strain, major energy price increases may push that city
over the brink into a fiscal crisis.

The best available data on municipal governments
which permits a fairly close examination of the impact
of energy prices on expenditures clearly support the
assertion that energy prices have placed considerable

pressure on local government expenditures. In Figure
10.1, annual changes in operating and non-operating
expenditures are compared to annual changes in the
producer price index for fuels.

FIGURE 10.1
Annual Rates of Change: Energy Prices, Municipal Operating
Expenditures, and Municipal Non-operating Expenditures

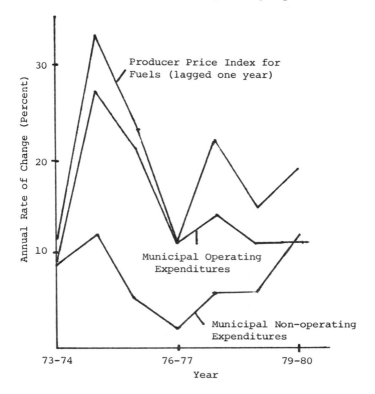

Source: U.S. Bureau of the Census, City Government Finances,
          selected years.

          U.S. Bureau of Labor Statistics, Producer Price Index

Operating expenditures, as we have defined them in
Figure 10.1, include all non-wage, non-capital direct
expenditures. Energy expenditures would constitute
between one-quarter and one-half of operating expen-

ditures thus defined and would be the single largest
operating expense.4/ This is the best indicator of
municipal energy costs in the available data.

In Figure 10.1, the producer price index is lagged
one year -- i.e., the 1972-73 change in energy prices is
plotted against the 1973-74 change in municipal
expenditures. The lag is introduced for two reasons.
First, municipal fiscal years tend to lead calendar
years; for many local governments, fiscal year 1979-80,
which is treated as 1980 in our analysis, covers part of
1979 and most of 1980. Second, it takes time for price
increases to be reflected fully in municipal expenditures.

The increases in operating expenses track the
increases in the producer price index for fuels up to
the end of the period. The average annual increase in
fuel prices was 18 percent (nominal, compounded) for an
overall increase of about 240 percent. The average
annual increase in operating expenses was 14.9 percent
(nominal, compounded), for an overall increase of about
165 percent. By contrast, the average annual increase
in non-operating expenses was 7.7 percent (nominal,
compounded), for an overall increase of 68 percent.

In addition, the annual changes in fuel prices and
operating expenses track one another closely until
1978-80. Figure 10.1 shows that from 1978 to 1980
operating expenses ceased tracking energy prices so
closely. The conceptual model in Chapter 2 predicted
this pattern would be seen over time. That is, we would
expect some loosening of the relationship as an
increasing number of measures are taken to reduce energy
expenditures and as these measures begin to take effect.

Thus, it should be readily apparent that in the
period between 1973 and 1979 there was considerable
pressure placed on local government finances by rising
energy prices. These pressures were felt in the form of
escalating operating expenses. If governments were to
maintain services, they had to respond to these major
cost increases.

They could raise expenditures to offset increasing
costs or they could cut back services, either across-
the-board or by realigning spending priorities or by
doing both. We turn next to an analysis of the patterns
of response.

EXPENDITURES

Aggregate Expenditure Analysis

For local governments coping with the pressure of
rising energy prices, the first possible response is to
reduce total real spending for non-energy items. That
is, faced with the need to pay much more for fuel, local

governments could cut back their purchases of all other
goods and services to offset the increased energy costs.
In part, this was the case. Figure 10.2, which shows
real expenditures between 1973 and 1980, using 1973 as
the base year, demonstrates that cities have managed to
keep total expenditures quite close to the general inflation rate, despite large increases in energy prices.
Spending is nearly level in constant dollars -- having
increased by only 6 percent (real) over the period.
Note that total real spending declined during the first
and second oil price shocks.

Figure 10.3 shows that the patterns observed for
cities are repeated, generally, for all local government
entities taken together -- cities, counties, towns, and
school districts. In the somewhat longer period of
1972-80, for the all-inclusive category of local governments, aggregate spending increased by 12 percent
(real). As a basis of comparison, it might be noted
that real GNP increased by 25 percent over the same
period and real disposable personal income grew by 26
percent. Thus, real expenditures by local governments
were growing at a very moderate rate. Here, too,
spending declined during the first and second oil price
shocks.

Given the fact that total expenditures have increased much less in real terms than energy prices,
which increased by 130 percent (real), we would expect
to see some realignment within the categories of
expenditures. That is, let us assume that energy
constitutes 10 percent of total expenditures for local
governments. This would certainly be the case where
utility expenditures are considered part of total
expenditures as in Figures 10.2 and 10.3. With an
increase of 130 percent between 1973 and 1980 in real
energy costs, total expenditures would have to increase
13 percent (1.30 x .10 = .13) if no cuts took place in
non-energy expenditures. Neither cities nor all governments taken together achieved this rate of increased
spending. Therefore, cuts or realignments were
necessary. Neither cities only nor all local governments could have managed to avoid realignment.

The general pattern of realignment is also shown in
Figures 10.2 and 10.3. Figure 10.2 shows total city
expenditures broken into broad categories: operating
costs, salaries, capital outlays, public assistance
payments, and miscellaneous expenditures. All expenditures are in real terms. Operating costs and utilities
have soared in a striking fashion. Assistance payments
have plummeted, although this spending is not a very
large portion of the total.5/ Other categories tend to
hover quite close to the inflation rate, with capital
outlays and salaries losing some ground.

Figure 10.3 shows a similar set of budget items for

FIGURE 10.2
Government Expenditures by Category, [1] Cities Only

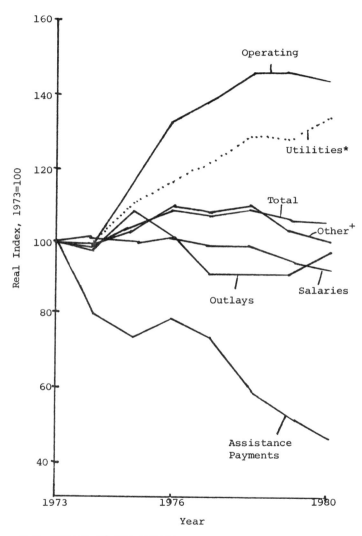

Source: U.S. Bureau of the Census

[1] Does not include intergovermental expenditures.
+   Includes interest on debt and insurance benefits.
*   This expenditure is included in salaries, operating costs and
    outlays.

FIGURE 10.3
Government Expenditures by Category, All Local Governments

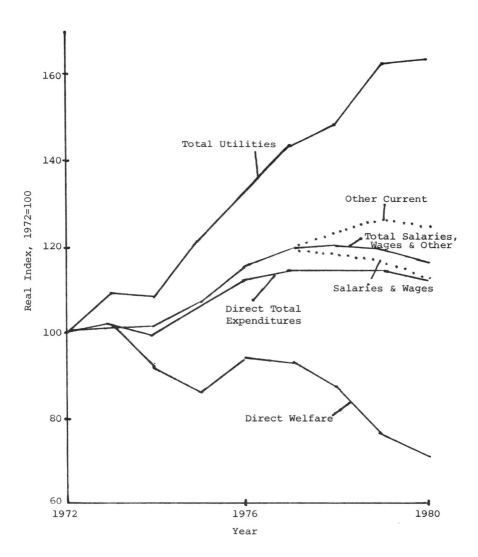

Source: U.S. Bureau of the Census

170

all local governments. The pattern for this all-
inclusive set of local governments is quite similar to
that for cities. Total real expenditures have increased
slightly. Utility expenditures have increased most
rapidly while welfare expenditures have declined
dramatically. Thus, there have been major trade-offs in
the use of resources to cope with the increase in
operating expenses.

Net Expenditure Analysis

A key question raised by Figures 10.2 and 10.3 is:
Who loses? Knowing that there has been a realignment
among salaries, capital, energy, and other expenses does
not indicate which types of services suffered. The
startling drop-off in assistance payments suggests that
spending may have been funneled into energy-intensive
areas at the expense of programs that redistribute
resources and are of crucial importance to low and
moderate income people.

In order to understand the extent to which local
spending decisions have conformed to our conceptualization of service delivery in the face of fiscal stress,
a more detailed empirical analysis is necessary. This
analysis must take into account spending for each type
of service by all local levels of government, as well as
federal and state categorical funds which are simply
funneled through local governments. To do this we have
used unpublished national aggregate data compiled by the
Bureau of the Census. The data provide a comprehensive
view of local government finances arranged by Standard
Metropolitan Statistical Area (SMSA) rather than by
governmental jurisdiction. The data contain detailed
information on intergovernmental revenues, user charges,
and expenditures by functional categories. In this
particular data it is not possible to distinguish cities
from all local governments. Therefore, in this net
expenditure analysis, that distinction is dropped.

Table 10.1 divides public services into the broad
categories of allocative and redistributive programs
discussed in Chapter 9. Expenditures for those services
are also broken down into two categories. "Total
expenditures" represent the total amounts disbursed by
local governments. "Local expenditures" are net of
intergovernmental revenues and charges collected in
exchange for the service. That is, they reflect only
local resources from general revenues expended for each
service. Compounded annual rates of <u>real</u> change for the
period from 1972 to 1980 are calculated for each
spending category and a weighted average rate of
increase is also presented.

The pattern of spending changes over the 1972-80
period is consistent with our hypothesis. In the total

TABLE 10.1
Allocative Versus Redistributive Expenditures for All Local
Governments
(Average Real Compounded Percent Change Per Year [Real,
Compounded])

Services	Total Expenditures	Local Expenditures
Allocative		
Fire	1.5	1.5
Police	1.7	1.7
Libraries	-8.7	-8.7
Parks and Recreation	1.7	1.5
Parking	.33	*
Highways	.25	1.8
Sewerage	3.6	.26
Sanitation	.94	.91
Water Transport	1.4	-.73
Airports	-3.1	-5.4
Average	.82	.29
Redistributive		
Welfare	-4.2	-2.6
Housing	.72	-8.4
Hospitals	2.1	-2.1
Education	.58	-2.1
Average	.15	-2.3

Source: U.S. Bureau of the Census.

*   No subsidy during some years.

expenditure column, allocative expenditures increased annually by an average of .82 percent, ranging from -8.7 percent for libraries to 3.6 percent for sewerage. Redistributive programs showed an average annual increase of only .15 percent, ranging from -4.2 percent for welfare to 2.1 percent for hospitals. As a point of comparison, both real GNP and real disposable personal income increased by about 2.8 percent during the same period.

In the local spending column, the results are even more clear-cut. Allocative expenditures increased by .29 percent and redistributive expenditures decreased by 2.3 percent. Expenditures for only two of the allocative items, airports and libraries, changed at a rate below the average for redistributive programs, and none of the redistributive programs grew at a rate above the average for the allocative group. In the local spending column, all of the redistributive services failed to keep pace with inflation.

These data clearly show that spending for redistributive programs has lagged behind most other expenditures. When the data are presented across time in constant dollars, these trends are confirmed (see Table 10.2).

Almost without exception, the cumulative changes in spending for public safety and public works, which constitute over 70 percent of the non-redistributive expenditure categories, exceed the spending levels for the redistributive services by extremely large margins. Expenditures for education and hospitals hover near the general rate of inflation until the end of the time series, when they fall sharply.

The cases of housing and welfare expenditures are far more striking. These services experience major losses during the 1972-80 period, falling significantly during or after the oil price shocks of both 1973-75 and 1978-80. All four redistributive programs suffer net losses over the period.

The "other transportation" category, which consists of commercial transit services, including spending for airports, parking, and water transport, behaves somewhat erratically. This is largely because these are toll goods which lost subsidies during the period. The sums involved are also very small.

The empirical evidence leaves little doubt that expenditures for those public services on which low and lower middle income groups rely most heavily have been significantly cut in real terms, imposing a disproportionate burden upon these groups. Although this reallocation of expenditures cannot be directly attributed to fiscal stress caused by energy price increases, there is, to say the least, a remarkable coincidence between budget retrenchment and surges in energy prices.

TABLE 10.2
Public Service Expenditures by Functional Category, All Local Governments
Net of User Charges and Intergovernmental Revenues (Real Index, 1972=100)

	1972	1973	1974	1975	1976	1977	1978	1979	1980
Total Expenditures	100	101	100	105	111	111	111	109	107
Public Safety[a]	100	105	102	107	115	118	121	117	114
Public Works[b]	100	95	96	109	115	109	106	111	108
Other Transportation[c]	100	65	40	42	31	15	11	31	41
Hospitals	100	68	98	107	104	93	95	84	85
Education	100	100	91	97	101	100	97	88	84
Housing	100	205	118	78	18	33	47	64	49
Welfare	100	47	97	60	81	81	100	92	81

a Police and Fire
b Parks, Sewerage, Sanitation, Public Buildings, and Highways
c Parking, Airports, and Water Transport

Source: U.S. Bureau of the Census.

REVENUES

The other side of the budgeting equation consists of income or revenues. Local government expenditures overall have increased by 12 percent in real terms from 1972 to 1980, creating a significant need for increased revenue. Moreover, there is no assurance that revenues have kept pace without realignment.

Local governments received about 40 percent of their revenue from other governments in 1980 (intergovernmental revenue). The balance of income comes from four primary local sources: property taxes, sales taxes, user charges, and income taxes. Utility operations are frequently funded from separate revenue pools, with some subsidy from general revenues.

We expect that a local government faced with the need for increased revenue is likely to turn first to other levels of government for funds. In the aggregate, intergovernmental revenues have remained constant as a percentage of total local revenue since the 1973 oil price shock, although there was considerable growth in the early 1970s prior to the first oil shock.6/ Therefore, local governments have been able to tap other levels of government only enough to maintain their relative level of support.

Local revenues, on the other hand, have undergone major changes during the decade. Figure 10.4 shows the composition of local revenues in the 1972-80 period for all local governments. The most notable change over the period is a 19 percent decline, in real terms, in the property tax. As a result, property taxes dropped from 61 to 49 percent of total local revenues. Sales taxes and user charges, on the other hand, have increased significantly in real terms -- 45 percent and 33 percent, respectively. Taken together, they have risen from 34 percent to 45 percent of local revenues. User charges account for the larger part of this increase and sales taxes represent only a small portion of revenues (less than 10 percent).7/ Income taxes, on the other hand, have increased only 13 percent in real terms. Moreover, they represent a very small portion of revenues, increasing only from 3 percent to 4 percent.

The sources of revenue for cities exhibited only slight differences from the sources for all local government entities. Property taxes declined as a percentage of total revenue. Sales taxes and user fees increased, while income taxes remained fairly constant.

Given the broad sentiment that sales taxes and user charges are the most regressive forms of taxation, and property and income taxes the most progressive, or at least proportional, it is clear that the response to increasing fiscal pressure on the revenue side has been disproportionately burdensome to low and moderate income

FIGURE 10.4
Locally Generated Revenues by Category, All Local Governments

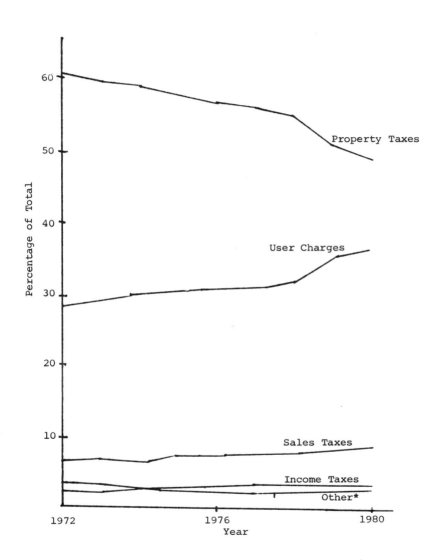

*Licenses and unallocable taxes.

people.

A separate source of local revenue comes from user
charges for municipal utilities, including electric
generation, natural gas distribution, water systems, and
mass transit. In the analysis of expenditures, we saw
that the increases for these services exceeded all
others, including operating expenses. The reason is
that utilities are, by their very nature, overwhelmingly
energy-intensive. Therefore, energy price increases are
likely to translate almost directly into utility expenditure increases. However, since these expenditures are
largely funded by user fees and frequently operated as
separate fiscal entities, the important question is
whether local governments pass through these cost
increases to consumers in the form of higher user fees
or absorb them in the form of increasing subsidies.

Figure 10.5 shows utility revenues as a percentage
of expenditures for four primary utility services for
all local governments. The level of subsidy varies
significantly among the utilities, with gas utilities
showing a net surplus of revenues, while transit services are heavily subsidized. The data clearly show
that local governments have not curtailed their subsidies for these utility services in response to rising
energy prices. In fact, it appears that user charges
have not increased nearly as rapidly as expenditures,
thereby increasing the subsidy level. This pattern is
especially striking for electric and transit services.
A similar pattern holds for the expenditures for these
services among city governments only.

Local levels of subsidy for utility services have
clearly not been compromised during the period 1972-80.
However, it should also be noted that these subsidies
did not shield the public from the ravages of inflation.
The simple fact is that energy prices were pushing up
the cost of these services so rapidly that both
households (in the form of increasing user fees) and
local governments (in the form of increasing subsidies)
bore a very heavy burden. User fees for these utilities
as a group increased at extremely rapid rates. For all
local governments, these utilities, taken together,
increased by 170 percent (nominal) between 1972 and
1980, with mass transit having the lowest rate -- 65
percent -- and natural gas the highest -- 283 percent.
User charges for all of these utilities except mass
transit increased faster than the general rate of
inflation over the period, which was slightly less than
97 percent. The pattern for city utilities is similar.

We have shown that during the decade of energy price
shocks, local governments held down spending for redistributive programs in favor of more "public" or
"allocative" goods and services such as public safety
and public works. Two of the redistributive services --

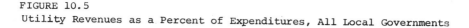

FIGURE 10.5
Utility Revenues as a Percent of Expenditures, All Local Governments

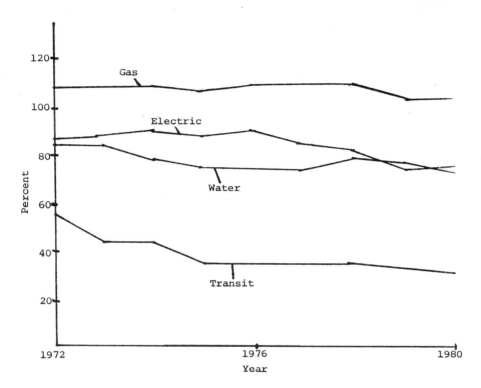

Source: U.S. Bureau of the Census.

welfare and housing -- lost significant ground in real
terms during the decade. The other redistributive
services -- education and hospitals -- fared well until
the second oil price shock, after which they suffered a
net loss.

Table 10.3 presents relative spending levels for
four redistributive services. It shows total levels
disbursed through local governments, total net of user
charges and local expenditures net of both user charges
and intergovernmental revenues (i.e., local subsidies
only). These breakdowns enable us to state the dynamic
changes in redistributive services with more precision.

In the case of education, it is clearly the inter-

TABLE 10.3
Redistributive Expenditures by Functional Category, All Local Governments (Real Index, 1972=100)

	1972	1973	1974	1975	1976	1977	1978	1979	1980
Education									
Total	100	102	101	107	111	110	110	108	105
Total without charges	100	102	100	107	110	110	110	108	106
Local without charges	100	100	91	97	101	100	97	88	82
Hospitals									
Total	100	101	104	107	110	111	112	116	119
Total without charges	100	95	96	106	94	85	80	73	72
Local without charges	100	68	98	107	104	93	95	84	85
Welfare									
Total	100	101	92	86	94	93	86	76	70
Local	100	47	96	60	81	81	100	92	81
Housing									
Total	100	100	94	87	77	82	83	95	107
Total without charges	100	100	96	86	72	78	79	93	110
Local without charges	100	205	118	78	18	33	47	64	49

Source: U.S. Bureau of the Census.

governmental revenues that permitted the spending levels
to be maintained during the second oil price shock. For
hospitals, the major factor permitting spending increases to exceed the rate of inflation seems to have
been user fees. In the case of welfare, intergovernmental revenues were used effectively to maintain
expenditures until the second price shock, when both
total and local spending declined significantly.
Housing expenditures were heavily dependent on
intergovernmental revenues, with very large gaps between
local spending and total spending. In addition, there
was a major falloff following the first oil price shock,
but we see a recovery by the end of the decade.

QUALITATIVE MEASURES OF THE
DETERIORATION OF PUBLIC SERVICES

We have used non-wage, non-capital expenditures as a
proxy for energy costs to show that rising energy prices
placed significant financial stress on local governments. We have also shown that during the period in
which this financial stress was evident, changes in
expenditures and revenue sources of local governments
occurred which can logically be expected to have had a
disproportionately adverse impact on lower income
households.

Some direct evidence on the actual impact of these
expenditures and revenue changes is available. This
evidence, which shows a deterioration of local public
services, is available for this period of rising energy
prices and is quite consistent with our argument.[8] It
presents a rather striking picture of the deterioration
of the quality of life of the lower income population.
Two types of evidence are available. The first is the
subjective evaluation of local public services by local
inhabitants. The second consists of more objective
evaluations of the general condition of urban areas.

Subjective Evaluation[9]

The HUD Annual Housing Surveys have included comparable systematic questions on a range of local public
services since 1973. As Table 10.4 shows, there are
specific as well as general questions on the adequacy of
services. Of the nine specific neighborhood conditions
referred to in the survey, five are easily identifiable
as local public services -- i.e., litter collection,
street repair, public transit, schools, and crime pre-
vention. The other four are more general neighborhood
conditions -- noise, odors, commercial/industrial
activities in residential areas, and abandoned buildings. These reflect general local responsibilities --
such as code enforcement for purposes of noise abatement

TABLE 10.4
Perceived Quality of Public Services
(Percent of Households Reporting Inadequate Services)

Service	OWNERS Lower 1973	Lower 1979-80	Non-lower 1973	Non-lower 1979-80	RENTERS Lower 1973	Lower 1979-80	Non-lower 1973	Non-lower 1979-80
Litter	12.8	17.5	10.3	13.9	16.1	24.9	13.3	17.0
Streets in Need of Repair	16.6	24.6	14.5	20.8	12.8	21.3	11.7	18.2
Schools	4.0	4.1	6.4	6.1	4.3	5.1	5.5	4.0
Crime	9.2	14.3	11.8	16.4	17.0	24.4	17.2	24.0
Mass Transit	32.9	57.3	37.4	55.5	23.8	39.1	24.8	27.6
Abandoned Buildings	6.3	4.2	4.4	2.1	8.5	13.8	6.3	8.2
Commercial/Industrial Activity	11.7	18.8	9.4	15.9	20.4	34.7	18.9	33.3
Odors/Smoke	12.1	8.9	11.6	8.4	11.9	12.1	11.8	10.1
Noise	44.5	37.0	44.4	34.6	47.4	53.7	48.4	34.3
Generally Poor Services	2.5	2.2	1.4	1.2	5.9	6.7	5.1	3.3
Number of Categories with Deterioration, 1973 to 1979-80	6		5		9		6	
Number of Categories with Improvement, 1973 to 1979-80	3		5		0		3	
Average Deterioration (Change in Percent Reporting Inadequate Services), 1973 to 1979-80	4.1		2.6		7.4		2.0	

Sources: U.S. Department of Housing and Urban Development, Annual Housing Survey: 1973, Number 1: Financial Characteristics by Indicators of Housing and Neighborhood Quality (Washington, D.C.: March 1976), Table 4.

U.S. Department of Housing and Urban Development, Annual Housing Surevy: 1979, Part B: Indicators of Housing and Neighborhood Quality by Financial Characteristics (Washington, D.C.: February 1982), Table A-3.

U.S. Department of Housing and Urban Developemnt, Annual Housing Survey: 1980, Part C: Financial Characteristics of the Housing Inventory (Washington, D.C.: November 1981), Table A-1.

and/or maintenance of air quality and/or the separation
of commercial and residential developments.

Taken together, the evidence clearly shows that
lower income households, in general, and lower income
renters, in particular, suffered a major deterioration
in the quality of their public services.

A higher percentage of lower income renters reported
inadequate or unsatisfactory services in 1979-80 than in
1973, in all nine of the service areas listed. There
was a 7.4 percentage point increase in those reporting
such conditions. In addition, lower income renters were
the only group to show an increased incidence (one percentage point) in the rating of neighborhood services,
in general, as poor.

Among lower income owners, a higher percentage
reported inadequate or unsatisfactory service in 1979
than in 1973 for six of the nine services. The average
increase was 4.1 percentage points. There was a slight
decline in those who reported their services were poor
in general.

Non-lower income renters responding to the survey
showed an increase in unsatisfactory or inadequate
conditions in six services. Non-lower income owners
showed an increase in five services. The increase in
respondents reporting unsatisfactory services was only 2
percentage points for renters and 2.6 for owners. There
was also a decline in those reporting poor service in
general, with non-lower income renters showing a large
decline in percentage points.

These responses reflect perceived changes in the
quality of service and the neighborhood environment.
They would reflect both changing levels of services and
changing expectations about service on the part of the
respondents.

Objective Evaluation

A recent study by the Brookings Institution provides
a different measure of the quality of the urban environ-
ment.10/ It addresses another aspect of the general
problem discussed in this and earlier chapters. The
authors of the study constructed an index of city
distress reflecting the following factors: 1975 unemployment rate, 1975 violent crime rate, percentage of
housing built before 1940, percent of population that
was poor in 1969, and the tax disparity between the city
and the surrounding SMSA in 1971. They also created an
index of city decline reflecting the following variables: change in the unemployment rate between 1970 and
1975, change in the violent crime rate between 1970 and
1975, change in city government debt burden between 1971
and 1975, and percent change in population income
between 1969 and 1974.

At least some of these factors, such as crime, city debt, tax burden, and old buildings, are directly relevant to the arguments made in this chapter as well as the HUD survey evidence just discussed. Indeed, the general thrust of the arguments made earlier would suggest that unemployment and income are closely related to changes in energy prices. In short, even though the indices only reflect conditions in the early 1970s, there should be a correlation between urban distress, urban decline, and energy price increases.

In order to examine this hypothesis we define two variables as follows: (1) Urban health is a measure we have created by taking the sum of the distress and decline indices. (2) Energy cost burden is estimated by taking non-wage, non-salary, non-capital, non-debt expenditures expressed as a percentage of locally generated local government revenues in 1979, the first year for which the data is available. Cities have not changed their energy use characteristics that much over the decade, so we are assuming that the 1979 index of energy intensity is a good indicator of the relative energy intensity of cities throughout the 1970s. A complete listing of each of the cities and their scores is contained in the Methodological Appendix, Section 5.

A simple linear least squares correlation coefficient between energy burden and urban health is -.45, indicating a moderate negative relationship. The higher the burden, the worse the state of health of the city. A correlation between urban decline and energy burden was -.41. The correlation between urban distress and energy burden was -.21.

Although the underlying factor would appear to be climate, with the warmer South and West exhibiting less energy burden and "healthier" urban circumstances, we also examined the relationship between energy burden, urban health, and urban decline on a state-by-state basis. In 17 of the 28 states that provided a test of the relationship between energy burden and urban health, the direction of the relationship was as predicted in our argument. In 17 of 30 states that provided a test of the relationship between energy burden and urban decline, the direction of the relationship was as predicted in our argument. (The remainder of the states had one or fewer cities in the sample or had no differences in the dependent [health/decline] and/or the independent [energy burden] variables.)

Certainly, there are many other factors at work in the determination of public service delivery and urban health, but we believe that energy costs should be considered among the more important ones, both because of their direct effects on local services as discussed in this chapter and their direct effects on housing and households as discussed in earlier chapters.

CONCLUSION

The fiscal impact of the energy price shocks on local governments has not been studied extensively heretofore. However, recent interest in the impact of external fiscal shocks on local governments, prompted by the "New Federalism," has produced analyses which, for the most part, predict what we have already observed in the context of energy.11/ Presented with budget imbalances, local governments will cut back on services and maintain those that are defined as vital at the expense of redistributive programs. Revenue needs will be met by increases in the most regressive forms of taxation -- sales taxes and user fees. In this fashion, rising energy prices will have a major indirect effect in eroding the living standard of lower income households.

11
The End of the Decade

On January 21, 1981, within moments of being inaugurated, President Ronald Reagan enacted the "final" decontrol of oil prices. That Executive Order (the second of his Administration) has become generally identified in public opinion as the decontrol of oil prices, an image that the Administration has labored strenuously to create.1/ Yet, that is not the case. Decontrol actually began in June 1979, by Executive Order of President Carter. By the time President Reagan arrived on the scene, decontrol was essentially completed. Domestic crude oil prices tell the real story of decontrol (see Figure 11.1).

On June 1, 1979, when the decontrol process began, the average price paid by refiners for oil produced in the U.S. was approximately $13.00/bbl. On January 21, 1981, when President Reagan stepped in to accelerate the end of the process, refiner acquisition cost for U.S. oil had already risen to about $33.00/bbl. Oil prices moved upward slightly for several months and then stabilized through the end of the year at approximately $33.50/bbl. Thus, almost the entire increase in domestic oil prices had taken place prior to President Reagan's action. In fact, his action only compressed into two months the price increases that the Carter Administration had programmed for the final nine months of decontrol.

With the stabilization of oil prices in late 1981 and the onset of a downward trend in 1982, culminating in a modest price break in early 1983, the national energy psychology changed dramatically. In the media, Congress, and academia, discussions of the benefits of falling energy prices became prominent.2/ Now that prices were falling, many who had spent little or no time considering the impact of rising prices suddenly discovered the strong link between energy prices and economic activity.

Thus, the end of the first decade of the energy

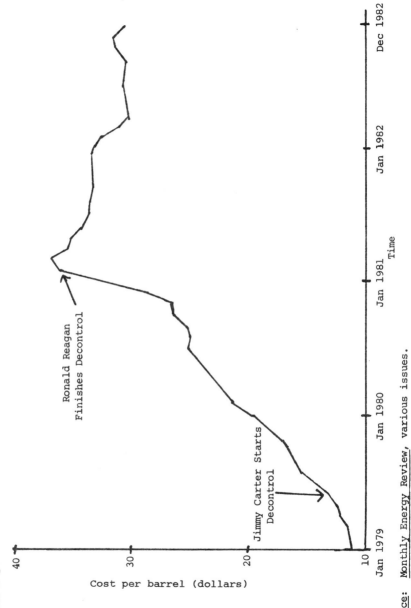

FIGURE 11.1
Refiner Acquisition Cost for Domestic Crude Oil, January 1979 to December 1982

Source: Monthly Energy Review, various issues.

crisis was filled with rather optimistic speculation
about the end of the crisis -- speculation that was at
odds with the thrust of concerns during the decade
itself and much of the analysis in this work. Most of
the detailed impact data utilized in the previous chapters ends in early 1981, at precisely the moment that
oil prices halted their precipitous rise. A question
may arise as to how the downward trend in crude oil
prices may affect our assessment of the burden that has
been placed on low and lower middle income households by
rising energy prices. Does the optimism currently being
expressed about falling prices extend to those segments
of the population? This chapter shows that, through the
early part of 1983, there had been no actual price
relief for lower income households and not much for the
economy as a whole. Further, it would take at least a
decade of very soft energy markets and sustained
economic growth to undo the damage that has been done to
lower income households and to the national economy.

ENERGY PRICE TRENDS

Figure 11.2 depicts the energy prices paid directly
by consumers for the period January 1979 to February
1983. It shows clearly that using crude oil prices as a
guide to residential and household energy prices can be
extremely misleading. Electricity and natural gas
prices have shown almost no response to the flattening
of crude oil prices. Using March 1981 -- the final
month covered by the Residential Energy Consumption
Survey of 1980-81 and, coincidentally, the peak of oil
prices -- as the point of reference, we observe that
electric and natural gas prices rose at rates of about
25 and 13 percent per year, respectively, during a
period in which crude oil prices declined by almost 20
percent.

Even more notable is the fact that heating oil and
gasoline prices showed only moderate responsiveness to
crude oil prices. Gasoline prices declined by only 8
percent and heating oil by only 6 percent in the period
when crude oil prices were declining by 20 percent. As
a result of these factors, home energy prices, measured
as the fuels component of the Consumer Price Index,
increased by almost 18 percent in current dollars between March 1981 and February 1983 (see Figure 11.3).

It is also notable that the energy component of the
Producer Price Index behaved rather differently than the
energy component of the CPI. It peaked in early 1982
and declined slightly through early 1983. For the entire period it decreased by 5 percent. In part, as we
show in the next section, this reflects the fact that
industrial energy consumption was much more sensitive to
the recessionary impact of the second energy price

188

FIGURE 11.2
Residential Energy Prices, 1979 to 1983

Source: Bureau of Labor Statistics, Consumer Price Index.

FIGURE 11.3

Indices of National Income, Personal Income, Energy Component of the
Producer Price Index, and Fuels Component of the Consumer Price Index

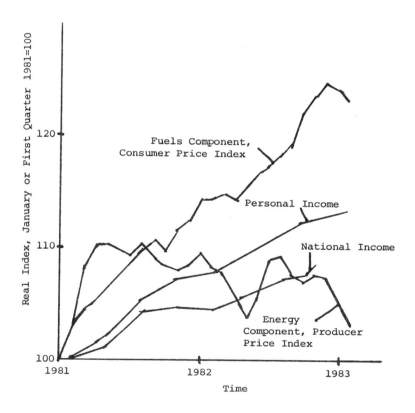

Source: U.S. Bureau of Labor Statistics.

shock. With industrial demand dropping sharply, the downward pressures on energy prices in the non-residential sectors were much stronger.

To put these changes in perspective we should note that home energy price increases were slower than in previous years. However, they were still well above the non-energy rate of inflation, which was only 12 percent during that period. More importantly, these increases were well above the rate of increase in national income. In nominal terms, national income increased by only 7.8 percent over the period between March 1, 1981 and the last quarter of 1982. Personal income, which would be a better measure of household income, as used throughout the earlier chapters, increased by 13.4 percent. Viewing prices and income, it appears that both the absolute and the relative burden grew in the two years between March 1981 and March 1983.

ENERGY CONSUMPTION, ENERGY BILLS, AND
THE BURDEN ON HOUSEHOLDS AND THE ECONOMY

In order to estimate the impact of price trends on household energy bills, it is necessary also to examine trends in energy consumption. As pointed out in Chapter 4, conservation can go a long way toward offsetting the burden of rising energy prices.

Figures 11.4 and 11.5 show that, in the case of the residential sector, conservation did not offset the recent price increases. Total consumption in the residential/commercial sector was higher in 1982 than in 1980, in part due to a colder winter. Per capita consumption was up slightly as well.

In contrast, both industrial and transportation energy consumption were down. This was true for total consumption and consumption per unit of output as well.

The implications of these trends, with respect to the size and distribution of the national energy bill, clearly suggest a heavier burden on lower income households and a continuing drag on the national economy. A specific estimate of the impact of these price changes across income groups, absent actual survey data, would necessarily be imprecise. In order to derive an estimate, several simplifying assumptions would be necessary.

Three straightforward assumptions would be as follows:

1. Income increases are spread equally across income groups;
2. Energy consumption per household is constant across income groups; and
3. Price increases are equivalent across income groups.

FIGURE 11.4
Energy Consumption by Sector

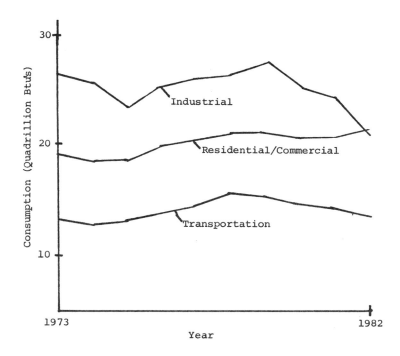

Source: U.S. Department of Energy, <u>Monthly Energy Review</u>, various
issues.

192

FIGURE 11.5
Standardized Energy Consumption by Sector

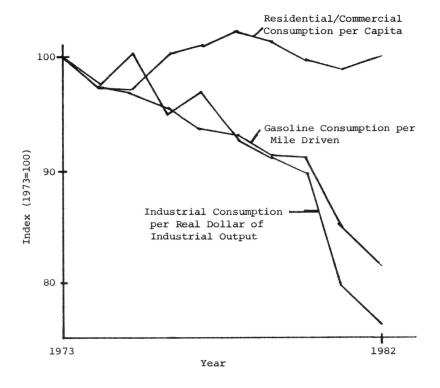

Sources: U.S. Department of Energy, <u>Monthly Energy Reveiw,</u>
           various issues,

           U.S. Bureau of the Census, for population figures.

Making these assumptions underestimates the relative
burden placed on the lower income population because:

1. Their income has tended not to keep up during
   recessionary periods (especially with cuts in
   federal income transfer programs);
2. They have not been able to hold consumption down
   as readily as non-lower income households; and
3. Price increases have been neutral at best.

However, even using these conservative assumptions
leads to the conclusion that in the two years between
March 1981 and February 1983, home energy price
increases consumed about 2 percent more of the income of
low income households, bringing expenditures for home
energy to 25 percent of income (see Table 11.1). They
consumed about 1 percent more of the income of lower
middle income households, pushing them above 10 percent.
In contrast, they consumed less than .3 percent more of
the income of non-lower income households, leaving them
just below 4 percent. Thus, the burden of rising home
energy prices has increased for lower income households
through early 1983.

Since gasoline prices increased only slightly over
the period, we find that the burden declined as a percentage of income. Low income households were devoting
about 11.5 percent of their income to gasoline expenditures in 1982-83 (down from 13.4 in 1980-81). Lower
middle income households were devoting 8.2 percent (down
from 9.3) and non-lower income households devoted 3.9
percent (down from 4.5). Thus, by early 1983, it
appears that total direct energy expenditures were constant as a percentage of income for low income households, at 36.6 percent, but had declined for lower
middle income households from 19.2 in 1980-81 to 18.6 in
1983. For non-lower income households they had declined
from 8.0 to 7.7 percent. The burden had become more
skewed toward lower income households. Insofar as indirect energy consumption is distributed in a relatively
even pattern across income groups, the softening of
producer energy prices would be neutral in impact on the
various income groups.

Of equal importance to the pattern of household
bills is the pattern of movement in the total national
energy bill and what that means in terms of resource
drain on the economy. As noted in Chapter 3, the energy
bill expressed as a percentage of GNP is the best
measure of the drag on the national economy. Expressing
the energy bill in this way also overcomes the illusion
that tracking month to month crude oil prices creates.
Because oil prices peaked in early 1981 and stabilized
in the second half of the year, it is easy to overlook
the fact that the average price for 1981 was well above

TABLE 11.1
The Increase in Direct Energy Expenditures: 1980-81 to 1982-83

Income Group	Average Household Income (dollars)		Average Home Energy Expenditures (dollars)		Average Gasoline Expenditures (dollars)		1982-83 Energy Expenditures as a Percent of Household Income		
	1980-81[a]	1982-83[b]	1980-81[a]	1982-83[b]	1980-81[a]	1982-83[b]	Home	Gasoline	Total Direct Energy
Low	3,274	3,840	759	964	440	443	25.1	11.5	36.6
Lower Middle	8,414	9,870	813	1,033	800	806	10.5	8.2	18.6
Non-Lower	28,914	33,916	1,012	1,285	1,301	1,311	3.8	3.9	7.7

[a] U.S. Department of Energy, Residential Energy Consumption Survey: Consumption and Expenditures, April 1980 through March 1981, Part I: National Data (Washington, D.C.: September 1982), Table 1.

[b] See text.

that of 1980. Indeed, even with falling oil prices in
1982, the 1982 national oil bill was higher than the
1980 bill and much higher than the 1979 bill.
    Table 11.2 shows an estimate of the national energy
bill as a percent of GNP for the entire decade after the
energy price shock of 1973. The point is clear. The
full impact of the run-up in energy prices was not felt
until 1981. The 1982 energy bill was only slightly
lower in absolute terms than the 1981 bill, while it was
.85 percentage points smaller as a percent of GNP. As a
percentage of GNP, the 1982 bill was about the same as
the 1980 bill and almost 2 percentage points higher than
the 1979 bill. The rule of thumb derived in Chapter 3
suggests that an increase in the national energy bill of
that size reduces the growth of GNP by 2 to 3 percentage
points.

TABLE 11.2
National Energy Bill as a Percent of GNP
(Billions of Dollars)

Year	Energy Bill[a]	GNP[b]	Energy Bill as a Percent of GNP
1973	115.24	1326.4	8.91
1974	145.77	1434.2	10.16
1975	167.78	1549.2	10.83
1976	192.77	1718.0	11.22
1977	221.74	1918.3	11.56
1978	241.00	2163.9	11.14
1979	303.53	2417.8	12.55
1980	385.08	2633.1	14.62
1981	445.14	2937.7	15.15
1982	437.56	3059.3	14.30

[a] See Tables A-5 and A-6.
[b] U.S. Bureau of Economic Analysis.

    By the most important measure, energy expenditures
as a percentage of household income or gross national
product, the national energy burden had marked time in
the period between early 1981 and early 1983. At best,
it was slightly lighter; at worst, it had been
redistributed toward lower income households.

PROSPECTS FOR THE SECOND DECADE OF THE ENERGY PROBLEM

The stabilizing of the energy burden and prospects of a moderate price decline in 1983 present a problem akin to that of evaluating a half full glass. The optimist, noting that the glass is half full, will say that the prospects of constant real energy prices could be very good news for the national economy. The period between 1976 and 1978 was marked by fairly flat energy prices (especially expressed as a percent of GNP) and real economic growth of 5.4 percent per year was achieved. By this reasoning, the transitional adjustment costs to higher prices work their way through the economy in a few years. The level at which expenditures for energy stabilize does not matter. If the economy does get the price shock out of its system (i.e., rigid markets finally adjust), there could be 2 to 3 percentage points of growth due to the end of the shock period.

The pessimist, noting that the glass is half empty, will point to the fact that energy expenditures as a percent of GNP are now fully 7 percentage points higher than they were at the start of the first decade of the energy problem. They will argue that this is a drag on the economy that will slow growth in a permanent and continuing fashion. The period of strong growth in the mid 1970s was not sustained, nor was it very high compared to prior economic recoveries. The simple arithmetic of that much drag on the economy and household budgets suggests a meandering recovery at best. It would take more than a decade of constant real energy prices and 5 percent real economic growth to return energy expenditures, as a percent of GNP, to their 1972 levels. The burden on households would require a similar miracle to be undone. Almost no one expects that such a level of growth, or such a pattern of prices, could be sustained for that long a period of time.

From this point of view, the conclusion one must reach is troubling. With respect to the first decade of the energy crisis, it is clear that an awesome price was paid and that it fell most heavily on low and lower middle income households. The social response was far from adequate to alleviate the human suffering imposed by rising energy prices. Having failed to meet the problem head on, it became inviting for those who would like to ignore it to use the period of flat prices to declare that the energy problem is solved, or that it never existed. Yet, the underlying damage to the living standard of lower income households and to the national economy remains, while vulnerability to future energy price shocks has been reduced little. Indeed, with energy playing such a large role in the economy, vulnerability has been increased. While the energy

crisis headlines have faded at the outset of the second
decade of the energy problem, the need for effective
policy responses has actually increased.

Methodological Appendix

SECTION 1: THE DESCRIPTION OF
THE LOWER INCOME POPULATION

Identifying the Lower Income Population

In order to describe the make-up of the lower income
population, we start with a calculation of the percentage of each age group that falls into each income category, for households as well as for unrelated individ-
uals.1/

The Poor. Table A.1 presents the poverty status and
age composition of the population with incomes below
$10,000 in 1979. The salient features, as discussed in
Chapter 2, are the fact that about 60 percent of
families and 40 percent of unrelated individuals with
incomes below $10,000 are officially defined as poor or
near poor. An additional 25 percent of families and
unrelated individuals are elderly or near elderly, but
not defined officially as poor or near poor.
Since we have defined the lower income population as
a population that warrants special social concern in the
context of energy price/policy decision-making, we
should examine further the make-up of the lower income
population that is not poor or near poor. The case for
concern about the poor or near poor can be taken at face
value, but what about the rest of the group we call
lower income? Is it a population at risk?

Those on Fixed Incomes: The Elderly and Near
Elderly. Because the elderly (age 65+) and near elderly
(55-64) make up such a large part of the lower income
population that is not defined as poor or near poor, we
should focus considerable attention upon this group.
Moreover, we should note (as discussed in Chapter 2)
that the Congressional concern expressed in the Crude
Oil Windfall Profit Tax Act extended to those on fixed

TABLE A.1
Age and Poverty Status of Households and Individuals with Incomes Below $10,000 in 1979
(Numbers in Millions)

Age	HOUSEHOLDS				UNRELATED INDIVIDUALS			
	Total	Poor	Near Poor	Other	Total	Poor	Near Poor	Other
15-24	1,320	697	217	406	3,186	1,141	295	1,750
25-44	4,133	2,539	940	604	2,838	805	276	1,757
45-54	1,285	726	306	253	1,154	481	107	566
55-64	1,444	561	251	632	2,056	929	39	1,088
65+	3,757	797	550	2,410	6,564	2,243	1,308	3,013
Total	11,939	5,320	2,264	4,355	15,798	5,599	2,025	8,179
PERCENT DISTRIBUTION								
15-24	11.0	5.8	1.8	3.4	20.2	7.2	1.9	11.0
25-44	34.6	21.3	7.8	5.5	18.0	5.1	1.7	11.1
45-54	10.8	6.1	2.6	2.1	7.3	3.0	.6	3.6
55-64	12.1	4.7	2.1	5.3	13.0	5.9	.2	6.9
65+	31.6	6.8	4.6	20.2	41.4	14.2	8.2	19.0
Total	100.0	44.4	18.9	36.5	100.0	35.4	12.6	51.8

Source: See Note 4.

incomes. This suggests a special social concern for retirees and disabled individuals, who are likely to fall into the group with fixed incomes.

A 1978 analysis of the income of the elderly shows that roughly 90 percent of all elderly married couples and unmarried individuals whose income was below $10,000 in 1978, but who were not defined as poor or near poor, were recipients of Social Security and its related benefits.2/ About one-third of all couples and individuals between 55 and 64 years of age with incomes below $10,000, but who were not officially defined as poor or near poor, were recipients of Social Security and its related benefits. Clearly, the vast majority (75 percent) of elderly and near elderly individuals with incomes below $10,000 who were not poor or near poor were on relatively fixed incomes. A focus on these persons is consistent with the Congressional concern as well as the general position taken in this study.

The Infirm and Unemployed Young. A second group that must be examined, given our definition of lower income and the context of social concern over energy price policy, is that group composed of individuals who are not poor or near poor and not elderly or near elderly.

Approximately 2.3 million persons between the ages of 15 and 54, who were not employed at all in 1979, and who were not defined as poor, stated that the reason for their unemployment was illness, disability, or an inability to find work.3/ These individuals also merit social concern.

Summary Description. If we make several simple, moderate assumptions -- 1) that 90 percent of those defined as poor or near poor had incomes below $10,000; 2) that 80 percent of those who could not find work had incomes below $10,000; and 3) that all elderly and near elderly families with incomes below $15,000 are two person households -- we arrive at a description of the lower income population which clearly suggests that this population is one that warrants special social concern. The breakdown of the population is as follows: 31.6 million poor or near poor persons, 11.6 million elderly on Social Security, 1.8 million near elderly on Social Security and 1.8 million involuntarily unemployed persons who are below age 55. A large part (46.8 out of 50.8 million -- or more than 90 percent) of the lower income population as we have defined it is, in fact, under considerable economic stress in its income-earning capacity -- it is poor, elderly, on fixed incomes, infirm, or involuntarily unemployed.

Reconciling Income Groups in Various Data Sets

Having identified income groups as the object of our analysis, we encounter a major difficulty in estimating the percentage of income spent on energy. The Department of Energy categorizes households according to income in the previous year but gives current year expenditures on energy.4/ That is, families are sorted into income groups according to their 1978 income, but 1979 energy expenditures are shown.

If 1978 income data is used with 1979 energy expenditures to estimate energy expenditures as a percent of income, a serious overestimation will be made. This occurs because, on average, income increased by 10 percent (nominal) between 1978 and 1979.

On the other hand, if 1979 income data from a different source is used as a base, there is some possibility of a misestimation, since the income categories defined by 1978 data would not be identical to those defined by 1979 data. For example, some households categorized as making less than $5,000 in 1978 would make more than $5,000 in 1979. Similarly, some households that fall in the $5,000 to $9,999 range in 1978 would fall above that range in 1979. Since the households are actually wealthier than they appear in the 1978 classification, the average consumption of energy in the group would be higher than if a proper 1979 classification had been used.

Looking at both DOE and Census data, we see that the average income in each of the categories is higher in 1979 than 1978 -- 3 percent higher in the low income category, .5 percent in the lower middle income category and 7 percent in the non-lower income category.5/ If 1978 income (taken from a separate source) is used with 1979 expenditures, the percentage of income devoted to energy would be overestimated by between .5 and 7 percent.

If we use the average expenditure on energy in 1979 by households categorized by 1978 income, we will overestimate expenditures as a percentage of income. The overestimate will reflect the marginal amount of additional consumption of the relatively wealthier group defined by the 1978 income data.

The question is, by how much would the average expenditure in each of the income categories (as we have defined them) be due to this slippage of a year in classification? When we examine the actual energy expenditure in the narrowest income categories available, we find that there is likely to be little overestimation (see Table A.2). Note that in the income categories around the critical cutting points -- $5,000 and $10,000 -- the difference in expenditures tends to be small -- around 10 percent. Insofar as the number of

TABLE A.2
Energy Expenditures in Income Groups Around Critical
Cutting Points

| | Climate Zones | | | | | | |
Income	Zone 1	Zone 2	Zone 3	Zones 4 & 5	Zone 6	Zone 7	National Average
$3,000 to $4,999	722	754	767	543	674	470	738
$5,000 to $7,999	701	771	743	577	590	541	680
$8,000 to $9,999	845	739	752	531	652	594	676
$10,000 to $11,999	866	772	815	628	650	753	748

Source: U.S. Department of Energy, Residential Energy Consumption Survey, Data Tapes.

households misclassified is likely to be small (about 15 percent of each category) the misestimation is likely to be less than two percent (.10 x .15 = .015). These differences are quite small. Throughout the analysis, we have simply used the average 1979 income coupled with the 1979 consumption based on 1978 income categories. This introduces an upward bias in the estimates that is extremely small.

Comparing Data from Various Years

Having chosen to match 1972-73 with 1979-80 because of the closeness of fit between the income categories, as described in Chapter 2, it becomes necessary to adjust the 1978-79 and the 1980-81 data, if they are to be compared to the 1979-80 data. We adopt an extension of the above reasoning to reconcile these years with the 1979-80 data set.

The group of households defined as having incomes below $5,000 in the 1978-79 survey is larger and, on average, richer than the group having incomes below $5,000 in the 1979-80 survey. The estimate of their consumption and expenditures should be adjusted downward if it is to be consistent with the 1979-80 data. In contrast, the group identified as having incomes below $5,000 in the 1980-81 survey is smaller and poorer than its 1979-80 counterpart. The estimates of its consumption and expenditures should be adjusted upward to render it consistent with the 1979-80 survey.

The size and nature of the necessary adjustment depends on where one thinks one is on the income/consumption curve. If one believes that these income groups fall on the relatively flat portions of the curve, as defined in Chapter 4 and Figure A.1a, then little or no adjustment is necessary. If one believes that these income groups lie on a section of the curve in which the slope is changing, then a fairly large, but non-linear, adjustment is necessary, as in Figure A.1b.

Lacking detailed data to make such adjustments, we have adopted a simple semi-linear interpolation (see Figure A.2). First, we calculate the average income in real, 1979 dollars for each of the income groups. In essence, this is what the income would have been in each of the groups if they had been matched in terms of real purchasing power, rather than nominal income. Second, we calculate the linear income elasticity of demand for energy (as measured by expenditures for energy) that is observed between each of the group means in the actual data. We then interpolate along the group specific income elasticity line.

The resulting adjustments, as shown in Table A.3, are quite consistent with the theoretical income/expenditure curve, for the 1980-81 period, but not earlier years. The income elasticity is lower at the low and high ends of the income distribution and higher in the middle. The pattern for earlier years suggests that lower income groups still had relatively higher elasticities. This shifting pattern would be consistent with the hypothesis that lower income households have been "pushed up against the consumption wall" as a result of the second oil price shock.

Be that as it may, the adjustments are relatively minor, with the highest adjustments of only 6 percent occurring in the higher income categories. The figures used in the text for 1980-81 are adjusted in all cases. Note that these adjustments work against our argument.

Adjustments to the consumption figures would be extremely small. There would be no adjustment in the bottom three income categories and adjustments of less than five percent in the four upper income categories. Because they are small and because they would work in favor of our arguments, we have not made these adjustment to the data reported in the text.

FIGURE A.la
Consumption and Expenditures Adjustment, 1978 to 1979

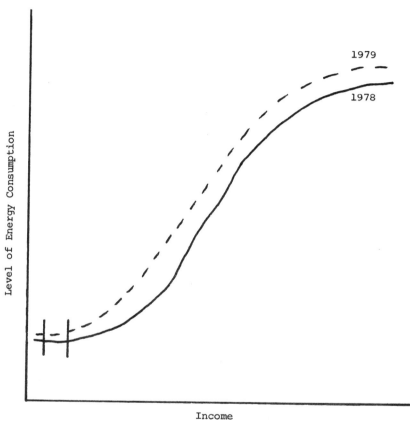

FIGURE A.1b
Consumption and Expenditures Adjustment, 1978 to 1979

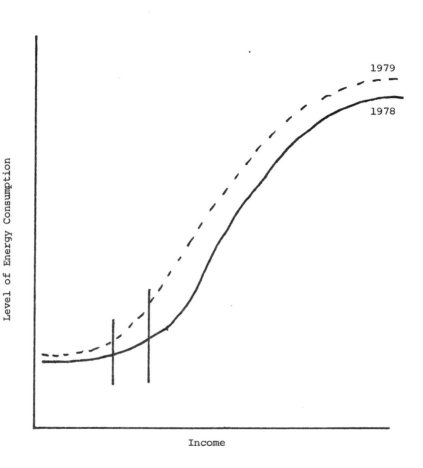

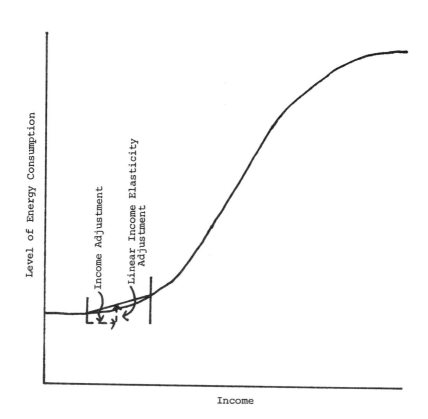

207

FIGURE A.2
Consumption and Expenditures Adjustment

208

TABLE A.3
Adjusting the 1980 Data to be Consistent with the 1979 Data

Income Category	Percent of Population		1980 Income		1980 Home Energy Expenditures		1980 Gasoline Expenditures	
	Actual	Adjusted	Actual	Adjusted	Actual	Adjusted	Actual	Adjusted
Less than $5,000	11.8	13.2	2,872	3,274	754	759	413	440
$5,000 to $9,999	15.8	16.4	7,381	8,414	807	813	712	800
$10,000 to $14,999	14.9	15.9	12,315	14,039	837	856	1,130	1,155
$15,000 to $19,999	13.3	14.1	17,348	19,777	900	942	1,202	1,333
$20,000 to $24,999	12.2	12.4	22,300	25,422	986	994	1,407	1,448
$25,000 to $34,999	16.5	15.7	27,347	33,456	1,005	1,044	} 1,372	1,346
$35,000 or more	15.7	12.4	50,441	57,503	1,206	1,273		

Source: See text.

SECTION 2: THE DERIVATION OF THE
INCREASE IN THE NATIONAL ENERGY BILL

Lost purchasing power was defined as the additional
cost of purchasing energy over the base year 1972. It
was calculated as the increase in price for each type of
energy, over the base year, multiplied by the total
consumption of that energy type. The calculations were
done separately for the residential, commercial,
industrial, and transportation (excluding household
gasoline) sectors.

Within each sector, consumption figures for each
major energy type were derived for the years 1972 to
1981. To do this, we used: 1) U.S. Department of
Energy, State Energy Data Report 1960 through 1980
(SEDR)6/ and 2) U.S. Department of Energy, Monthly
Energy Review (MER), various issues.7/ Each figure was
converted into quadrillion BTUs, using conversion
factors from the MER.

Next, an average price for each type of fuel was
derived. In some cases, it was necessary to interpolate
prices for some of the early years, before consistent
time series data were being kept. To derive prices, we
used: 1) U.S. Department of Energy, Energy Information
Administration, Annual Report to Congress, 1978, Volume
3 (ARC);8/ 2) U.S. Department of Energy, Monthly Energy
Review, various issues; 3) U.S. Bureau of Labor Statistics, components of the Consumer Price Index (CPI);9/
and 4) American Gas Association, Gas Facts, 1979
(AGA).10/

Table A.4 gives the sources for each component of
the estimate (price and quantity). Tables A.5 and A.6
give the actual numbers used.

The flat base loss for each energy type was
calculated as the increase in price over the base year
multiplied by consumption. The loss above CPI was
calculated by taking the difference between the base
year price adjusted by the general inflation rate, as
measured by the CPI, and the actual price. This
difference was then multiplied by consumption.

SECTION 3: ESTIMATING GROSS RENT,
UTILITY COSTS, CONTRACT RENT, AND INCOMES
OF LOWER AND NON-LOWER INCOME HOUSEHOLDS

Rent

Piecing together a long-term data series on
microeconomic variables such as gross rent, contract
rent, and incomes of specific groups of households can
be a difficult task. Unlike macroeconomic variables,
there is no routine monitoring mechanism in place for
quarterly or monthly reporting. Fortunately, however,

TABLE A.4
Sources for Loss of Purchasing Power Calculations

	Consumption Source	Conversion Factor	Price Source
Residential Sector			
Elec-	1972-80: SEDR, p. 15 1981-82: 2/83 MER, p. 24, broken out by 1979-80 ratios	kWh/3,412 BTUs	1972-82: 2/79 MER, p. 93; 2/83 MER, p. 92: "Average Residential Electric Utility Prices"
Fuel Oil	1972-80: SEDR, p. 15 1981-82: 2/83 MER, p. 24, broken out by 1979-80 ratios	42 gallons/5,825,000 BTUs	1972: ARC, Table 17.2 1973: interpolated 1974-82: 2/79 MER, p. 88; 2/83 MER, p. 88: "Average Selling Price to Residential Customers"
LPG	same as above	42 gallons/3,700,000 BTUs	1972: ARC, Table 17.2 1973-74: interpolated 1975-82: 2/79 MER, p. 92; 2/83 MER, p. 83: Average of Propane and Butane Prices
Natural Gas	same as above	ft^3/1,019 BTUs	1972: ARC, Table 17.2 1973-82: 2/83 MER, p. 91: "Average Residential Heating"
Motor Gasoline	1972-80: SEDR, p. 18 1981-82: 2/83 MER, p. 26, broken out of petroleum column using 1979-80 ratios in SEDR	42 gallons/5,253,000 BTUs	1972: ARC, Table 20.4 1973: CPI for last quarter 1974-82: 2/83 MER, p. 86

Commercial

Fuel		Conversion	
Electricity	1972-80: SEDR, p. 16 1981-82: 2/83 MER, p. 24, broken out by 1979-80 ratios	kWh/3,412 BTUs	1972: ARC, Table 18.1 1973-82: 2/83 MER, p. 92: "Commercial Average"
Petroleum	same as above	42 gallons/6,056,000 BTUs	1972: ARC, Table 18.1 1973-82: 2/83 MER, p. 88: "Distributor's Average Price"
Natural Gas	same as above	ft³/1,019 BTUs	1972-80: AGA, Table 94 1981-82: 2/83 MER, p. 91, broken out by AGA 1979-80 ratios

Industrial

Fuel		Conversion	
Electricity	1972-80: SEDR, p. 17 1981-82: 2/83 MER, p. 23	kWh/3,412 BTUs	1972: ARC, Table 19.1 1973-82: 2/83 MER, p. 92: "Industrial"
Petroleum	same as above	42 gallons/6,287,000 BTUs	1972: ARC, Table 19.1 1973-75: interpolated 1976-82: 2/83 MER, p. 90: "Retail"
Natural Gas	same as above	ft³/1,019 BTUs	1972-80: AGA, Table 94 1981-82: 2/83 MER, p. 91, broken out using AGA 1979-80 ratios
Coal	same as above	N.R.	1972: ARC, Table 19.1 1973-82: 2/83 MER, p. 92: "Coal Prices Delivered to Steam Electric Utilities"

TABLE A.4 (cont'd)

	Consumption Source	Conversion Factor	Price Source
Transportation			
Motor Gasoline	see Motor Gasoline section under Residential Consumption		
Distillate Fuel	1972-80: SEDR, p. 18 1981-82: 2/83 MER, p. 26	42 gallons/5,825,000 BTUs	1972: ARC, Table 20.4 1973-75: interpolated 1976-82: 2/83 MER, p. 83: #2 Diesel - Average Price Retail
Jet Fuel	same as above	42 gallons/5,670,000 BTUs	1972: ARC, Table 20.4 1973-75 interpolated 1976-82: 2/83 MER, p. 87: Kerosene-Type Retail Price
Residuel Fuel	see Petroleum section under Industrial Consumption		
Natural Gas	same as above	ft^3/1,019 BTUs	1972: ARC, Table 20.2 1973-82: 2/83 MER, p. 91: "Price Delivered to Electric Plant"

TABLE A.5
Breakdown of Purchasing Power Lost in the Non-Residential Sector
(Quantities In Quadrillion BTUs) (Prices Per Million BTUs)

	1972	1973	1974	1975	1976	1977	1978	1979	1980	1981	1982
TOTAL											
Total Consumption	38.86	40.64	39.13	36.70	38.80	39.53	40.43	41.48	39.38	37.61	34.97
Average Price	1.32	1.49	1.86	2.35	2.64	3.06	3.28	4.10	5.52	6.83	7.12
Loss above CPI	-	4.14	12.02	23.36	32.31	44.88	48.71	74.04	113.38	144.00	142.36
Flat Base Loss	-	7.33	21.26	37.49	50.88	68.48	78.86	114.94	164.64	203.61	202.83
COMMERCIAL											
Total Consumption	5.80	5.90	5.71	5.61	6.00	5.94	6.09	6.19	6.00	6.01	5.98
Average Price	2.23	2.64	3.34	4.06	4.44	5.19	5.58	6.27	7.99	9.95	10.56
Loss above CPI	-	1.63	4.05	6.64	8.44	11.62	12.80	14.79	21.58	28.55	32.34
Flat Base Loss	-	2.42	6.34	10.27	13.26	17.58	20.40	25.01	34.56	44.23	49.81
INDUSTRIAL											
Total Consumption	24.96	26.21	25.19	22.92	24.25	24.65	24.88	25.45	23.63	22.06	19.74
Average Price	1.01	1.09	1.40	1.77	2.05	2.44	2.66	3.31	4.39	5.48	5.87
Loss above CPI	-	.51	5.24	10.71	16.40	24.05	26.98	39.51	56.72	72.54	69.82
Flat Base Loss	-	2.10	9.82	17.42	25.22	35.25	41.05	58.54	79.87	98.61	95.94
TRANSPORTATION											
Total Consumption	8.10	8.53	8.23	8.17	8.55	8.94	9.46	9.84	9.75	9.54	9.25
Average Price	1.60	1.93	2.22	2.80	3.05	3.35	3.44	4.79	6.75	7.97	7.57
Loss above CPI	-	2.00	2.73	6.01	7.47	9.21	8.93	19.74	35.08	42.91	35.83
Flat Base Loss	-	2.81	5.10	9.80	12.40	15.65	17.41	31.39	50.21	60.77	55.22

Source: See text.

TABLE A.6
Breakdown of Purchasing Power Lost in the Residential Sector
(Quantities In Quadrillion BTUs) (Prices Per Million BTUs)

	1972	1973	1974	1975	1976	1977	1978	1979	1980	1981	1982
TOTAL (Excl. Gasoline)											
Total Consumption	10.09	9.84	9.51	9.58	9.99	9.85	9.95	9.78	9.34	9.40	9.31
Average Price	2.14	2.54	3.15	3.61	3.94	4.60	5.06	6.02	7.61	8.92	9.96
Loss above CPI	–	2.67	5.94	8.14	10.29	14.75	17.13	22.46	31.70	40.20	46.70
Flat Base Loss	–	3.94	9.61	14.08	17.98	24.23	29.05	37.95	51.09	63.73	72.80
ELECTRICITY											
Total Consumption	1.84	1.98	1.97	2.01	2.07	2.20	2.30	2.33	2.45	2.47	2.56
Average Price	6.60	7.44	9.09	10.29	10.93	11.87	12.63	13.60	15.71	18.17	20.13
Loss above CPI	–	.88	2.56	3.57	4.04	5.06	5.37	4.93	6.63	9.50	12.50
Flat Base Loss	–	1.66	4.91	7.42	8.96	11.59	13.87	16.31	22.32	28.58	34.64
FUEL OIL											
Total Consumption	2.24	2.17	1.97	1.92	2.14	2.11	2.06	1.73	1.42	1.49	1.41
Average Price	1.26	1.88	2.50	2.72	2.93	3.31	3.56	4.73	7.05	8.69	8.46
Loss above CPI	–	1.18	2.00	2.10	2.60	3.13	3.28	4.39	6.49	8.87	7.82
Flat Base Loss	–	1.35	2.44	2.80	3.57	4.33	4.74	6.00	8.22	11.07	10.15
LPG											
Total Consumption	.63	.60	.55	.53	.55	.53	.52	.58	.54	.43	.41
Average Price	1.18	1.52	1.87	2.22	2.41	2.86	2.67	4.27	5.98	6.11	6.05
Loss above CPI	–	.16	.26	.37	.44	.61	.43	1.29	1.97	1.53	1.36
Flat Base Loss	–	.20	.38	.55	.68	.89	.77	1.79	2.59	2.12	2.00

NATURAL GAS

Total Consumption	5.26	4.98	4.90	5.02	5.15	4.91	4.98	5.05	4.87	4.78	4.83
Average Price	1.15	1.06	1.23	1.51	1.81	2.22	2.57	3.17	3.87	4.47	5.33
Loss above CPI	—	-.79	-.62	.13	1.27	2.71	3.86	5.90	7.81	9.44	12.91
Flat Base Loss	—	-.45	.39	1.81	3.40	5.25	7.07	10.20	13.25	15.87	20.19

MOTOR GASOLINE

Total Consumption	9.54	9.97	9.78	9.99	10.49	10.77	11.14	10.58	9.90	9.65	9.36
Average Price	2.82	3.28	4.40	4.70	4.86	5.15	5.21	7.05	9.76	10.82	10.24
Loss above CPI	—	2.90	10.48	10.62	10.75	11.42	9.03	22.66	41.64	45.35	34.50
Flat Base Loss	—	4.58	15.45	18.78	21.39	25.09	26.63	44.74	68.74	77.18	68.71

Source: See text.

the combination of several national censuses, conducted
by the Bureau of the Census, and the Annual Housing
Surveys, sponsored by the Department of Housing and
Urban Development, provides a firm basis for making
estimates in the decade after 1969. Moreover, the
estimates derived from those data sources appear to be
quite consistent with other surveys and analyses done
separately.

Table A.7 presents the estimates of median gross
rent, utility payments, and contract rent from the
Annual Housing Surveys. In addition, mean contract rent
for the early 1970s drawn from other sources is shown.
It can be seen that these data provide a consistent set
of estimates.

Although the base year for the median rent in the
Annual Housing Surveys and the means in two other
surveys appear consistent, Table A.7 also shows that the
rate of increase in median rents over the period after
the first energy price shock appears to be somewhat
higher than in other analyses. The difference is not
great and may reflect the more comprehensive coverage of
the housing survey. Since we have used numerous other
pieces of information from the Annual Housing Survey, we
have chosen to simply use the data on gross rent,
contract rent, and utilities from that series, as it is,
in order to maintain consistency.

Making estimates for low income renters is somewhat
more difficult. Because we have defined the lower
income group as the bottom third of the income
distribution, we are forced to combine several smaller
income groups that appear in the published data. Table
A.8 shows the groups, with their median gross rent in
1973 and 1979, as well as other estimates for the early
years.

There are two possible approaches to combining the
groups. One possibility is to interpolate the median
directly. We identify the median group of the combined
three income categories and interpolate linearly. A
second possibility is to take a weighted average of the
medians. The two approaches lead to reasonably consistent results. Since our central concern in using these
estimates is the rate of change between 1973 and 1979,
the difference between the two estimates is quite small.
The average annual rate of change for the interpolation
is 8.96 percent per year. The average annual rate of
change for the weighted average is 8.46 percent per
year.

The ratio of gross rent of lower income households
(as we have defined them) to the national median is
about .85 to 1. This is consistent with the other
available evidence. The estimates for 1972-73 of lower
and national average contract rent based on both the
survey of Five Thousand American Families and the

TABLE A.7
Comparison of Gross Rent, Contract Rent, and Utility Costs
(in Dollars)

| Year | Median | | | Mean |
	Gross Rent	Contract Rent	Utilities	Contract Rent
1969[a]	108	89	19	–
1973[b]	133	116	17	119[c]-122[d]
1980[b]	241	203	38	–

Average Annual Percentage
Change, 1973-80

AHS Median[b]	8.8	8.3		
Lowry (urban only)[e]				
Unadjusted	7.6	6.3		
Adjusted	8.3	7.1		
BLS (urban only)[f]	—	6.4		

[a] U.S. Bureau of the Census, Census of Housing: 1970, HC 7-4 (Washington, D.C.: 1973).

[b] U.S. Department of Housing and Urban Development, Annual Housing Survey, various years.

[c] Richard D. Coe, "A Comparison of Utility Payments and Burdens Between 1971 and 1977," in James N. Morgan and Greg S. Duncan (eds.), Five Thousand American Families: Patterns of Economic Progress, Vol. VIII (Ann Arbor: Institute for Social Research, 1980).

[d] U.S. Bureau of Labor Statistics, Consumer Expenditure Survey: Interview Survey, 1972-73, Average Annual Income and Expenditures for Commodity and Service Groups Classified by Family Characteristics Report 455-4 (Washington, D.C.: 1977).

[e] Ira S. Lowry, Rental Housing in the 1970s: Searching for the Crisis (Santa Monica, Cal.: The Rand Corporation for the U.S. Department of Housing and Urban Development, January 1982).

[f] U.S. Bureau of Labor Statistics, "Urban Residential Rent."

Table A.8
Low Income Rent (in Dollars)

Year	Three Lowest Income Groups			Interpolated Median	Weighted Average of Medians	Mean
	Lowest Income	Next Group	Next Group			
1969[a]	–	–	–	80	–	–
1972-73[b]	84	100	112	–	–	94-97[c]
1973[d]	92	115	130	113	111	–
1980[d]	179	187	222	206	195	–

[a] U.S. Bureau of the Census, Census of Housing: 1970, HC 7-4 (Washington, D.C.: 1973).

[b] U.S. Bureau of Labor Statistics, Consumer Expenditure Survey: Interview Survey, 1972-73 Average Annual Income and Expenditures for Commodity and Service Groups Classified by Family Characteristics, Report 455-4 (Washington, D.C.: 1977), Table 1.

[c] $94 is from Richard D. Coe, "A Comparison of Utility Payments and Burdens Between 1971 and 1977," in James N. Morgan and Greg J. Duncan (eds.), Five Thousand American Families: Patterns of Economic Progress, Vol. VIII (Ann Arbor, Mich.: Institute for Social Research, 1980).

[d] U.S. Department of Housing and Urban Development, Annual Housing Survey, various years.

219

Consumer Expenditure Survey yield a ratio of .78 to 1.
An estimate for New York in 1979 also yields a ratio of
.78 to 1.11/ The ratio of lower income gross rent to
national average gross rent should be slightly higher
than the ratio for contract rent since energy costs are
a large component of lower income gross rent.

To maintain consistency with other analyses, we
utilize the interpolated median gross rent. Not only is
this consistent with the other choices, but it enables
us to link the analysis of rent directly to income as
discussed below.

Income

Since a large part of the discussion of the crisis
in rental housing turns on the question of the relative
rate of increase in rents and income, it was necessary
to estimate a median income for lower income rental
households. We judged that the most reasonable approach
was to find the interpolated median of the low income
categories. In this way, our estimates of gross rent
and median income would be internally consistent and
linked.

Table A.9 gives the estimate of median income per
household and median income per capita for the lower
income group and the national average. It should be
stressed that we have used the medians only to calculate
rates of change -- not to represent the absolute burden
of rent (i.e., rent as a percent of income). Medians
would overstate absolute burdens because they are
smaller than the mean. Therefore, we have used the
Annual Housing Survey direct estimates of rent as a
percent of income for the purpose of discussing the
burden of rent as a percent of income. Table A.9 also
shows the rough estimate of per capita income adjusted
for changes in the make-up of the population. In this
instance we have adjusted 1979 income to the 1973 base.

As an indication of the rate of change in income,
the medians are reasonably reliable. We have compared
mean and median incomes for renters in 1975 and 1979 and
estimate the average annual rate of change for each.
The year 1975 is the first year for which comparable
data in the Census and the Annual Housing Survey is
available, while 1979 is the most recent year for which
such data is available. The average annual change,
compounded, was 6.1 percent for the median income and
6.3 percent for the mean.

The net effect of these estimating procedures used
in Chapter 8 -- the use of medians in particular -- is
probably to overstate rent increases slightly and
understate income increases very slightly. However, the
misestimations are quite small and certainly would not
reverse any of the conclusions reached in the text.

TABLE A.9
Median Income Estimates (in Dollars)

Income Category	Median Income Per Household	Median Income Per Person	Median Income Per Person Adjusted for Population Change
Lower Income			
1973	3,616	1,674	-
1980	5,793	2,401	2,707
1973-80 Average Annual Change	5.1	5.3	7.1
National Average			
1973	7,200	2,915	-
1980	11,269	4,549	4,836
1973-80 Average Annual Change	5.7	6.6	7.5

Source: U.S. Department of Housing and Urban Development, Annual Housing Survey, various years.

Furthermore, we believe that utilizing one set of data
-- rather than patching together a synthetic data set --
renders the analysis more consistent.

Operating Expenses and Energy
Expenses for Rental Housing

Estimating operating costs and energy costs as a
percent of operating costs for rental units, for the
purposes of comparing costs between the public and
private sectors and estimating the burden of energy
prices on operating revenues in the private sector,
presents a major problem. Little actual data is
available. Studies of operating expenses are typically
restricted to case studies or small geographic areas.12/
National data is not readily available and that which
is, is self-selected and does not provide a sound basis
for estimating the relationship between gross rent,
contract rent, and operating costs.13/
In general, a rule of thumb has emerged that
operating expenses run about 50 and 60 percent of total

expenses. Total expenses are taken as equal to contract
rent (with profit included) to derive net operating
returns.14/ Operating expenses are deemed to be
somewhat higher at present for low income units -- 60-70
percent of contract rent -- and somewhat lower for
non-lower income units -- well below 60 percent.15/
    However, in a time when operating costs have been
rising more rapidly than rents, a static rule of thumb
will be misleading. Operating costs have been rising
relative to total costs and total revenues.
    Table A.10 presents a number of recent estimates of
operating costs as a percentage of rent and energy costs
as a percentage of operating costs. The estimates are
fairly close and, on the basis of these, we have
estimated operating and energy costs for 1969, 1973, and
1980 as discussed in the text.

SECTION 4: CLASSIFICATIONS OF PUBLIC
SERVICES: AN ALTERNATIVE REVIEW

    In Chapters 9 and 10 we evaluated which services
would be cut back and which taxes raised as a response
to the resource crisis created by rising energy prices.
To demonstrate that these changes will have a particularly negative effect on low and lower middle income
households, we used an analytic framework drawn from the
"public goods" literature. A brief review of that
literature and the reasoning we applied to it follows.

A Framework for Analyzing Public Services Cutbacks

    Basic Approaches. Public service delivery,
especially at the local level, has become one of the
most intensely analyzed aspects of public policy
research. The intensity of interest has been generated
from three different vantage points: 1) a philosophical
debate over the nature of public goods;16/ 2) court
actions stipulating the criteria for evaluating the
equity of service delivery;17/ and 3) economic analysis
of the efficiency of service delivery.18/
    Each of these three perspectives has stimulated an
extensive body of research literature. The literatures
exhibit a diversity of theoretical and methodological
approaches and are marked by intense analytical as well
as political debate. However, in spite of these
differences, if we focus on the question of service
cutbacks in times of fiscal stress, useful generalizations and common conclusions can be drawn from each of
the research literatures.19/
    At the risk of making an extreme oversimplification,
we can distinguish the questions and issues analyzed in
each of these three areas.
    The literature on the nature of public goods ("pub-

TABLE A.10
Energy as a Percent of Operating Costs

	Energy as a Percent of Operating Costs					Operating Costs as a Percent of Rental Revenue		
	National[a] OTA	Indiana[b]	New York[c]	Public[d] Sector	New Jersey[e]	New York[c]	National[b] Rand	New Jersey[e]
1970	14–17	–	–	30	8	–	45	46
1974	–	22	–	36	11	–	50	49
1977	–	29	36[a]	–	15	–	–	64
1979	30–31	–	–	–	–	49	56	–
1980	39	–	–	36–38	–	–	58	–

a   U.S. Congress, Office of Technology Assessment, Energy Efficiency of Buildings in Cities (Washington, D.C.: 1982), Table 30.

b   David Scott Lindsay and Ira S. Lowry, Rent Inflation in St. Joseph County, Indiana, 1974–78 (Santa Monica, Cal.: The Rand Corporation, November 1980), Table 3.4.

c   Peter D. Salins, The Ecology of Housing Destruction: Economic Effects of Public Intervention in the Housing Market (New York: New York University Press for the International Center for Economic Policy Studies, 1980), Table 13.

d   See text, Chapter 8.

e   George Sternlieb and James W. Hughes, "Rent Control's Impact on the Community Tax Base," in George Sternlieb and James W. Hughes (eds.), America's Housing: Prospects and Problems (New Brunswick, N.J.: Rutgers University, Center for Urban Policy Research, 1980). 1974 is 1973; 1977 is 1976.

("public choice") addresses the following question: "What services are not likely to be provided by the private sector, even though it is in the best interest of each individual to have those services provided?" The underlying task is to identify those characteristics of each type of desirable service which prevent individual suppliers from capturing the adequate benefit (return) in the marketplace required to provide the service on their own.

The literature on distributive equity addresses the following question: "What services ought to be provided by the local public sector and how shall they be distributed in order to ensure social justice?" Distributive equity may address only "fair" distribution of general public services -- e.g., garbage collection -- or it may include compensating distribution of specific services to target groups -- e.g., public assistance (welfare) which redistributes wealth.

The literature on the economic efficiency of service distribution asks the following questions: "What is the most cost effective manner for delivering services and how can society maximize the public good by minimizing cost?" The crux of this issue appears to be the choice of the optimal mix of services to be provided and/or economies of scale, although there are other economies in service delivery (administrative costs, overuse, or congestion costs, etc.) that can be addressed.[20]/

We will briefly examine a sample of each approach to the analysis of public services to derive generalizations about the pattern of expected cutbacks during times of fiscal stress, as well as to gain insight into which services are most vital to the low and lower middle income population.

Public Choice. In an analysis conducted by Ostrom and Ostrom, two characteristics of goods (or services) are considered critical in defining their nature. These are the characteristics of exclusion and jointness. Exclusion pertains to the ability to package or control access to a good:

> Exclusion has long been identified as a necessary characteristic for goods and services to be supplied under market conditions...
> Exclusion occurs when potential users can be denied goods or services unless they meet the terms and conditions of the vendor. If both agree, goods and services are supplied at a price. A quid pro quo exchange occurs. The buyer acquires the good and the seller acquires the value specified. Where exclusion is infeasible, anyone can derive benefits from the good...[21]/

The second characteristic of goods, critical for a determination of their nature, is jointness of use or consumption:

No jointness of consumption exists when consumption by one person precludes its use or consumption by another person. In that case consumption is completely subtractible. A loaf of bread consumed by one person is not available for consumption by another; it is subtracted from the total that was originally available. A good having no jointness of consumption and with which exclusion is feasible is defined as a purely private good. Jointness of consumption, on the other hand, implies that the use or enjoyment of a good by one person does not foreclose its use or enjoyment by others; despite its use by one person, it remains available for use by others in undiminished quantity and quality. A weather forecast is an example of a joint consumption good.22/

Utilizing these two characteristics, Ostrom and Ostrom define four types of goods:

1. Purely public goods are non-exclusive and joint.
2. Toll goods are exclusive and joint.
3. Common pool resources are non-exclusive and non-joint.
4. Private goods have no jointness of consumption and are exclusive.

The classic example of a public good is a mosquito abatement program. It is impossible to exclude specific citizens from the benefit of the program or to charge them according to their benefit (i.e., their use of the program). As a purely public good, mosquito abatement is not likely to be undertaken by private suppliers because they cannot charge for it -- and thereby recover the cost -- and they will get the benefit if anyone else takes the action. Private action is unlikely and, unless public action is taken, society is likely to be deprived of the good.

It is important not to confuse the manner in which a public good is provided with its essential nature as a public good. It may be possible to achieve effective mosquito abatement by having each individual agree to spray his or her personal property (assuming no common or public areas) so long as all agree to do so. It is the necessary covenant -- the agreement by all -- which defines the mosquito abatement program as a public good and makes the societal benefit possible.

Toll goods are goods which are exclusive and joint. Individuals can be excluded from the benefit of the good or made to pay for their exact share of the benefit. The service, however, has a joint nature such that the enjoyment of the good by one individual does not preclude others from enjoying it. The classic example is a toll road. Access can be restricted, but the use by one does not subtract from the potential use by others (within the limits set by congestion).

A "common pool resource" is a non-exclusive, non-joint good. Individuals cannot be excluded, but benefits or costs are non-joint. The classic example is a ground water pool. Drawing on the pool reduces the available pool of resources and precludes others from enjoying that part of the pool which has been consumed. Common pool resources have little relevance to local public services as discussed below.

Private goods have no jointness of consumption and are exclusive. Their value is easily calculated and collected in private transaction. Under standard assumptions about competitive markets and free flowing information, we can expect individuals to provide exactly the optimum level of these goods through private action.

Table A.11 lists the four categories of goods, including the examples given by Ostrom and Ostrom. It is our hypothesis that during times of fiscal stress, goods which are less "public" would be subject to greater reduction in expenditures or subsidies (i.e., fees would be increased to cover the full cost of use). Moreover, we believe that non-exclusion would take precedence over jointness in commanding resources during times of fiscal stress. Thus, we hypothesize that decreases in subsidies (cuts in services or increases in fees) for private goods will be greater than those for toll goods, which in turn will be greater than for public goods. Where relevant, common pool resources would fall between toll goods and public goods.

The Equity of Local Service Distribution. Dimond, Chamberlain, and Hillyerd identify three types of goods in their discussion of the equity of public services distribution.23/ The definitions of these goods are derived largely from interpretations of Supreme Court decisions. Goods are defined by the level of protection which society must offer citizens in the acquisition of them -- minimal protection, equality, or unregulated free market risk.

Minimum protection guarantees the basic level of a service:

Deprivation of basic public services, below the minimum society has determined necessary for survival, to persons who lack the wherewithal to secure such services elsewhere (through user fees,

226

TABLE A.11
A Public Goods Categorization Of Services

	Joint	Non-joint
	Public Goods	**Common Pool Resources**
Non-ex-clusive	Peace and Security Mosquito Abatement Fire Protection Air Pollution Control	Ground Water Crude Oil Fishing Grounds
	Toll Goods	**Private Goods**
Exclu-sive	Toll Roads Cable Television Libraries Telephone Services/ Utilities	Bread Shoes

Source: Vincent Ostrom and Elinor Ostrom, "Public Goods
and Public Choices," in E.S. Savas (ed.),
Alternatives for Delivering Public Services
(Boulder, Col.: Westview Press, 1977).

special assessments, private purchase or residential relocation) is unacceptable.24/

Equality is defined as providing compensatory
services. That is, beyond fair access, it can be argued
that society must "maximize the welfare of the worst off
representative man."25/ This requires that "social and
economic inequalities are arranged so that they are ...
to the greatest benefit of the least advantaged."26/
Goods and services for which society need not make
special provisions in their distribution are defined as
being subject to "market risk." That is, they are
services which society allows to be distributed wholly
by the market, placing individuals at the risk of not
acquiring those services, depending upon the outcome of
the whole range of market transactions.
Since Dimond, et al., are interested in minimum
protection only, they do not provide a detailed categorization of services. They define minimally adequate
education, health, welfare, and shelter as goods and
services subject to the minimum protection principle.

227

do not, however, discuss the possibility that the provision of certain levels of services might be adequate to meet the minimal protection principle, but higher levels of the same services for certain individuals might meet the equality principle. That is, one might define the fair provision of public education as minimally adequate but require compensatory education to meet the equality principle.

Table A.12 presents a list of services, arranged with those that are easily identified as subject to the minimum protection principle at the top. The middle of the list would represent services which are subject to the minimum protection and equality principles. Toward the bottom are services which are subject to the equality principle only, or, at the very bottom, to market risk.

Again, it is our hypothesis that during times of fiscal stress, services are cut from the bottom to the top. Note that this list is quite consistent with the list derived from the earlier discussion of public choice, although the underlying principle is significantly different.27/

Economic Efficiency. The literature on economic efficiency is multifaceted, including purely economic concerns with the optimal provision of services, analysis of urban decay associated with suburban flight, and cost-cutting analysis associated with the "taxpayer revolt" of the 1970s.28/ Although there are many aspects to this literature, for the purposes of our analysis we will look only at the study of urban decay and its antecedents in the analysis of the optimal provision of public goods.29/ The central issue in the analysis of the optimal provision of public services is the question of how and why specific services are provided by certain communities in close proximity to each other in order to maximize the welfare of residents of each community. In the urban decay analysis, the central issue is to discover how and why services and revenue bases are distributed among communities, to the detriment of central cities.

Boskin utilizes a distinction between two types of goods -- those which enhance the value of property and those which are redistributive -- to explain patterns of service distribution:

It is convenient to view local governments as providing two distinct types of public goods. On the one hand, they provide goods, such as education and police and fire protection, which increase the services from real property (the only thing which must remain) within their jurisdiction. On the other, they provide services, such as welfare and bilin-

228

TABLE A.12
An Equity Categorization of Public Services

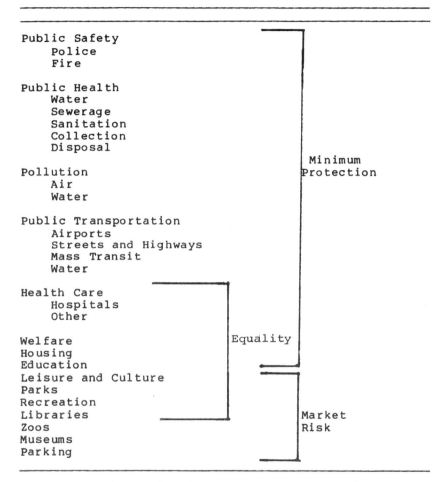

Public Safety
    Police
    Fire

Public Health
    Water
    Sewerage
    Sanitation
    Collection
    Disposal

Pollution
    Air
    Water

Public Transportation
    Airports
    Streets and Highways
    Mass Transit
    Water

Health Care
    Hospitals
    Other

Welfare
Housing
Education
Leisure and Culture
Parks
Recreation
Libraries
Zoos
Museums
Parking

Minimum
Protection

Equality

Market
Risk

Source: Paul R. Dimond, Constance Chamberlain, and
        Wayne Hillyerd, A Dilemma of Local Govern-
        ments (Lexington, Mass.: Lexington Books,
        1978).

gual programs in schools, which redistribute the command over resources. While each local government positively values increased internal redistributive services, the competing governments attempt to induce both an in-migration of wealthy individuals and business ... and an out-migration of recipients of redistributive programs.30/

This distinction, based on economic considerations tied to land values and the fiscal viability of local governments, parallels the equity discussion quite closely. Note, in particular, the implicit distinction between minimal provision of a certain service, such as education, which may be considered to contribute to property values (by enhancing the quality of life within the jurisdiction), and provision of a higher level of that service (bilingual education), which is considered redistributive. This parallels our earlier distinction between minimal protection and equality.

Without actually defining categories of goods, Boskin's analysis hypothesizes that local governments, anxious to preserve the wealth of their population, will emphasize services such as police and fire protection at the expense of welfare and special education. While the purpose of preserving these services is the maintenance of a wealthy population, the results coincide with the two categorizations described above. That is, services such as police and fire protection coincide with the services that will be cut last in the other analyses. Welfare and special education coincide with those that will be cut first.

Other Categorizations of Public Services. All three of the approaches to public service analysis discussed above suggest underlying distinctions between categories of local level goods and services -- distinctions that transcend simple issues of efficiency and address more fundamental issues of the basic nature of services.

Given this fundamental similarity in the categorization of services, it should not be surprising that some authors have chosen to synthesize the various approaches. Muth, as discussed in text, divides public services into two broad categories -- allocative and redistributive.31/ Allocative goods parallel public goods. Redistributive goods, as defined by Muth, parallel the broader definition of equity we have used above.

Moreover, Muth divides allocative goods into two categories, "area-wide" and "local." This would seem to encompass a distinction from the economic efficiency literature of economies of scale.

In Table A.13 we see the resulting categorization of services, which is consistent with the earlier lists developed from the separate literatures. We hypothesize

TABLE A.13
Categorization of Services

Area-Wide Allocative Services
    Streets and Highways
    Sewerage and Sanitation
    Water Transport
    Airports

Local Allocative Services
    Fire
    Police
    Libraries
    Parks and Recreation
    Parking

Redistributive Services
    Education
    Hospitals
    Health
    Housing
    Welfare

Source: Richard Muth, Urban Economic Problems
         (New York: Harper and Row, 1975).

---

that during times of fiscal stress, cutbacks would occur first at the bottom of the list and move towards the top.[32]/

Additional Evidence on Rankings of Public Services. It is worth noting that these analytic concepts of different categories of public services are reasonably consistent with survey and other evidence on public attitudes toward services. For example, in one recent survey, 21 public services were ranked by two groups of respondents -- one which was given an estimate of the cost of each service to the municipality and one which was not.[33]/
The results show that certain services received high levels of support by both groups. These are clearly the most "public" services as we have defined them -- fire, police, streets, water, sewers. A second group of services received high levels of support from those who were told the price. In the main, these are toll goods -- museums, parks, ambulance service, animal shelters, public health. Finally, redistributive goods -- welfare

and education -- received the lowest level of support
from both groups. These public valuations of service
appear to be consistent with the rankings of services
presented earlier. We can conclude that the general
public, like local governments, will support cuts in
redistributive services first, toll goods second, and
public services last.

In this regard, we can also note that the extent to
which services are actually provided by local governments seems to reflect public opinion.34/ Although
somewhat dated, Liebert's analysis of the percentage of
local governments which provided each of 12 services in
1962 is noteworthy. Ten of the twelve included in the
historical analysis were also included in the survey
mentioned above. Table A.14 shows the services as
ranked in the survey and the number of local governments
providing the service in 1962. As Table A.14 shows,
there is a strong correlation between attitudinal
support for specific services (expressed in the late
1970s) and actual delivery of those services two decades
earlier.

Thus, we believe that the classifications used in
Chapter 9 to categorize services is well grounded in the
intellectual debate over the nature of public services,
as well as the empirical reality of public opinion
about, and the actual provision of, services.

SECTION 5: URBAN HEALTH, URBAN DECAY, URBAN
DISTRESS, AND ENERGY BURDEN FOR 150 CITIES

Table A.15 gives the scores on the urban health,
urban decay, urban distress, and energy burden variables
used to examine the relationship between local
government energy burden and urban characteristics.

TABLE A.14
Evidence on the Coincidence of Public Support for the Provision of
Public Services and the Actual Provision of Public Services
(Percentage of Local Governments Providing Specific Services)

Category from Survey	Service	Percent of Local Governments Providing Service in 1962
High Support With and Without Price Specified	Police	100
	Fire	100
	Streets	100
	Sewers	60
	Libraries	--
	Water	--
High Support Only With Price Specified	Parks	89
	Public Health	70
	Parks	--
	Ambulance Service	--
	Animal Shelters	--
High Support Only Without Price Specified	Garbage Collection	22
	Courts	12
	Mental Health	--
	Elections Office	--
	Tax Office	--
Low Support With and Without Price Specified	Education	22
	Welfare	24
	Coliseum	--
	Sheriff	--
	Schools	--
	Registry of Deeds	--

"--" indicates services which were not included in the 1962
analysis.

Sources: Thomas S. Arrington and David D. Jordan, "Willingness to
          Pay Per Capita Costs as a Measure of Support for Urban
          Services," Public Administration Review, March/April
          1982.

          Roland S. Liebert, Disintegration and Political Actions:
          The Changing Functions of City Governments in America
          (New York: Academic Press, 1976).

TABLE A.15
Measures of Local Energy Burden and Urban Health

State	City	Energy Burden[a]	Urban Health[b]		
			Distress	Decline	Health
Alabama	Birmingham	.27	−3	0	−3
	Huntsville	.33	+3	+1	+4
	Mobile	.26	0	+1	+1
	Montgomery	.26	+1	+4	+5
Arizona	Phoenix	.46	+1	+1	+2
	Tucson	.39	+1	−2	−1
Arkansas	Little Rock	.24	−1	0	−1
California	Anaheim	.42	+2	−2	0
	Berkeley	.91	−3	−1	−4
	Fremont	.30	+5	+2	+7
	Fresno	.26	−1	+1	0
	Garden Grove	.53	+4	−2	+2
	Glendale	.35	+4	0	+4
	Huntington Beach	.26	+3	0	+3
	Long Beach	.50	−2	−1	−3
	Los Angeles	.15	−2	0	−2
	Oakland	.40	−3	−2	−5
	Pasadena	.44	−1	0	−1
	Riverside	.36	+3	−3	0
	Sacramento	.25	−1	0	−1
	San Bernadino	.25	−3	−2	−5
	San Diego	.38	+3	0	+3
	San Francisco	.03	−2	+1	−1
	San Jose	.31	+3	+2	+5
	Santa Ana	.50	+2	−1	+1
	Stockton	.66	−2	+2	0
	Torrance	.24	+5	+2	+7
Colorado	Colorado Springs	.49	+2	0	+2
	Denver	.38	−1	+1	0
Connecticut	Bridgeport	.71	−1	−2	−3
	Hartford	.89	−4	−5	−9
	New Haven	.52	−3	−1	−4
	Stamford	.33	+1	−2	−1
	Waterbury	.67	+1	−2	−1
District of Columbia	Washington	.76	−1	0	−1
Florida	Ft. Lauderdale	.23	−1	0	−1
	Hialeah	.23	+1	+1	+2
	Hollywood	.27	+1	−1	0
	Jacksonville	.35	+2	+1	+3

TABLE A.15 (cont'd)

State	City	Energy Burden[a]	Urban Health[b]		
			Distress	Decline	Health
Florida	Miami	.31	+4	0	+4
	St. Petersburg	.46	-3	-1	-4
	Tampa	.28	-3	-1	-4
Georgia	Atlanta	.28	-4	-3	-7
	Columbus	.42	+2	0	+2
	Macon	.52	0	+2	+2
	Savannah	.76	-3	0	-3
Hawaii	Honolulu	.35	+2	0	+2
Illinois	Chicago	.41	-1	+1	0
	Peoria	.18	0	-1	-1
	Rockford	.55	+1	-2	-1
Indiana	Evansville	.49	-1	-1	-2
	Fort Wayne	.35	0	+1	+1
	Gary	.60	-2	-3	-5
	Hammond	.59	+2	+1	+3
	Indianapolis	.73	+2	-2	0
	South Bend	.49	0	+1	+1
Iowa	Cedar Rapids	.24	+4	0	+4
	Des Moines	.41	+3	+1	+4
Kansas	Kansas City	.77	-1	0	-1
	Topeka	.32	+2	+2	+4
	Wichita	.36	+4	+4	+8
Kentucky	Lexington-Fayette	.41	-1	+3	+2
	Louisville	.71	-3	+1	-2
Louisiana	Baton Rouge	.54	0	+1	+1
	New Orleans	.29	-1	+3	+2
	Shreveport	.21	+1	+2	+3
Maryland	Baltimore	.69	-3	+1	-2
Massachusetts	Boston	.49	-5	-4	-9
	Cambridge	.50	-2	-4	-6
	Springfield	.89	-3	-3	-6
	Worcester	.69	-1	-3	-4
Michigan	Dearborn	.59	+1	+1	+2
	Detroit	.51	-3	-3	-6
	Flint	.37	-3	-2	-5
	Grand Rapids	.43	-2	-1	-3
	Lansing	.15	0	0	0
	Warren	.65	+4	-1	+3
Minnesota	Duluth	.36	+2	+2	+4
	Minneapolis	.55	0	0	0
	St. Paul	.66	+2	0	+2
Mississippi	Jackson	.62	+2	+1	+3

TABLE A.15 (cont'd)

State	City	Energy Burden[a]	Urban Health[b] Distress	Decline	Health
Missouri	Independence	.10	+4	+2	+6
	Kansas City	.58	−1	0	−1
	St. Louis	.53	−4	0	−4
	Springfield	.01	+2	+1	+3
Nebraska	Lincoln	.26	+4	+2	+6
	Omaha	.46	+3	+3	+6
Nevada	Las Vegas	.70	−1	−4	−5
New Jersey	Camden	.94	−4	−2	−6
	Elizabeth	.67	−1	−2	−3
	Jersey City	.75	−3	−4	−7
	Newark	.38	−5	−3	−8
	Trenton	.52	−4	−4	−8
New Mexico	Albuquerque	.37	+1	−1	0
New York	Albany	.88	+1	+1	+2
	Buffalo	1.10	−2	−1	−3
	N.Y. City	.62	−3	−3	−6
	Rochester	.76	−2	−3	−5
	Syracuse	1.10	0	−1	−1
	Yonkers	.56	+3	−2	+1
North Carolina	Charlotte	.35	0	+1	+1
	Greensboro	.50	+1	+2	+3
	Raleigh	.45	+2	+4	+6
	Winston Salem	.30	−3	0	−3
Ohio	Akron	.51	−2	−2	−4
	Canton	.43	−3	−2	−5
	Cinncinati	.48	−3	−1	−4
	Cleveland	.52	−5	−4	−9
	Columbus	.48	0	+1	+1
	Dayton	.53	−4	−4	−8
	Toledo	.58	0	−2	−2
	Youngstown	.47	−3	−1	−4
Oklahoma	Oklahoma City	.25	+1	−2	−1
	Tulsa	.26	+3	+2	+5
Oregon	Portland	.34	−3	−1	−4
Pennsylvania	Allentown	.49	+3	0	+3
	Erie	.64	+2	+1	+3
	Philadelphia	.50	−4	−3	−7
	Pittsburg	.67	−3	−1	−4
	Scranton	.65	−2	+1	−1
Rhode Island	Providence	.41	−2	0	−2
South Carolina	Columbia	.32	−1	+1	0

236

TABLE A.15 (cont'd)

State	City	Energy Burden[a]	Urban Health[b]		
			Distress	Decline	Health
Tennessee	Chattanooga	.79	-2	+1	-1
	Knoxville	.32	-1	0	-1
	Memphis	.50	+1	0	+1
	Nashville-Davidson	.21	+2	+3	+5
Texas	Amarillo	.27	+4	+2	+6
	Austin	.24	+2	+3	+5
	Beaumont	.14	0	+2	+2
	Corpus Christi	.15	+2	+3	+5
	Dallas	.15	+1	+1	+2
	El Paso	.12	+2	0	+2
	Fort Worth	.22	+3	+1	+4
	Houston	.25	+3	+3	+6
	Lubbock	.22	+3	+4	+7
	San Antonio	.25	+2	+3	+5
Utah	Salt Lake City	.21	+1	+2	+3
Virginia	Alexandria	.47	+3	+2	+5
	Hampton	.50	+5	+3	+8
	Newport News	.50	+2	+2	+4
	Norfolk	.55	-1	0	-1
	Richmond	.68	-2	+2	0
	Virginia Beach	.43	+5	+3	+8
Washington	Seattle	.09	0	0	0
	Spokane	.57	-1	0	-1
	Tacoma	.45	-2	+2	0
Wisconsin	Madison	.38	+4	+2	+6
	Milwaukee	.44	+1	-1	0

[a] U.S. Department of Commerce, City Government Finances in 1979-80 (Washington, D.C.: September 1981), Table 5.

[b] Katharine L. Bradbury, Anthony Downs, and Kenneth A. Small, Urban Decline and the Future of American Cities (Washington, D.C.: The Brookings Institution, 1982), p. 52.

Footnotes

CHAPTER 1

1. One fairly complete listing of research in the energy area can be found in U.S. Department of Energy, Technical Information Center, Energy Abstracts for Policy Analysis (Washington, D.C.: first published November 1974).

2. "The Leverage of Lower Oil Prices," Business Week, March 22, 1982, p. 66. It should be noted that the popular press and many academics only came to acknowledge the awesome impact of energy prices when the prospect of a moderation in price increases or an actual decline in prices was at hand. In that context, they were ready to talk about a boost to the economy through lower energy prices. Many of these analysts had earlier denied or ignored the negative effects of rising prices. An objective analysis must recognize the impact of energy prices both when they rise and when they fall. The Consumer Energy Council of America has always argued that rising energy prices have a massive impact on the economy.

For example, in April 1979, in discussing crude oil decontrol, the first issue we addressed was the economic issue ("Questions and Answers on Crude Oil Decontrol," [Washington, D.C.: Consumer Energy Council of America, April 30, 1979]): "We must ask ourselves whether we really want the administration, the oil companies and the cartel to price us into a depression as a device for cutting energy use and whether this constitutes sound public policy." Although some accused CECA of over-stating the economic impact of decontrol at the time, this statement hardly seems any more extreme than Business Week's recent retrospective appraisal. The data presented in Chapter 3 document the fact that, since CECA's statement was made, we have entered the longest and deepest recession since the depression of the 1930s -- especially when the downturn is measured by unemployment.

3. Daniel Yergin and Martin Hillenbrand (eds.), Global Insecurity: A Strategy for Energy and Economic Renewal (Boston: Houghton Mifflin, 1982), p. 3.

4. See Chapter 3.

5. Our analysis of the resources at stake and the potential impact can be found in the Consumer Energy Council of America Research Foundation, Natural Gas Decontrol: A Case of Trickle-Up Economics (Washington, D.C.: January 28, 1982), The Past as Prologue I: The Underestimation of Price Increases in the Decontrol Debate: A Comparison of Oil and Natural Gas (Washington, D.C.: February 1982), The Past as Prologue II: The Economic Effects of Rising Energy Prices: A Comparison of the Oil Price Shock and Natural Gas Decontrol (Washington, D.C.: March 1982).

Differing points of view on the potential impacts can be found in the U.S. Department of Energy, A Study of Alternatives to the Natural Gas Policy Act, Appendix A: Two Market Analysis of Natural Gas Decontrol, Appendix C: Macroeconomic Consequences of Natural Gas Decontrol (Washington, D.C.: November 1981) and Glenn C. Loury, An Analysis of the Efficiency and Inflationary Impacts of the Decontrol of Natural Gas Prices (Washington, D.C.: Natural Gas Supply Association, April 1981). An evaluation of ten studies of decontrol (not including CECA's), can be found in Foster Associates, Inc., A Comparison and Appraisal of Ten Natural Gas Deregulation Studies (Washington, D.C.: Chemical Manufacturers Association, February 16, 1982).

6. Our analysis of the potential impact of energy taxes can be found in Consumer Energy Council of America Research Foundation, A Comprehensive Analysis of the Impact of a Crude Oil Import Fee: Dismantling a Trojan Horse (Washington, D.C.: April 1982). Other analyses of these taxes can be found in Congressional Budget Office, Memorandum: Oil Import Fees, (Washington, D.C.: March 22, 1982); Oil Import Tariff: Alternative Scenarios and their Effects (Washington, D.C.: April 1982); Bernard A. Gelb and Everson W. Hall, Revenue and Macroeconomic Impacts of an Oil Import Tax: A Brief Review (Washington, D.C.: Congressional Research Service of the Library of Congress, April 6, 1982).

7. Yergin and Hillenbrand, Global Insecurity..., pp. 130-131.

CHAPTER 2

1. Juxtaposing social, technical and economic considerations is frequently suggested, but rarely carried out. As discussed in Chapter 1, it is the social side of the equation that is usually given short shrift. For these reasons, we emphasize the social

issue in this work. However, in the past, we have analyzed the economic and technical aspects of the energy issue in a balanced fashion and suggested a framework for integrating the various aspects of the analysis. See, Consumer Energy Council of America, Energy Conservation in New Buildings: A Critique and Alternative Approach to the Department of Energy's Building Energy Performance Standards (Washington, D.C.: April 1980), Chapter 13; Consumer Energy Council of America Research Foundation, A Comprehensive Analysis of the Costs and Benefits of Low Income Weatherization and Its Potential Relationship to Low Income Energy Assistance (Washington, D.C.: June 2, 1981), Chapter III, A Comprehensive Analysis of a Crude Oil Import Fee...; Mark Cooper, "Energy Policy and Jobs: The Conservation Path to Fuller Employment," a paper presented to the Conference on Energy and Jobs, Industrial Union Department, AFL-CIO, May 5, 1980.

For example, Sam Schurr, et al., Energy in America's Future: The Choices Before Us (Baltimore: Johns Hopkins University Press for Resources for the Future, 1979), p. 13, discuss the economic, thermodynamic, and ethical, equity or environmental dimensions and stress the economic to the exclusion of the other aspects.

2. Bibliographic references can be found in U.S. Department of Energy, Fuel Oil Marketing Advisory Committee (FOMAC), Low Income Energy Assistance Programs (Washington, D.C.: July 1979, July 1980); Meg Power and Joel Eisenberg, Low Income Energy Assistance in the 1980s: The Needs and the Choices (Washington, D.C.: Northeast Coalition for Energy Equity, March 1, 1982).

3. A number of works have recently been devoted to analyzing and recounting the history of the policymaking process. See, for example, Craufurd D. Goodwin et al., Energy Policy in Perspective: Today's Problems, Yesterday's Solutions (Washington, D.C.: The Brookings Institution, 1981); Joseph Kalt, The Economics and Politics of Oil Price Regulation: Federal Policy in the Post-Embargo Era (Cambridge, Mass.: MIT Press, 1981), Chapters 6 and 7; M. Elizabeth Sanders, The Regulation of Natural Gas Policy and Politics, 1938-1978 (Philadelphia: Temple University Press, 1981).

4. The two primary interventions in the marketplace that became the central topic of the energy policy debate were crude oil and natural gas price controls. Crude oil price controls appear to have been a "hangover" from the Nixon wage and price controls, while natural gas controls were longstanding. There were, of course, other forms of intervention in the form of tax incentives and subsidies for production. As pressures built to decontrol prices, intervention in the marketplace shifted to incentives for conservation,

energy assistance and allocation controls. These were embodied in a series of laws in the mid-late 1970s, including the Energy Policy and Conservation Act of 1975, the Energy Conservation and Production Act of 1976, the Public Utilities Regulatory Policy Act of 1978, the Fuel Use Act of 1978, and culminating in the Crude Oil Windfall Profit Tax Act (1980).

5. The Crude Oil Windfall Profit Tax Act made this an explicit statement. A body of testimony that seems to have paved the way for this policy conclusion can be found in U.S. Congress, Senate, Special Committee on Aging, Hearings on the Impact of Rising Energy Costs on Older Americans, 95th Cong., 1st. sess., April 1977; U.S. Department of Energy, Office of Hearings and Appeals, Fuel Oil Evidentary Hearing (August 1978); FOMAC, Low Income Energy... (1979).

Some believed at the time, and still do, that energy need not be defined in this special manner; or, that even if it is so defined, there is no need for such a special commitment, since existing income transfer programs are more than adequate to cope with the problem (Thomas C. Schelling, Thinking Through the Energy Problem [New York: Committee for Economic Development, 1979]). Others took, and still take, the contrary point of view, arguing that an even broader and more specific commitment to alleviate the burden of rising energy prices is necessary (FOMAC, Low Income Energy...). Nevertheless, the prevailing view was to define energy as a uniquely vital commodity and to make a specific moral commitment to cushion the burden that rising energy prices place on fixed, low, and lower middle income households.

6. U.S. Congress, Crude Oil Windfall Profit Tax Act of 1980, Conference Report, 96th Cong., 2nd sess., May 7, 1980, pp. 64-65.

7. Ibid., p. 117.

8. Each of the past three Administrations has exercised its executive powers to decontrol part of the domestic energy industry and used the efficiency argument as its basic reason (Ford, heating oil [April 1976]; Carter, crude oil [June 1979]; Reagan crude oil [January 1981]). The reasoning was set forth in policy analyses and/or testimony before Congressional Committees and/or public pronouncements. See, for example, U.S. Congress, House, Interstate and Foreign Commerce Committee, Testimony of Gorman Smith, 94th Cong., 2nd sess., June 22, 29, 1976, H.R. Doc. No. 914-131, in the matter of heating oil decontrol; U.S. Congress, Joint Economic Committee, Energy Subcommittee, Testimony of Charles L. Shultze, Chairman, Council of Economic Advisors, 96th Cong., 1st sess., April 25, 1979, in the matter of crude oil decontrol; and the comments of David Stockman in "Decontrol of Oil Prices

Expected Today," The Wall Street Journal, January 28,
1981, in the matter of gasoline decontrol. Congress,
for its part, legislated the phased decontrol of natural
gas in 1978.

The support for decontrol in the intellectual
community is best reflected in a series of influential
books published in the late 1970s. Most prominent among
them are: Robert Stobaugh and Daniel Yergin (eds.),
Energy Future: The Report of the Energy Project at the
Harvard Business School (New York: Random House, 1979);
Hans Landsberg, ed., Energy: The Next Twenty Years: A
Report Sponsored by the Ford Foundation and Administered
by Resources for the Future (Cambridge, Mass.:
Ballinger, 1979); National Research Council, National
Academy of Sciences, Energy in Transition 1985-2010:
Final Report of the Committee on Nuclear and Alternative
Energy Systems (San Francisco: W.H. Freeman and Company,
1980); Schurr, et al., Energy in America's Future....

9. The earliest piece of survey evidence that
addressed the issue of the difficulty of cutting back on
energy consumption by various income groups appears to
have been gathered in mid-1974 by the Survey Research
Center at the University of Michigan (see Richard T.
Curtin, "Consumer Adaptation to Energy Shortages,"
Journal of Energy and Development, 2:1, Autumn 1976).
Much higher proportions of lower income than higher
income consumers said they could not adjust their
heating easily to energy shortages. The difficulty of
adjustment of electricity consumption was more even
across income categories, although lower income
households still said more frequently that they could
not easily adjust. With respect to gasoline, the
reverse was true. Higher income households said they
could not easily adjust.

Commenting on the general pattern of survey
evidence, an official of the Department of Energy
involved in conducting research into the attitudes of
the public toward energy told the Energy Research
Advisory Board:

> Electricity is generally considered by the pub-
> lic to be a basic human right rather than a commod-
> ity. Underlying this attitude, historically, is
> the notion that it's the government's responsibili-
> ty to assure that adequate power supplies are
> available to consumers (Inside Energy, June 11,
> 1982, p. 6).

10. Conducted by Cambridge Reports, Inc., (N.D.).

11. A Survey of the Psychosocial and Economic
Effects of Inflation and Natural Gas Deregulation on
Residential and Commercial Customers, prepared by
Stockton State College, November 1981.

12. The Community Development Program, College of Human Development of the Pennsylvania State University for the Bureau of Consumer Services of the Public Utility Commission of the Commonwealth of Pennsylvania, Residential Utility Consumer Payment Problems: A Study of Customer, Company and PUC Interactions, Vol. II: Consumer and Company Responses to Impending Utility Terminations (May 1982).

13. Barbara C. Fahrar, et al., Public Opinion About Energy: A Literature Review (Washington, D.C.: U.S. Department of Commerce, National Technical Information Service, June 1979), p. 117.

14. Ibid., pp. 87-89. Daniel Yergin, "America in the Strait of Stringency," in Yergin and Hillenbrand, Global Insecurity..., pp. 132-133, points out that there may be deep-seated psychological reasons for these responses that go beyond simple economics.

15. June 26, 1982.

16. "Burden Allocation and Electric Utility Rate Structures Issues and Options in the TVA Region," presented at A Conference on Higher Energy Costs: Assessing the Burden, organized by Resources for the Future and the Brookings Institution, October 9-10, 1980, p. 2.

17. Ibid., p. 5.

18. Ibid., p. 7.

19. A recent issue of the Journal of Social Issues (37:2, 1981) includes a series of articles on the topic of energy conservation which deals with responses to rising prices and contains an extensive bibliography. For additional bibliographic references, see C. Dennis Anderson and Gordon H.C. McDougall, Consumer Energy Research: An Annotated Bibliography (Canada: Consumer Research and Evaluation Branch of Consumer and Corporate Affairs, July 1980).

20. See note 8 above.

21. The corollary was occasionally stated, although not emphatically and not analyzed in detail (see Schurr, et al., Energy in America's Future... and Schelling, Thinking Through..., pp. 58-60). Only when the equity issue is seen as a major obstacle to market pricing does it appear to have received close attention. See Committee for Economic Development and the Conservation Foundation, Energy Prices and Public Policy (New York: Committee for Economic Development, July 1982), Chapter 2, in which the equity issue receives roughly equal attention as other issues and is given a prominent place in the discussion, which is in marked contrast to the earlier analysis done by the Committee for Economic Development. Yergin, "America in the Strait...," pp. 122-123, presents a most interesting analysis of the factors that enabled the efficiency argument to triumph over the equity argument, or at least to diffuse it ade-

quately to clear the way for decontrol of energy prices.
22. We have in mind the statistical concept of the
risk associated with creating a Type I or Type II error.
A Type I error occurs in hypothesis testing when the
null hypothesis is true and we consider it false. A
Type II error occurs when the null hypothesis is false
and we consider it true. The label of Type I or Type II
depends on how the social scientist wants to test his or
other estimates.

Our hypothesis is that there is a large disproportionate impact on lower income households caused by
rising energy prices. The null hypothesis would be that
there is little or no disproportionate burden. For the
purposes of this study we have chosen to minimize the
possibility of a Type II error. We want to especially
avoid accepting the null hypothesis (no disproportionate
burden) when it is actually false, because the policy
consequences are so dire. Wrongly believing that there
is little or no disproportionate burden, we underfund
social responses and place the most vulnerable part of
the population at extreme risk. (For a discussion of
the null hypothesis that makes this point in more
technical terms, see William L. Hayes, _Statistics_ [New
York: Holt, Rinehart and Winston, 1963].)

23. U.S. Department of Energy, Energy Information
Administration, _Residential Energy Consumption Survey:
Consumption and Expenditures, April 1978 through March
1979_ (Washington, D.C.: July 1980), _1979-1980 Consumption and Expenditures, Part I: National Data_ (Washington, D.C.: April 1981), _1978-1980 Consumption and
Expenditures, Part II: Regional Data_ (Washington, D.C.:
May 1981). _Consumption and Expenditures, April 1980
through March 1981_ (Washington, D.C.: September 1982).

We have chosen to utilize survey-based data, rather
than several available synthetic sets of data, since the
assumptions that go into synthesizing the data leave
them subject to doubt, even though they are rendered
more comprehensive (e.g., it is possible to link home
energy and gasoline consumption). See the discussion in
U.S. Department of Energy, Energy Information Administration, _A Distributional Analysis of the 1985 Energy
Projections for the Annual Report to Congress of the
Energy Information Administration_ (Washington, D.C.:
June 1978).

24. U.S. Department of Commerce, Bureau of the
Census, U.S. Department of Housing and Urban Development
(Sponsor), _Annual Housing Survey: Current Housing Report
Series H-150: Parts A-F_, various issues.

The Parts utilized throughout this study are _Part A:
General Housing Characteristics for the United States
and Regions_, _Part B: Indicators of Housing and Neighborhood Quality by Financial Characteristics for the United
States and Regions_, _Part C: Financial Characteristics of_

244

the Housing Inventory for the United States and Regions, Part F: Energy Related Housing Characteristics for the United States and Regions (1978 and after).

25. Our primary source has been U.S. Department of Labor, Bureau of Labor Statistics, Consumer Expenditure Survey: Interview Survey, 1972-73, Average Annual Income and Expenditures for Commodities and Service Groups Classified by Family Characteristics Report 455-4 (Washington, D.C.: 1977). For the analysis of appliance and automobile ownership we have used the same source, the report entitled, Inventories of Vehicles and Selected Household Equipment, 1973 Report 455-5 (Washington, D.C.: 1978).

26. Richard D. Coe, "A Comparison of Utility Payments and Burdens Between 1971 and 1979," in James N. Morgan and Greg S. Duncan (eds.), Five Thousand American Families: Patterns of Economic Progress, Vol. VIII (Ann Arbor: Institute for Social Research, 1980), pp. 339-380.

27. U.S. Department of Energy, Energy Information Administration, Residential Energy Consumption Survey: Consumption and Expenditures, April 1978 through March 1979 (Washington, D.C.: July 1980), and Characteristics of the Housing Stock and Households (Washington, D.C.: February 1980).

28. U.S. Department of Transportation, Federal Highway Administration, 1977 Nationwide Personal Transportation Study, Reports 1-7 (Washington, D.C.: various dates).

29. U.S. Department of Commerce, Bureau of the Census, City Government Finances (Washington, D.C.: various dates). The city government data is published annually. Data for all local governments is not published but is available in the form of computer printouts.

30. The regions are as follows: Northeast (Maine, Vermont, New Hampshire, Connecticut, Massachusetts, Rhode Island, New Jersey, New York, and Pennsylvania), South (Maryland, Delaware, District of Columbia, Virginia, West Virginia, North Carolina, South Carolina, Georgia, Florida, Alabama, Mississippi, Tennessee, Kentucky, Arkansas, Oklahoma, Louisiana, and Texas), North Central (North Dakota, South Dakota, Minnesota, Wisconsin, Michigan, Ohio, Illinois, Indiana, Missouri, Iowa, Kansas, and Nebraska), and West (Montana, Wyoming, Colorado, New Mexico, Idaho, Utah, Arizona, Nevada, California, Oregon, Washington, Alaska, and Hawaii).

31. U.S. Department of Labor, Bureau of Labor Statistics, Consumer Expenditure Survey: Interview Survey 1972-73....

32. U.S. Department of Commerce, Bureau of the Census, Money Income of Families and Persons in the United States, 1979 (Washington, D.C.: 1981).

CHAPTER 3

1. Daniel Yergin, "Crisis and Adjustment: An Overview," in Yergin and Hillenbrand, Global Insecurity..., p. 6.

2. The methodology entails (1) calculating the average annual real rate of growth in the eight years prior to the first oil price shock, (2) estimating what real GNP would have been if that rate of growth had obtained in the years after the oil price shock, and (3) subtracting the actual GNP from the projected GNP. The difference between projected and actual GNP is lost GNP. This approach attributes the entire loss to energy price increases.

3. U.S. Department of Energy, The Interrelationships of Energy and the Economy (Washington, D.C.: 1981), Chapter 2.

4. Basic, technical discussions of the impact of energy prices can be found in the following articles: George Perry, "The United States," in Edward R. Friede and Charles L. Schultze (eds.), Higher Oil Prices and the World Economy: The Adjustment Problem (Washington, D.C.: The Brookings Institution, 1975); Robert J. Gordon, "Alternative Responses of Policy to External Supply Shocks," Brookings Papers on Economic Activity 1, 1975; Edmund S. Phelps, "Commodity-Supply Shocks and Full-Employment Monetary Policy," Journal of Money, Credit and Banking 10:2, May 1978; William D. Nordhaus, "Oil and Economic Performance in Industrial Countries," Brookings Papers on Economic Activity 2, 1980. Somewhat more accessible discussions can be found in Robert S. Dohner, "Energy Prices, Economic Activity, and Infla- tion: A Survey of Issues and Results," in Knut Anton Mork (ed.), Energy Prices, Inflation, and Economic Activity (Cambridge, Mass.: Ballinger, 1981); Robert S. Gordon, "Postwar Macroeconomics: The Evolution of Events and Ideas," in Martin Feldstein, (ed.), The American Economy in Transition, (Chicago: Chicago University Press, 1980).

5. The benefits of accommodative responses have been noted by Gordon, "Alternative Responses...;" Phelps, "Commodity-Supply Shocks...;" as well as Edward M. Gramlich, "Macro Policy Responses to Price Shocks," Brookings Papers on Economic Activity 1, 1979; Knut Anton Mork and Robert E. Hall, "Macroeconomic Analysis of Energy Price Shocks and Offsetting Policies: An Integrated Approach," in Mork, Energy Prices...; Perry, "The United States." Mork and Hall show that the accommodative response is not very inflationary, if it occurs early.

6. U.S. Department of Energy (A Study of Alterna- tives to the NGPA, Appendix C..., p. 23) notes interest rates explicit, as do Stephan Thurman and Richard

246

Berner, "Analysis of Oil Price Shocks in the MPS Model,"
in Mork, Energy Prices... and Perry, "The United
States."
    7. Empirically, estimates typically vary by a factor
of two in the magnitude of projected impacts. Nordhaus
("Oil and Economic Performance," p. 346) states that the
impact may last from one to four decades for the long
run.
    8. Arthur Okun, Prices and Quantities: Macroeconomic
Analyses (Washington, D.C.: The Brookings Institution,
1981), pp. 56-59 in regard to labor and pp. 200-203 in
regard to capital.
    9. The impact of rising energy prices on productiv-
ity has received considerable attention. Discussion of
specific aspects of this impact by those who estimate
small impacts can be found in George L. Perry,
"Potential Output: Recent Issues and Present Trends,"
Brookings Reprint, 336, 1978; E. Denison, "Explanations
of Declining Productivity Growth," Survey of Current
Business, 59, 1979; William Fellner, "The Declining
Growth of American Productivity: An Introductory Note,"
in William Fellner (ed.), Essays on Contemporary Economic Problems (Washington, D.C.: American Enterprise
Institute, 1979).
    Those who estimate the impact of rising energy
prices to be large include R. Rasche and J. Tatom,
"Energy Prices and Potential GNP" and "The Effects of
the New Energy Regime on Economic Capacity, Production
and Prices," Federal Reserve Bank of St. Louis Review
(1977); Dale W. Jorgenson, "Energy Prices and Productivity Growth," Data Resources Inc. (1979); E.A. Hudson
and D.W. Jorgenson, "Energy Prices and the U.S. Economy
1972-1976," Natural Resources Journal, 18, 1978; J.
Tatom, "Energy Prices and Capital Formation" and "The
Productivity Problem," Federal Reserve Bank of St. Louis
Review (1979); Martin Neil Baily, "Productivity and the
Services of Capital and Labor," Brookings Paper on
Economic Activity 1, 1981.
    There is little disagreement on the conceptual
causes of declining productivity. Rather, the disagreement centers on the elasticity of substitution between
energy and other factors of production which leads to
disagreement about how big the impact is and how long it
lasts. An interesting exercise to demonstrate the
striking difference in the impact on GNP depending on
the assumptions made about the elasticity of substitution has been conducted by W. Hogan and Alan Manne,
"Energy-Economic Interactions: The Fable of 'The Elephant and the Rabbit'," in Robert S. Pindyck (ed.),
Advances in the Economics of Energy and Resources: The
Structure of Energy Markets, Vol. I (Greenwich, Conn.:
JAI Press, 1979).
    10. The graphic language seems to be related to the

economist's terminology which identifies factors outside the economy that can have a major impact on the economy as external shocks. Thus, one of the earliest econometric studies of rising energy prices after the oil embargo of 1973 listed oil prices as one of many such shocks (James L. Pierce and Jared J. Enzler, "The Effects of External Inflationary Shocks," Brookings Papers on Economic Activity 1, 1974, pp. 13-14):

> The economy is always vulnerable to a variety of external influences or shocks that have important impacts on income, employment, and prices. While these external shocks are unforeseeable and unavoidable, economic policy must somehow deal with their consequences.
>
> Lately an alarming number of upward jolts to prices have come from sources beyond the normal interaction of production, wages, and prices. One was the relative decline in the value of the dollar following the abandonment of the system of fixed exchange rates, which raised the prices of imported goods and contributed to the rise in farm prices as exports competed with domestic consumption. A number of other events shook the economy at about the same time. Crop failures in the Soviet Union resulted in a gigantic sale of American grain. The Peruvian anchovy catch mysteriously dropped, contributing to a worldwide protein shortage and higher prices for feedstocks. Then floods in the Midwest destroyed part of the soybean crop, driving feedstock prices still higher. Late in 1973, a cartel of oil producers got the upper hand over the buyer cartel and forced fuel prices drastically upward. Finally, the dismantling of domestic price controls may undo whatever downward pressures the program had on the price level. Because these inflationary surges have substantial effects on real income and on relative prices, their implications for economic stabilization policy deserve examination.
>
> The consequences of the recent upward price shocks to prices will be analyzed under the assumption that they are permanent, even though they may be overshadowed by downward disturbances from other sources, or even partly reverse themselves (anchovies may reappear off the coast of Peru and soybean fields may yield a bumper crop, for example). This assumption permits analysis of the longer-run consequences of external disturbances that are not quickly reversed.

Energy has certainly outlasted the others in not being reversed and therefore requiring analysis of its

248

longer run consequences.

11. These are the two dominant fuels, accounting for about two-thirds of all energy consumed in the United States. They are also the dominant household fuels (i.e., fuels used in the home or for personal transportation).

12. Here we should also note the relationship between recession, unemployment, in particular, and oil imports. After the 1979-81 surge in prices, oil imports dropped dramatically and this has frequently been claimed as one of the beneficial effects of crude oil decontrol. Figure F.1 shows the close correlation between imports and unemployment. A simple rule of thumb that can be derived directly from the figure is that for every 1 million people put out of work, imports will decline by three-quarters of a million barrels per day.

13. A rule of thumb that has been used is that for every 1 percentage point of inflation caused directly by energy price increases, an additional one-half to one percentage point is caused indirectly through the impact on the production of goods and services. See, Consumer Energy Council of America Research Foundation; The Past as Prologue II..., pp. 8-13.

14. A. Bradley Askin (ed.), How Energy Affects the Economy (Lexington, Mass.: Lexington Books, 1978) has a general review of differences in models. U.S. Department of Energy, A Study of Alternatives to the NGPA, Appendix C... and ICF Incorporated, Preliminary Analysis of the Macroeconomic Impacts of Natural Gas Decontrol: The Structure and Behavior of the DRI and Wharton Models (draft, April 20, 1981) contain extensive comparisons of the two most frequently used models.

15. Otto Eckstein (The Great Recession: With a Postscript on Stagflation [New York: North Holland, 1978], p. 5) has called econometric modeling "an exercise in contemporary cliometrics." Cliometrics can be defined as the study of economic history through the construction of quantitative, contrafactual scenarios which test the causal importance of specific historical facts. For example, if there had been no energy price increase in 1979-80, what would the course of economic activity have been? Cliometrics, as an approach to economic history, has been the subject of considerable controversy. One of the most important controversies centers on the specification of the counterfact to be tested. If one specifies the incorrect counterfact, the analysis loses its logical basis (see, for example, Stefano Fenoalta, "The Discipline and Theory: Notes on Contrafactual Methodology and the New Economic History," Journal of European Economic History, 2:3, 1975). In this case, the failure to take account of monetary policy may be a misspecification of the counterfact if energy prices and restrictive monetary policy are inseparable.

FIGURE F.1
Changes in Unemployment and Changes in Imports

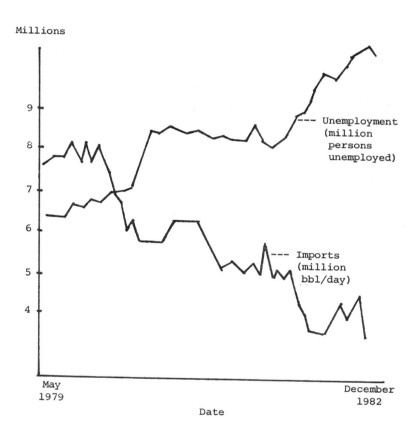

Source: Economic Report of the President, 1982;

Monthly Energy Review, various issues.

250

16. Typically, sensitivity or test cases are chosen
to augment base case analyses. These test cases
generally examine values for critical variables that are
10 to 20 percent higher and lower than the base case.
As will be seen in Table 3.2 the estimates generated by
various models fall within 15 percent of the mean of the
estimate. That is, the coefficient of variation which
is calculated by dividing the standard deviation by the
mean is generally about .15 or less.

17. Most of the models -- especially the major ones,
such as DRI and Wharton -- are continually undergoing
refinement, updating and modification in order to
improve their predictive power. The DRI model listed
for the early price shock was probably significantly
modified by the time DOE used it to analyze the entire
decade. Additional runs of these models have been
reviewed in Consumer Energy Council of America Research
Foundation, The Past as Prologue II....

18. Hudson and Jorgenson, "Energy Prices and the
U.S...."

19. Pierce and Enzler, "External Inflationary
Shocks...."

20. David E. Serot, "The Energy Crisis and the U.S.
Economy, 1973-1975," in Askin, How Energy Affects....

21. Ibid., p. 23. See also, Otto Eckstein, "Shock
Inflation, Core Inflation, and Energy Disturbances in
the DRI Model," in Mork, Energy Prices..., pp. 78-79.

22. DOE, The Interrelationships..., p. 24; and
Eckstein, "Shock Inflation...," pp. 78-79.

23. Denison, "Explanations of Declining...;" Tatom,
Energy Prices and Capital Formation...; and Baily,
"Productivity...".

24. DOE, The Interrelationships..., pp. 21-23; and
Eckstein, "Shock Inflation...," pp. 78-79.

25. DOE, The Interrelationships..., p. 19 and
Eckstein, "Shock Inflation...," pp. 78-79.

26. Nordhaus ("Oil and Economic Performance...") has
much lower estimates for a pooled set of OECD countries.
It is not clear whether the pooled estimate has any
relevance to the individual countries, the United States
in particular, since the U.S. has such radically
different energy consumption patterns than the other
major industrialized countries.

Further, we would point out that the most recent
studies of productivity, using classical growth
accounting techniques, identify a large number of
factors, all of which account for between 5 and 20
percent of the change in productivity growth. Only
capital/labor substitution is much higher (see, for
example, John Kendrick's "International Comparisons of
Recent Productivity Trends," in William Fellner [ed.],
Essays in Contemporary Economic Problems [Washington,
D.C.: American Enterprise Institute, 1981]). The

econometric results presented above would certainly rank
energy very high on the list of factors. Moreover, as
Baily ("Productivity...") has pointed out, energy may be
playing a significant role in the capital/labor
substitution effect:

> The most important cause of the growth slowdown
> in recent years seems to be a decline in the ser-
> vices of capital, caused by obsolescence and by the
> diversion of some part of capital spending to sav-
> ing energy or product conversion . . .
> A decline in capital services relative to the
> capital stock of 2 percent a year in 1968-78 is
> sufficient to explain the productivity slowdown.
> This paper argues that structural change in the
> economy, in part in response to higher energy
> prices, has been the underlying cause of the in-
> creased rate of capital obsolescence (pp. 48-49).

27. Economic Report of the President (Washington,
D.C.: January 1981), p. 51.
28. Ibid., p. 190. Similarly, Mork and Hall
("Macroeconomic Analysis...,") show that accommodative
policies can easily absorb half of the macroeconomic
impact of the price shock.
29. See Note 15, above.
30. Eckstein, The Great Recession..., Chapter 9, and
DOE, The Interrelationships..., Tables 2 and 3.
31. DOE, The Interrelationships..., Tables 2 and 3.
32. Ibid.
33. Ibid., pp. 19-22.
34. Yergin ("Crisis and Adjustment...," and "America
in the Strait...") stresses the political implications
of these shifts.

CHAPTER 4

1. Mark Cooper, "Comment on the Impact of High
Prices," in Hans H. Landsberg (ed.), High Energy Costs
-- Assessing the Burden (Washington, D.C.: Resources for
the Future, 1981).
2. Charting energy consumption from the early to the
late 1970s proves to be a difficult task, much more
difficult than charting energy expenditures. Energy
consumption is a highly specialized issue which requires
special measurement and surveys, whereas energy expenditures are part of overall expenditures and tend to be
captured in general surveys. See Harold Beebout, Gerald
Peabody, and Pat Doyle, "The Distribution of Household
Energy Expenditures and the Impact of High Prices," in
Landsberg (ed.), High Energy Costs..., pp. 28-39, for a
brief discussion. Their figures appear to be derived
from average expenditures and prices, rather than a

direct measurement of actual consumption. See also, The
Energy Policy Project of the Ford Foundation, A Time to
Choose (Cambridge, Mass.: Ballinger, 1974), pp. 116-125.
     3. See, for example, State of Ohio, Office of
Consumers' Counsel, Characteristics of Residential
Electric and Gas Customers (Columbus, Ohio: June 1979).
     It is important not to confuse changes in thermostat
settings with the absolute level of the thermostat
setting. Most data on thermostat settings is gathered
in conjunction with retrofit activities since monitoring
is necessary to establish the cost-effectiveness of the
retrofit. However, lower income households frequently
are found to turn their thermostats up after a retrofit.
This apparently anomolous behavior can lead to erroneous
conclusions about thermostat-setting behavior. Most
reports of the incidence of thermostat-raising after
retrofit do not point out that even after raising they
are lower than for non-lower income households. A
plausible explanation for the fact that lower income
households raise their thermostats after retrofits is
that the retrofits decrease their energy bills and increase their relative income. With the additional purchasing power, the household chooses to buy more thermal
comfort (i.e., more energy). Moreover, because the
household has been forced to endure very low levels of
consumption, additional units of energy consumption have
relatively high marginal utilities and the household
devotes a large part of the additional income to it.
     4. Eric Hirst, et al., Residential Energy Use and
Conservation Actions: Analyses of Disaggregate Household
Data (Oak Ridge, Tenn.: Oak Ridge National Laboratory,
March 1981); U.S. Department of Energy, Energy Infor-
mation Administration, The National Interim Energy
Consumption Survey: Exploring the Variability in Energy
Consumption (Washington, D.C.: July 1981).
     5. For a discussion of the constraints on the
conservation activities of lower income households, see
U.S. Congress, Office of Technology Assessment (OTA),
Residential Energy Conservation (Washington, D.C.: 1979)
Vol. I, Chapter 10; Energy Efficiency of Buildings in
Cities (Washington, D.C.: 1982), Chapter 5; FOMAC, Low
Income Energy... (1980), Chapter VIII.
     6. Mark Cooper, "Comments on the Impact..."
     7. DOE, Residential Energy Consumption Survey:
1979-80....
     8. HUD data in the Annual Housing Survey..., yields
similar estimates of expenditures, but gives less
precise estimates of the percentage of income spent on
energy because only median incomes are available in
published data.
     9. This estimate is slightly lower than those in

FOMAC, <u>Low Income Energy...</u> (1980), which were based on
extrapolation of trends from 1978, rather than 1979-80
survey data. They are also lower than the estimates in
The Grier Partnership, <u>Too Cold...Too Dark</u> (Washington,
D.C.: for the Community Services Administration, 1981).
They are very close to those in National Council of
Senior Citizens, Project Energy Care, <u>Seared Hopes and
Frozen Promises</u> (Washington, D.C.: June 30, 1982).

10. Earlier studies of the impact of rising energy
prices have avoided this problem by estimating the
percentage of income spent on energy for families at the
mean of a given income category (e.g., the mean of the
poverty population). Since these social definitions are
constantly changed to reflect inflation, these studies
are, in fact, adjusting their income estimates.

11. The personal income deflator was used (with a
base of 1972).

12. It can be argued that even adjusting income for
the rate of inflation would not account fully for the
change in energy expenditures of low income households.
In the period between 1972 and 1979, real incomes were
rising. GNP increased by 25 percent in real terms in
those seven years, as did personal income. If a family
with $3,000 income in 1972 kept up with the increase in
GNP, it would have $3,750 in real income in 1979.
Similarly, a family with $11,000 in income in 1972 would
have $13,750 in real income in 1979 if it kept up with
the national average increase in GNP.

Assuming that each has kept up with the national
average shifts the curve of expenditures as a percent of
income inward (i.e., indicating lower expenditures for
each household). If each household had kept up with the
national trend in income, the percentage of income that
low income households ($3,000 a year) devoted to energy
would have risen from about 7.5 percent in 1972 to about
12.5 percent in 1979. The percentage of income which
the middle income household ($11,000 a year) devoted to
energy would have risen from about 3.2 percent to about
4.7 percent. Again, this adjustment reduces the
absolute percentage loss of income due to rising energy
expenditures, but maintains or even increases relative
differences between low and middle income households.

One note of caution should be added. By and large,
as Chapter 6 shows, low income households have not done
as well as the nation in maintaining their incomes
relative to inflation. Thus, low income households have
probably been forced to devote much more than an
additional 5 percent of their real income to rising
energy prices for home energy expenditures.

Prior studies have not explicitly taken real growth
into account. Those that chart the mean income of a
specific group (e.g., the poverty population) would have
to take growth into account by estimating the size of

the group (i.e., the percent of the population which would fall into the category), since the percentage of households below the poverty line would, in all probability, fall as real incomes rose. This is not frequently done.

Furthermore, the method of handling inflation and real growth by plotting the mean and size of specific groups suffers from the vagaries of social definitions, i.e., they tend not to be simple arithmetic calculations. Our approach, which identifies groups as a percent of the population and makes adjustments for inflation and growth in simple mathematical terms, avoids these problems in the calculation and estimation of burden. It is open to the charge that identifying the bottom third of the population is arbitrary and implicitly an evaluative approach. It defines households with $10,000 in income in 1979 as lower income and therefore the object of social concern.

If the income distribution were very much narrower, or the country very much richer, this approach would be subject to question. For example, if the upper limit of the bottom third of the income distribution were $20,000, in real 1979 purchasing power, it would be difficult to justify a great deal of concern about a household at that level of income as being lower income. Given the make-up of the population as discussed in the Methodological Appendix, we believe that the basis for a social concern with the lower income population is well-established.

CHAPTER 5

1. The general policy pieces cited in Note 8 Chapter 2 were particularly extreme in this regard. Because a large part of gasoline is consumed by middle and upper income households and, in many respects, the energy problem is a liquid fuel problem, what little concern for social equity these studies did express was never voiced with regard to gasoline.

2. FOMAC, Low Income Energy..., mentions it briefly in its calculation of total household expenditures. Congressional Budget Office, The Decontrol of Domestic Oil Prices: An Overview (Washington, D.C.: May 1979), Chapter VII; Low Income Energy Assistance: Issues and Options (Washington, D.C.: June 1981), Chapter II, has typically devoted equal attention to gasoline and home energy consumption. In addition, the equity impacts have been discussed by J.P. Strucker and T.F. Kirkwood, The Economic Impact of Automobile Travel Cost Increases on Households (Santa Monica, Cal.: The Rand Corporation, July 1977); Daniel Hill, "The Relative Burden of Higher Gas Prices," in Morgan and Duncan (eds.), Five Thousand American Families..., Vol. VIII; Greg Duncan, "Some

Equity Aspects of Gasoline Price Inflation," in Morgan
and Duncan (eds.), Five Thousand American Families...,
Vol. VI.

3. Note that this category is larger than the
category of households with incomes below $5,000 in
1979.

4. Although this data does not explicitly identify
single occupant usage (since it is possible that the
differences observed in the table could arise from
extreme differences in the number of passengers per
trip), apparently the raw data shows that the difference
is, in fact, due to single occupant trips. See John
Pucher, Chris Henderson and Sue McNeil, "Socioeconomic
Characteristics of Transit Riders: Some Recent
Evidence," Traffic Quarterly, 35:3, July 1981, p. 466.

5. The bulk of the difference in the percentage of
heads of household who drive to work is due to the fact
that a much larger portion of the lower income group is
not employed. However, even if we restrict our
attention to those heads of households who drive to
work, we still find that lower income households choose
to drive their automobiles to work (when alternative
transportation is available) less than non-lower income
households do. Of the 17.5 percent of lower income
heads of households who drive to work, one-quarter (4.2
percent) do so even though they indicated there was
adequate public transportation within walking distance
of their home. Among the non-lower income heads of
households who drive to work, however, one-third (21.7
percent out of 67 percent) chose to drive even though
there was adequate public transportation available
within walking distance of their home. The fact that so
few lower income heads of household drive to work in the
first instance and such a small proportion of them chose
to do so when public transportation was available
demonstrates the striking contrast between lower and
non-lower income households in the discretionary use of
automobiles to commute to work. One might be surprised
that one-quarter of those low income heads of households
who drive to work could have used public transportation.
However, we would stress the fact that five times as
large a proportion of non-lower income household heads
chose to drive to work even though public transportation
was available as most indicative of the basic nature of
vehicles as commodities in the various income groups.

6. Hans H. Landsberg and Joseph M. Dukert (eds.),
High Energy Costs -- Uneven, Unfair, Unavoidable?
(Baltimore: Johns Hopkins Press for Resources for the
Future, 1981).

CHAPTER 6

1. The Energy Policy Project, A Time to Choose, p.

128, pointed this out early on in the energy/equity
debate. An alternative perspective taken on the same
set of numbers stresses the absolute amount of energy
consumption (see Stobaugh and Yergin, Energy Future...
[Second Edition], pp. 275-276).

2. The explanation for this change lies in the
increase in appliance ownership, see Chapter 4.

3. James P. Strucker, "The Impact of Energy Price
Increases on Households: An Illustration," Rand Paper
Series No. P-5585 (Santa Monica, Cal.: The Rand
Corporation, 1976); and Robert Herendeen, B. Hannon and
C. Ford, "An Energy Consuming Tax: How Large Should
Rebates Be?" (unpublished), both cited in Beebout,
Peabody and Doyle, "The Distribution of Household Energy
Expenditures...;" R. Herendeen and J. Tanaka, "Energy
Cost of Living," Energy, June 1976, cited in Stobaugh
and Yergin, Energy Future..., p. 276.

The evidence suggests that the most important
determinant of indirect energy consumption is overall
consumption itself. That is, indirect energy
consumption is roughly proportionate to consumption in
general, so that lower income groups, which consume
fewer goods and services, would consume less energy
indirectly.

The evidence also suggests that there may be a
slight skew to the pattern of indirect energy
consumption. Lower income people appear to consume
goods which embody, on average, less energy. That is,
lower income households consume less energy indirectly
both because they consume fewer goods and services in
general and because they consume less energy-intensive
goods and services.

Herendeen, et al., "An Energy...," calculates this
figure and shows that the middle ($11,000 in 1972-73)
and upper ($14,000 in 1972-73) income groups consume
between 15 and 30 percent more energy than the low
income ($2,000 in 1972-73) group. The Energy Policy
Project, A Time to Choose, shows a calculation which
contradicts this, but two thirds of the estimate is
based on the assumption that indirect energy is
distributed according to income.

There is an important factor which works in the
opposite direction, however, and cancels out the fact
that the poor consume less energy-intensive goods and
services. Although the poor consume less energy per
dollar of expenditure than the wealthy, they also tend
to spend a higher proportion of their income. That is,
they spend all of their total income, and sometimes more
than their total income (by drawing down savings and
going into debt). The upper income groups spend less
than their total income. Therefore, energy consumption
per dollar of income -- not per dollar of expenditure --
is lower in the higher income groups. The simple

arithmetic is as follows:

$$\frac{\text{Energy Expenditures}}{\text{Total Expenditures}} \times \frac{\text{Total Expenditures}}{\text{Income}}$$

$$= \frac{\text{Energy Expenditures}}{\text{Income}}$$

For example, in the 1972-73 Consumer Expenditure Survey, households in the bottom 13 percent of the income distribution scale had expenditures of about 150 percent of income, while the top 13 percent had expenditures of only 60 percent of income. This would more than offset the differences in the relative energy intensity of expenditures of the two groups.

Furthermore, it is important to note that the lower income population consumes certain commodities that are very energy-intensive. As Chapter 9 shows, they consume much more in transit services as a percentage of income than higher income groups. Transit services are very energy intensive.

On balance, the evidence from the 1972-73 Consumer Expenditure Survey suggests that indirect energy consumption is at best proportional among the income groups and probably slightly regressive towards the lower income group. Three different estimates have been made. One, which calculates indirect energy consumption per dollar of expenditure, shows that middle income households consumed about 12 percent more energy than low income households, while very high income households consumed 24 percent more. Adjusting these numbers to energy consumption per dollar of income would reverse the pattern, leaving lower income households consuming somewhat more. The second estimate, which calculates total indirect energy consumption per household, would lead to estimates of expenditures per dollar of income which would show an even larger burden falling on lower income households.

The Energy Policy Project, A Time to Choose, p. 126 shows much higher levels of indirect energy consumption because it allocates all energy, including that used for government services, to households. Since those services are assumed to be used equally by all groups, that would shift the burden toward lower income households (compared to the other types of indirect energy consumption). Furthermore, it distributes all energy consumption not elsewhere allocated to households, according to income. Insofar as the energy intensity of consumption rises with income, this may allocate somewhat too large a portion to lower income groups.

An estimate of expenditures for indirect energy consumption as a percent of total expenditures shows that lower income households spent 8.4 percent of their expenditures on indirect energy, while middle income households spent 7 percent and those in the upper income brackets spent slightly less than 7 percent. Calculated as a percentage of income, the burden of indirect energy expenditures on lower income households would be even higher. In sum, we can safely conclude that indirect energy expenditures certainly do not diminish and probably add to the disproportionate burden borne by low and lower middle income households.

4. FOMAC, Low Income... (1980), and the Committee for Economic Development and the Conservation Foundation, Energy Prices and Public Policy..., estimate lost purchasing power after inflation. There are other reasons we have not chosen to estimate lost purchasing power above the rate of inflation, although this is the approach taken most frequently.

First, to routinely factor in inflation leads to a distortion if a comparison between lost purchasing power and transfer payments is made. Low income energy assistance and inflation-indexed transfer payments are paid in current dollars, not real dollars. Payments made in 1978 dollars buy only what a 1978 dollar can buy, not what 1978 dollars adjusted to 1972 base prices can buy. Social programs appropriate current dollars, not real dollars. Policymakers and individuals think in terms of current dollars. Presenting lost purchasing power in real dollars, while transfer payment decisions are made in current dollars, distorts their relative magnitudes.

Second, because transfer payment programs are inadequately indexed to inflation, routinely factoring in inflation introduces distortions, which can be quite large in the estimates of real losses in purchasing power. To avoid any distortion, we calculate all losses and gains (through transfer payments) in current dollars.

Third, routinely factoring in inflation takes no note of the fact that lower income households spent a much larger part of their income on energy at the outset. By simply assuming the rate of inflation first, one assumes that the income of lower income households is eroded relative to other groups by the process of inflation.

Fourth, simply factoring in inflation takes no account of the fact that lower income households tend to be less able to maintain their incomes relative to inflation. Simply assuming the rate of inflation would mean a further erosion of the living standard of the lower income population.

Fifth, calculations after the rate of inflation also assume, implicitly, that the general rate of inflation indicates something about the burden of rising energy

prices. Yet, if the suggestion is that the burden is
similar across income categories, that is decidedly not
the case, since the commodity basket of various income
groups differs drastically as we have seen. This is the
factual error in such calculations.

Finally, it should also be recognized that
calculations of lost purchasing power above the rate of
inflation are really normative statements, not analytic
ones. That is, they implicitly assume that lower income
households should bear the burden of the general rate of
inflation. Yet, this is only one possible normative
judgment among many. For instance, a judgment that
would be more consistent with the premise of this study
would be to assert that lower income households should
be forced to devote no more of their income to energy
than non-lower income households. This would equalize
the burden of energy prices.

Statements about changes in real purchasing power
should be made after all factors are taken into account.
The general rate of inflation is only one factor.
Changes in income and the actual increase in the cost of
living borne by various groups are two other factors
that are critical to any estimation of changes in real
purchasing power. In this chapter, we begin with an
estimation of lost purchasing power in current dollars,
factor in assistance payments in current dollars, then
make an aggregate estimate of real purchasing power.

5. Congressional Budget Office, Low Income Energy
Assistance..., pp. 46-47, 52; and Consumer Energy
Council of America Research Foundation, "Oil Price
Decontrol and the Poor: A Social Policy Failure,"
(Washington, D.C.: for U.S. Congress, Joint Economic
Committee, February 2, 1981.

6. U.S. Executive Office of the President, Council
of Economic Advisors and Office of Management and
Budget, Report on Indexing Federal Programs (Washington,
D.C.: January 1981).

7. We have used the mean of the figures reported in
U.S. Department of Energy, The Interrelationships...,
Table 2.

8. A comparison between 1973 and 1979 of the
percentage of each type of transfer payment going to
each group of households (for families only) shows that
the lower income families accounted for almost the same
percentages of these payments going to families in the
two years. (See U.S. Department of Labor, Bureau of
Labor Statistics, Consumer Expenditure Survey: Interview
Survey, Average Annual..., Table 3; and U.S. Department
of Commerce, Bureau of the Census, Money Income of
Families..., Table 8.)

9. Robert P. Hagemann, Inflation and Household
Characteristics: An Analysis of Group Specific Price
Indexes, BLS Working Papers No. 10 (Washington, D.C.:

U.S. Bureau of Labor Statistics, December 1980).

10. Martin Duffy, et al., Inflation and the Elderly: Summary Report (Lexington, Mass.: Data Resources, Inc., April 1980); Benjamin Bridges, Jr. and Michael D. Packard, "Prices and Income Changes for the Elderly," Social Security Bulletin, 44:1, January 1981; U.S. General Accounting Office, A CPI for Retirees Is Not Needed Now but Could Be in the Future (Washington, D.C.: June 1, 1982).

11. Bridges and Packard, "Prices and Incomes...."

12. As discussed in Chapter 8, calculations of income per capita will be slightly different than calculations of income per household because the number of persons per household has declined. This calculation leads to a similar conclusion. In this calculation, there is some "over" counting since a part of the general rate of inflation was caused by energy price increases.

CHAPTER 7

1. U.S. General Accounting Office, Rental Housing: A National Problem That Needs Immediate Attention (Washington, D.C.: November 1979); Peter D. Salins, The Ecology of Housing Destruction: Economic Effects of Public Intervention in the Housing Market (New York: New York University Press for the International Center for Economic Policy Studies, 1980); George Sternlieb and James W. Hughes (eds.), America's Housing: Prospects and Problems (New Brunswick, N.J.: Rutgers University Center for Urban Policy Research, 1980); John Egan, John Carr, Andrew Mott, and John Roos, Housing and Public Policy: A Role for Mediating Structures (Cambridge, Mass.: Ballinger for the American Enterprise Institute, 1981).

2. Ira S. Lowry, Rental Housing in the 1970s: Searching for the Crisis (Santa Monica, Cal.: The Rand Corporation, for the Department of Housing and Urban Development, January 1982); The Pollyana Institute, Rental Housing: Two Decades of Progress (Washington, D.C.: 1980).

3. Salins, The Ecology of Housing....

4. More precisely, it would be the wrong form of intervention. The urban decay school would certainly fall into this category -- especially those who advocate various forms of government consolidation. (See, for example, Thomas G. Cowing and A.G. Holtman, The Economics of Local Public Service Consolidations [Lexington, Mass.: Lexington Books, 1976].) Advocates of rent control would fall into a similar category insofar as rent control is not predominant. (See John Ingram Gilderbloom, "Moderate Rent Control: Its Impact on the Quality and Quantity of the Housing Stock," Urban Affairs Quarterly, 17:2, December 1981, for a thorough

review of the literature and a lively exchange of
views.)
    5. Lowry, <u>Rental Housing in the 1970s...</u>, seems to
argue this for the past, but not the future. Daniel A.
Hicks (ed.), <u>Urban America in the Eighties: Perspectives
and Prospects</u> (New Brunswick, N.J.: Transaction Books,
1982) and Katharine L. Bradbury, Anthony Downs, and
Kenneth A. Small, <u>Urban Decline and the Future of
American Cities</u> (Washington, D.C.: The Brookings
Institution, 1982) would also fall in this category, in
the sense that they look to larger social forces outside
the housing market itself for the causes of much of the
crisis.
    6. Lowry, <u>Rental Housing in the 1970s...</u>, lays out
this set of arguments cogently.
    7. Ibid.
    8. Ibid.
    9. The adjustment for population shift is based only
on the largest shift, which is an increase in
multiperson households with female heads.
    10. Salins, <u>The Ecology of Housing...</u>, Egan, et al.,
<u>Housing and Public Policy....</u>
    11. Lowry, <u>Rental Housing in the 1970s...</u>, Bradbury,
Downs, and Small, <u>Urban Decline....</u>
    12. To some extent, Bradbury, Downs, and Small,
<u>Urban Decline...</u>, fall into this category, as does
Hicks, <u>Urban America...</u>, in the sense that strategies to
cope with the shifting of economic activity are called
for.
    13. The rent control advocates fall into this cat-
egory (e.g., Gilderbloom, "Moderate Rent Control...").
    14. To a significant extent, some of the differences
of opinion outlined above stem from differences in
definition of what is a "crisis." We use the word
"condition" to avoid the evaluative term "crisis." We
would define a crisis as the failure to satisfy basic
needs. Further, we would define basic needs in a broad
sense to include physical amenities, environmental
conditions and reasonable cost. Egan, et al., <u>Housing
and Public Policy...</u>, p. 2, offer the following succinct
discussion:

    In our view, housing needs should be defined
primarily in terms of basic physical amenities and
environmental decency at an affordable price. For
example, some 6.3 million families live in housing
without complete indoor plumbing or central heating
or in buildings in extreme disrepair. Families in
these circumstances have basic housing needs. But
our concern, in keeping with following the goals of
the 1949 Housing Act, is not limited to the simple
physical structure of the house. Two other issues
merit particular attention. In some cases, fami-

lies are able to find structurally sound housing, but at the cost of spending such a large percentage of their incomes that such essentials as food and health are neglected. Others find decent structures, but in environments undesirable for anyone. Housing must be viewed not only as a structure at a price, but in the context of goods and services and environmental concerns. These include streets, schools, water and sewers, crime, and cleanliness.

15. It should also be obvious from the above discussion that many of the "positions" taken by the participants in the debate are "mixed," in the sense that all recognize a number of factors. We subscribe to this eclectic approach, but, in pointing out a factor which has been neglected, we concentrate upon it and do not bother to mention or list the other factors.

16. See, for example, Cowing and Holtman, The Economics.... John Odland and Blanche Balzer, "Localized Externalities, Contagious Processes and the Deterioration of Urban Housing: An Empirical Analysis," Social and Economic Planning Sciences, 13, 1979, p. 87, summarize this process as follows:

> The deterioration process may be characterized as contagious if the spread of deterioration depends on interactions between a set of structures which have already entered a state of deterioration and a set of structures which are vulnerable to deterioration. Deterioration may occur in locational patterns which are similar to those produced by contagious processes even where these interactions are absent, however, since incidents of deteriorations may involve both contagious effects and other blighting effects which do not depend on the location of deteriorated structures but which are localized in the same vicinity.

17. Lowry, Rental Housing in the 1970s..., describes the market process of deterioration caused by a shortage of rental revenues due to an excess of supply over demand as follows:

> If an economist were asked what circumstances in a competitive market would lead producers to sell their output at less than long-run average cost, he would immediately answer, "Excess capacity." Could that explanation apply to rental housing in the 1970s?
> Certainly, the industry is technologically prone to excess capacity. Housing is capital-intensive, the capital is durable, and its location (except for mobile homes) is fixed. When a local market is

overbuilt or its renter population decreases, the owners of rental property are faced with high vacancy losses until demand catches up with supply or until supply is gradually diminished by demolition or conversion to nonresidential use. Competitive rent reductions may increase aggregate consumption by promoting household formation and shifting vacancies from large or high-quality dwellings to small or low-quality dwellings; but absent a rapid rate of household formation, there is no quick way to work off excess supply.

Salins, The Ecology of Housing..., argues that even where there is excess supply the real question is the manner and fashion in which the housing stock is reduced. That is, excess supply can lead to "healthy" patterns of reduced density, commercialization of buildings and neighborhoods, rather than the "pathological" patterns of decay, abandonment and destruction.

The argument that the lower income market would be most adversely affected must be specified carefully. With perfect markets, we would expect the vacancies to occur at the top of the market. Rising rents would force all renters to move to cheaper apartments if there is an income constraint operating. That is, each landlord would be able to find a downwardly mobile family to fill his or her vacant apartment and the only vacancy would occur in the most expensive apartment. There are two discontinuities in the rental market which concentrate the vacancies in the lower income market. First, the constraint on income is not evenly spread across households. As we have seen, in energy price-induced recessions, the lower income households suffer most. Therefore, middle income households will not be feeling as much pressure to move down in the market. Landlords of lower income housing will not as readily find potential tenants. Second, insofar as the middle class is feeling pressure on its income, it will have a wider range of choices about how to deal with those pressures in terms of adjusting its commodity basket. If it places a high priority on the quality of its housing, it will sacrifice other things before it moves down in the market. Its aversion to moving into lower class housing would be particularly strong.

These observations are tantamount to saying (1) that there are at least two market segments in the rental market, lower and middle; (2) that the pressure on resources from outside the market is greater on the lower income segment; and (3) that the refusal to cross segments concentrates vacancies or uncollectables at the top of the lower income segment.

Figure F.2 depicts this argument. The initial

264

FIGURE F.2
Shifts in the Demand Curve for Rental Units Within Market Segments

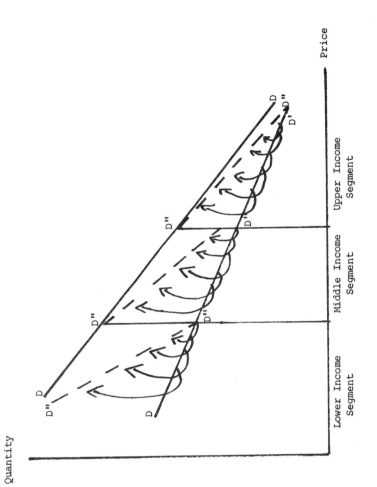

increase in the price of lower income rental housing
(which, as we shall see, is greater than non-lower
income housing) and the initial decrease in available
resources in the lower income population (which, as we
have shown, is greater for the lower income population
than the non-lower) are depicted as a downward shift in
the demand curve faced by landlords. The shift is
larger at the low income end. The initial downward
shift is offset at various points along the curve by
downward mobility. However, at the boundary between the
market segments, downward mobility does not occur,
producing the greatest downward shift in the demand
curve. In addition, in the middle income segment, we
assume some of the downward shift is absorbed by a
realignment of the commodity basket which places greater
priority on housing.

18. The difficulty of implementing conservation in
rental housing has been widely discussed, but little
researched. Basic conceptual issues are discussed in J.
Mackenzie, "Summary: Institutional Issues," and C.
Remmie, "Focusing on the Market for Residential
Retrofit: Present Opportunity and Future Prospects," in
Jeffrey P. Harris and Jack M. Hollander (eds.),
Improving Energy Efficiency in Buildings: Progress and
Problems, proceedings of the 1980 Summer Study organized
by the American Council for an Energy-Efficient Economy,
(University of California, Santa Cruz: August 10-22,
1980). A review of the available evidence, which
documents the problems, can be found in OTA, Energy
Efficiency of Buildings..., Alisa Gravitz, U.S.
Department of Energy, Office of Conservation Policy and
Evaluation, DOE Report on the Rental and Multi-Family
Housing Energy Efficiency Workshop: Memorandum for DOE
Multi-Family Task Force (January 30, 1981).

19. Egan, et al., Housing and Public Policy..., pp.
27-29, argue that owner-occupants value their residences
as commodities, not simply investments, and, therefore,
manage them more closely and have different motivations
to maintain them. The argument can be formulated in
terms of the "lumpiness" of marginal utilities. The
individual homeowner, faced with a decline in real
income due to a rise in energy prices, will cut back a
little all around -- do a little less maintenance, use a
little less energy, buy a little less food or entertainment, as marginal utilities dictate. In one sense the
tenant may have fewer choices -- either pay the rent or
not -- and the landlord may be forced to deal with the
residue of tenant decisions -- if tenants choose to
balance their personal accounts by going into arrears.
The landlord then has fewer ways to absorb the loss.

20. OTA, Energy Efficiency of Buildings..., Chapter
4; Egan, et al., Housing and Public Policy..., p. 27.
In fact, much of the discussion of landlord behavior

turns on financing schemes and the capitalization of
various attributes of the housing stock into the sale
price or finance terms. There is little doubt that the
landlord's economic parameters and criteria are very
different from those of the owner-occupant.
    21. PHAs generally agree to pay a fixed percentage
of their rental income to local governments in lieu of
property taxes. The extent to which these payments
actually cover the local services used varies
considerably. In New York City, for example, the city
government has provided aid to the PHA in the form of
separate security personnel and community centers. See
U.S. Congress, House, Government Operations Committee,
Manpower and Housing Subcommittee, Statement of John
Simon, General Manager, New York City Housing Authority,
97th Cong., 1st sess., May 19, 1981.
    22. Of course, the fiscal condition of PHAs impacts
all taxpayers due to the federal subsidies. In this
context, there has been a continual debate about the
fundamental nature of the public housing program and
repeated redefinition of the program. Anthony Downs,
"The Successes and Failures of Federal Housing Policy,"
The Public Interest, 34, Winter 1974, presents an
interesting typology of the program's history. Eugene
J. Meehan, The Quality of Federal Policymaking:
Programmed Failure in Public Housing (Columbia, Mo.:
University of Missouri Press, 1979), presents a somewhat
different typology and a penetrating critique of the
structure of the policy. The past half decade has
certainly been a period of reconsideration, with both
the Carter and Reagan Administrations determined to
consider, if not implement, basic changes. (See, for
example, Jill Khadduri, Katherine Lyall and Raymond
Struyk, "Welfare Reform and Housing Assistance: A
National Policy Debate," Journal of the American
Institute of Planners, 44:1, 1978; Raymond J. Struyk and
Jill Khadduri, "Saving the Housing Assistance Plan:
Improving Incentives to Local Governments," Journal of
the American Planning Association, 46:4, October 1980;
Robert D. Reischauer, "Federal Budget Reveals Political,
Economic Costs of Housing Assistance," Journal of
Housing, 38, March 1981; Edgar O. Olsen, "Housing
Programs and the Forgotten Taxpayer," The Public
Interest, 66, Winter 1982; John R. Nolan, "Reexamining
Federal Housing Programs in a Time of Fiscal Austerity:
The Trend Toward Block Grants and Housing Allowances,"
The Urban Lawyer 14:2, 1982; U.S. Congress, House,
Government Operations Committee, Manpower and Housing
Subcommittee, Testimony of Phillip Winn, HUD Assistant
Secretary for Housing, 97th Cong., 1st sess. [May 19,
1981].)
    23. For a thorough overview of the structure of HUD
subsidies to PHAs since 1969, see Abt Associates,

"Evaluation of the Performance Funding System" (Cambridge, Mass.: July 1981), draft report prepared for HUD; and Robert Sadaca, Morton Isler, and Joan DeWitt, The Development of a Prototype Equation for Public Housing Operating Expenses (Washington, D.C.: An Urban Institute Paper, 1975). The above studies focus on an evaluation of only one aspect of the public housing program -- its financial structure. There have been numerous analyses of other aspects of the program, with particular emphasis on costs and benefits. See, for example, William P. Sayre, "Subsidized Housing - Costs and Benefits," Federal Reserve Bank of Chicago, 111:3, 1979; Michael P. Murray, "Tenant Benefits in Alternative Federal Housing Programmes, Urban Studies, 17, February 1980; Jill Khadduri and Raymond Struyk, "Improving Section 8 Rental Assistance, Translating Evaluation into Policy," Evaluation Review, 5:2, 1981.

24. Currently, variations in utility consumption are shared on a 50/50 basis.

CHAPTER 8

1. Before we begin the analysis, we must point out that, given the available data, we are not able to distinguish between the low and lower middle income population as we have done in earlier chapters. We can, however, identify the lower income population as a whole and distinguish it from the non-lower income population. We draw upon several sources of data and the income categories from each are reasonably comparable.

In the 1960 Census, we can identify the lower income population as that group of households with incomes below $4,000. It constituted 49 percent of the renter population and 37.5 percent of the total population. The data covered metropolitan areas only.

In the 1970 Census, we identify the lower income population as those households with incomes below $7,000 per year. It constituted 55.4 percent of the renter population and 41.4 percent of the total population. These percentages are somewhat higher than the others because of the available classifications.

In 1973, the lower income population in the HUD Annual Housing Survey (AHS) can be identified as that group of households with incomes below $7,000. It constituted 48.5 percent of the renter population and 35.9 percent of the total population.

In the 1979 AHS, the lower income population can be identified as that group with incomes below $10,000. It represented 49.6 percent of the renter population and 33.1 percent of the total.

Again, in the 1980 AHS, the lower income population is identified as those households with $10,000 or less in income. It constituted 47.5 percent of the renter

population and 31.7 percent of the total population.
Since our central focus for the purpose of analyzing the
impact of rising energy prices is on the renter
population and on the data from 1973 to 1979-80, the
lower and non-lower income segments of the rental market
represent essentially similar percentages of the rental
market.
    2. U.S. Department of Housing and Urban Development,
Alternative Operating Subsidy System for the Public
Sector (Washington, D.C.: May 1982), Chapter 10, makes a
comparison between public sector and private sector
operating costs. From the point of view of our
analysis, the comparison suffers two weaknesses. First,
it consists of only one data point -- 1980. Second, it
makes no effort to distinguish operating costs in lower
and non-lower income households. This is in addition to
the problems that HUD notes with a self-selected sample
of data for the private sector. Nevertheless, the
estimates presented in this chapter, especially those in
Table 8.2, are within 10 percent of the private sector
data presented by HUD.
    3. David Scott Lindsay and Ira S. Lowry, Rent
Inflation in St. Joseph County, Indiana, 1974-78 (Santa
Monica, Cal.: The Rand Corporation for the U.S.
Department of Housing and Urban Development, November
1980), assert this, pp. 30-32. Salins, The Ecology of
Housing..., in presenting his estimates of typical
operating costs for marginal and viable housing, gives
estimates of energy expenditures as a percentage of
operating costs that are one-third higher for marginal
housing.
    4. Scott and Lowry, Rent Inflation in St. Joseph
County..., and James P. Strucker, Rent Inflation in
Brown County, Wisconsin, 1973-79 (Santa Monica, Cal.:
The Rand Corporation for the U.S. Department of Housing
and Urban Development, August 1978). The latter is
referred to in the former.
    5. Again, the recent Rand studies (Scott and Lowry,
Rent Inflation in St. Joseph County... and Strucker,
Rent Inflation in Brown County...) confirm these
estimates. Scott and Lowry attribute 70 percent of the
increase in gross rent to increases in fuel costs of
operating lower income rental housing. Furthermore, 61
percent of the increase in operating costs is attributed
to rising fuel costs. The somewhat higher estimate
probably stems from a closer accounting than the
aggregate figures. Moreover, the procedure used to
estimate the impact of rising energy prices leaves no
room for conservation to have reduced the magnitude of
the impact of rising energy prices.
    6. Salins, The Ecology of Housing..., in his
estimates shows this difference for the private sector.
This is also approximately the difference that HUD

269

(Alternative Operating Subsidy System...) shows between public sector housing, which is low income, and the private sector housing, which is, in the aggregate, middle income.

7. The reader may be struck by the fact that lower income households had more rooms per person in 1973, and non-lower income households only caught up by 1980. The explanation is simply that lower income households inhabit much smaller units, but also have smaller households.

Thus, even though the number of rooms per person for non-lower and lower income households was roughly the same in 1980, the important point is that changes in the quantity of housing services consumed by lower income households cannot account for increases in their rent between 1973 and 1980, since there was, in fact, no change at all.

This comparison of the increase in the number of rooms per person should not be confused with an evaluation of the actual space per person. The lower income household began the period with a greater number of rooms per household (1.73 compared to 1.53), which we assume were, in general, smaller. The very small increase in the number of rooms they occupy (from 1.73 in 1973 to to 1.75 in 1980) does not account for the much greater increase in the cost of rent. Nor do we have any reason to believe that the rooms occupied by the lower income population in 1980 were very much larger than they were in 1973.

8. This is true if one uses linear comparisons. However, marginal comparisons lead to the opposite conclusion. That is, if we calculate the percent improvement per year ($\Delta X/N$), we find that the percentage of households who lacked plumbing declined more each year between 1973 and 1980. However, if we calculate the rate of improvement ($\Delta X/X/N$), we find the opposite to be the case. The former is tantamount to saying the lack of complete plumbing declined X percentage points per year. The latter is tantamount to saying the lack of plumbing declined at a rate of X percent per year.

9. Taken together, these two sets of observations provide strong evidence of a filtering up or trickle down process (filtering up of lower income households into middle income housing or trickling down of middle income housing to lower income households) in the rental housing market. We clearly see that lower income house-holds are inhabiting housing which has more amenities, but is in worse condition. It turns out, in addition, that lower income housing was slightly older, on average, in 1980 than 1970, whereas non-lower income housing was slightly newer. That is, the percentage of lower income households living in buildings 30 years old or

older was higher in 1980 than 1970 (56.2 percent compared to 55.9 percent), but lower for non-lower income
households (43.3 percent compared to 44.7 percent). The
filtering up or trickle down theory of American urban
development argues that, so long as new units are being
added to the top or middle of the housing stock, a sort
of upwardly mobile musical chairs in the housing market
will occur. Middle and upper class households leave
their old housing to inhabit newer housing. The lower
income groups move up into the now vacant middle class
housing, which is deteriorating, but nonetheless preferable to existing lower income housing. We would expect
to see improvements in amenities, but could also see
deterioration in conditions.

The filtering up hypothesis has been a subject of
much discussion. Anthony Downs, Neighborhoods and Urban
Change (Washington, D.C.: The Brookings Institution,
1981), Chapter 4, defends its validity and provides a
recent bibliography. Salins, The Ecology of Housing...,
pp. 24-38, argues that, as a theory of the housing
market, it needs a great deal of qualification.

We should also note that some of the increase in
appliance ownership by lower income households,
documented in Chapter 4, could well be attributed to
filtering up. In many parts of the country, especially
in the rental market, major appliances stay with the
residence rather than move with the occupant. In
addition to central air conditioning and dishwashers,
which are all but fixed in place, this is certainly true
of refrigerators, room air conditioners, and clothes
washers and dryers.

10. This estimate results from an estimate of rent
per person per room derived from the gross rent estimates in the Methodological Appendix, Section 3, divided
by the rooms per person figures given in Table 8.3.

11. This estimate is derived from an examination of
the rate of change of median incomes, as described in
the Methodological Appendix, Section 3, divided by the
rooms per person figures given in Table 8.3.

12. Note that contract rents are smaller than gross
rent and would take a smaller percentage of income.

13. HUD maintains two data sets of interest in this
analysis. One, a PHA-by-PHA record of finances, suffers
from low response rates from PHAs and is therefore
skewed. The second is a sample of PHAs developed by the
Urban Institute (U.I.) and updated to 1980 on HUD's
computer. Repeated runs of this tape, which includes
data from 1977 to 1980, showed puzzling results and
fundamental incompatibility with the Abt sample. For
example, the following table shows selected national
expenditure data from both the 1977 Urban Institute

sample and the 1978 Abt Associates sample ($/PUM):

	1977 (U.I.)	1978 (Abt)
Total Expenditures	130.81	92.44
Utilities	44.54	34.43
Maintenance	39.87	24.83
G&A	36.14	26.45

The likely cause of these differences is the greater proportion of large PHAs in the U.I. sample. Large PHAs have higher operating costs, on average. However, even some individual PHA data in the Urban Institute printout is inconsistent with other sources. Data supplied by the New York City Housing Authority are compared below with a 1981 HUD memorandum on relative PHA costs, and with the U.I. sample ($/PUM):

	U.I.	NYCHA	HUD
Total	218.55	254.48	254.14
Utilities	66.33	91.89	97.37
Local income	130.46	140.84	--

The U.I. sample appears to include some 1979 data which are presented as 1980 figures. Most disturbing for our purposes is the trend in utility expenditures. The table below compares the change in the energy component of the Consumer Price Index to the change in PHA utility expenditures during the two oil price shocks. The Abt sample shows utility costs increasing slightly more than the CPI. The U.I. sample indicates that PHA utility expenditures increased at less than one-half the rate of the CPI. Clearly the two data sets are irreconcilable:

	1971-75 (Abt)	1977-80 (U.I.)
CPI-energy	58.8%	74.2%
PHA utilities	62.4%	33.3%

Our difficulties in reconciling data on PHA operations are similar to problems encountered by Abt Associates in evaluating the Performance Funding System. According to the HUD contract officer responsible for the Abt project, an unexpectedly large portion of the contract funds was devoted to "cleaning up" the data and creating the data base we use in this report.
14. The inflation factors are based on the following average percentage increases in PHA costs estimated on PFS worksheets. The data were provided by Joan DeWitt at HUD:

Year	Utility Expenditures	Non-Utility Expenditures
77-78	6.1%	6.5%
78-79	11.4	6.0
79-80	26.3	7.1
80-81	22.7	7.8

15. Abt, "Evaluation of the PFS...," pp. 75, 79.

16. Telephone conversation with Peggy Mangum, HUD, April 20, 1982. See, also, HUD memorandum from Philip Abrams, "Adjustment to the PFS allowable utilities consumption levels," March 16, 1982.

17. The 4 percent figure was provided by Wayne Sherwood of the Council of Large Public Housing Authorities (May 19, 1982). The 1981 CIAP and Modernization funds totaled $927.4 million according to U.S. Congress, House, Government Operations Committee, Manpower and Housing Subcommittee, Testimony of Phillip Winn..., p. 5.

18. See U.S. Congress, Senate, Banking, Finance and Urban Affairs Committee, Housing and Urban Affairs Subcommittee, Testimony of Lewis Spence, Council of Large Public Housing Authorities, 97th Cong., 2nd sess. (March 30, 1982).

19. Ibid., pp. 5-6.

20. Ibid., p. 15.

21. See U.S. Congress, House, Government Operations Committee, Manpower and Housing Subcommittee, Testimony of Phillip Winn..., pp. 12-14.

22. Telephone conversation with Chris Visher, National Housing Law Project, April 19, 1982. The Council of Large Public Housing Authorities has filed suit against HUD on this point.

23. Telephone conversation with Wayne Sherwood, CLPHA, May 19, 1982.

CHAPTER 9

1. S.M. Miller and Pamela Roby, The Future of Inequality (New York: Basic Books, 1970) entitle a chapter of their book "Basic Services: The Hidden Multipliers of Income." They describe these as follows:

> Income and assets are important components of the command over resources, but they do not include the increasingly important area of services. These services include education and training, health, neighborhood amenities, protection, social services, and transportation. In the high-income society, services comprise a great and increasing proportion of expenditures and furnish important segments of total satisfaction and well-being. (p. 84)

2. FOMAC, Low Income Energy... (1980). Technically, this is called incidence analysis which, in a more complete form, has been conducted for most public services, taking into account taxes, subsidies, and levels of consumption (see Note 12 below).

3. U.S. Department of Commerce, Bureau of the Census, Governments Division, data tapes maintained for the "Government Finances" series.

4. Robert G. Mogull, "Jurisdictional Spending for Public Welfare, Journal of Regional Science, 21:3, August 1981, Table 1.

5. A number of models of the response to fiscal stress or fiscal limitations have been proposed. The empirical studies have examined very broad categories, frequently emphasizing the revenue side. (See, for example, Richard A. Eribes and John S. Hall, "Revolt of the Affluent: Fiscal Controls in Three States," Public Administration Review, 41, Special Issue, January 1981; and James W. Danziger and Peter Smith Ring, "Fiscal Limitations: A Selective Review of Recent Research," Public Administration Review, January/February 1982. Andrew Glassberg, "The Urban Fiscal Crisis Becomes Routine;" Jerry McCaffery, "Revenue Budgeting: Dade County Tries a Decremental Approach;" Jeffrey D. Straussman, "More Bang for Fewer Bucks? Or How Local Governments Can Rediscover the Potentials [and Pitfalls] of the Market;" and Jerome B. McKinney, "Process Accountability and the Creative Use of Intergovernmental Resources," all in Public Administration Review, 41, Special Issue, January 1981.)

6. This is the distinction used by Richard Muth, Urban Economic Problems (New York: Harper and Row, 1975), p. 364.

7. Ibid., pp. 371-372.

8. Ibid., p. 364.

9. There is ample evidence that programs designed to aid the poor are dominated by politically powerful organizations. Dennis R. Judd and Robert E. Mendelson, The Politics of Urban Planning (Chicago: University of Illinois Press, 1973), after completing a literature review and a case study of East St. Louis, conclude "... urban planners have most often legitimated and implemented the interests of powerful political and economic groups (p. 176)." Stephen Therndenson, Poverty, Planning, and Politics in the New Boston: The Origins of ABCD (Boston: Basic Books, 1969), p. 180, reaches a similar conclusion. See, also, Kenneth Newton, Urban Political Economy (New York: St. Martin's Press, 1981); Robert L. Lineberry, Equality and Urban Policy (Beverly Hills: Sage, 1977); Robert L. Lineberry (ed.), The Politics and Economics of Urban Services (Beverly Hills: Sage, 1978); and L.H. Masotti and Robert L. Lineberry, The New Urban Politics (Cambridge, Mass.: Ballinger,

274

1976).

10. The analysis of the use of intergovernmental
revenues and their implications for local governments
has increased dramatically as fiscal stress and the
revenue limitation (taxpayer revolt) movements have
spread. See, for example, Catherine H. Lovell,
"Evolving Local Government Dependency," Public
Administration Review, 41, Special Issue, January 1981;
"Revenue-Raising Limitations on Local Government: A
Focus on Alternative Responses," Public Administration
Review, 41, Special Issue, January 1981; Roger L. Faith,
"Local Fiscal Crises and Intergovernmental Grants: A
Suggested Hypothesis," Public Choice 34, 1979, as well
as the references cited in Note 5, above.

11. See Note 9.

12. Keith Ray Ihlanfeldt, "The Incidence of the
Property Tax on Homeowners," National Tax Journal, 32:4,
December 1979; Kalman Goldberg and Robert C. Scott,
"Fiscal Incidence: A Revision of Benefits Incidence
Estimates," Journal of Regional Science, 21:2, May 1981;
Mark Schneider and John R. Logan, "Fiscal Implications
of Class Segregation: Inequalities in the Distribution
of Public Goods and Services in Suburban Municipali-
ties," Urban Affairs Quarterly, 17, September 1981.

13. Joseph Slavet, Katherine L. Bradbury, and Philip
I. Moss, Financing State-Local Services (Lexington,
Mass.: Lexington Books, 1975).

CHAPTER 10

1. International City Management Association, An
Assessment of Local Government Energy Management
Activities (Washington, D.C.: August 1980), p. 1.

2. David W. MacKenna, Jacilyn Walker, and P.D.
Creer, Jr., Energy and Local Government: The Price of
Crisis (Arlington, Texas: Institute of Urban Studies,
The University of Texas at Arlington, 1975), pp.
122-125. The lower figure excludes utility costs.

3. City of Los Angeles, Action Report prepared under
the Comprehensive Community Energy Management Program
(N.D.).

4. Energy is between 5 and 10 percent of total
expenditures. Operating expenses are about 20 percent
of all expenses.

5. Assistance payments were less than 2 percent of
total spending in 1979-80 according to the Census data.

6. International City Management Association, An
Assessment..., p. 1.

7. There was also a slight increase in other
miscellaneous categories, from 17 percent of total to 19
percent. These categories include interest earnings,
property sales, and unallocable categories.

8. The decline of infrastructure has received

considerable attention in the popular media. (See, for
example, "The Decaying of America," Newsweek, August 30,
1982.)
   9. There has been a debate over the relevance of
subjective evaluations to the process of planning the
delivery of public services. See, for example, Mark J.
Versel, "Zero-base Budgeting: Setting Priorities through
the Ranking Process," Public Administration Review, 38,
November 1978, as well as the opinion surveys discussed
in the Methodological Appendix, Section 4.
   10. Bradbury, et al., Urban Decline....
   11. See Ronald C. Fisher and Janet Kohlase, "Local
Government Revenue: Tax Reliance, Revenue Diversifi-
cation, and Metropolitan Finance," and Anthony Pascal,
"The Post Municipal City," both papers presented at the
Conference on Urban Development and Public Finance: The
Decade Ahead (Washington, D.C.: University of the
District of Columbia and the Department of Housing and
Urban Development, April 5-6, 1982).

CHAPTER 11

   1. The most obvious example of this effort is the
reference made by President Reagan in his Saturday radio
talk on March 5, 1983. In proposing decontrol of
natural gas prices he pointed to the success of his
decision to decontrol oil prices.
   2. The official recognition of falling prices came
in a study by the Congressional Budget Office entitled
The Economic and Budgetary Consequences of an Oil Price
Decrease: A Preliminary Analysis, March 1983
(Washington, D.C.).

APPENDIX

   1. U.S. Department of Commerce, Bureau of the
Census, Characteristics of the Population Below the
Poverty Level: 1979 (Washington, D.C.: 1981), Tables
43-46.
   2. U.S. Department of Health and Human Services,
Social Security Administration, Income of the Population
55 and Over, 1978, Staff Paper No. 41 (Washington, D.C.:
December 1981), Tables 12 and 42.
   3. U.S. Department of Commerce, Bureau of the
Census, Characteristics of the Population Below the
Poverty Level: 1979, Tables 27, 28, 43 and 44.
   4. This is true in all 3 years for which the
Residential Energy Consumption Survey has been
conducted.
   5. U.S. Department of Commerce, Bureau of the
Census, Money Income in 1978 of Households in the United
States (Washington, D.C.: 1980), U.S. Department of
Commerce, Bureau of the Census, Money Income of Families

276

and Persons in the United States: 1979, U.S. Department
of Energy, Residential Energy Consumption Survey:
Consumption and Expenditures, April 1978 through March
1979, U.S. Department of Energy, Residential Energy
Consumption Survey: 1979-1980 Consumption and
Expenditures, Part I.
     6. U.S. Department of Energy, Energy Information
Administration, State Energy Data Report: 1960 through
1980 (Washington, D.C.: September 1981).
     7. U.S. Department of Energy, Energy Information
Administration, Monthly Energy Review (Washington, D.C.:
various issues).
     8. U.S. Department of Energy, Energy Information
Administration, Annual Report to Congress, 1978
(Washington, D.C.).
     9. Economic Report of the President (Washington,
D.C.: February 1982).
     10. American Gas Association, Gas Facts, 1979
(Arlington, Va.: 1980).
     11. Salins, The Ecology of Housing..., p. 97.
     12. George Sternlieb (The Tenement Landlord [New
Brunswick, N.J.: Rutgers University Press, 1969] and
Sternlieb and Hughes, America's Housing...) is among the
most prominent of those who have used the case study
approach to estimate operating costs. Gilderbloom,
"Moderate Rent Control...," gives a thorough critique of
these case studies.
     13. See Note 2 in Chapter 8.
     14. Sternlieb, The Tenement Landlord; Sternlieb and
Hughes, America's Housing..., p. 274.
     15. OTA, Energy Efficiency of Buildings..., Chapter
V.
     16. A view of the various sides of the philosophical
debate would include, James M. Buchanan and Robert D.
Tollison (eds.), The Theory of Public Choice (Ann Arbor:
University of Michigan Press, 1972); E.S. Savas (ed.),
Alternatives for Delivering Public Services (Boulder,
Col.: Westview Press, 1977); Richard A. Musgrave and
Peggy B. Musgrave, Public Finance in Theory and Practice
(New York: McGraw Hill, 1980); Mancur Olson, Jr., The
Logic of Collective Action (Cambridge, Mass.: Harvard
University Press, 1965); Robert L. Bish, The Public
Economy of Metropolitan Areas (New York: Markham, 1971).
A sampling of recent empirical analysis in which much of
the earlier empirical work is referenced would include
Kenneth V. Greene and Thomas J. Parliament, "Political
Externalities, Efficiency, and the Welfare Losses from
Consolidation," National Tax Journal, 33:2, June 1980;
Jacob Meerman, "Are Public Goods Public Goods?," Public
Choice, 35, 1980; James B. Kan and Paul H. Rubin, "The
Size of Government," Public Choice, 36, 1981; Peter W.
Abelson, "Some Benefits of Small Local Government
Areas," Publius, Winter 1981. A more sociological/

historical perspective can be found in Roland J.
Liebert, Disintegration and Political Action: The
Changing Functions of City Governments in America (New
York: Academic Press, 1976).
    17. Recent general conceptualizations of the equity
of service delivery can be found in Paul R. Dimond,
Constance Chamberlain, and Wayne Hillyerd, A Dilemma of
Local Government (Lexington, Mass.: Lexington Books,
1978); Richard C. Rich, Analyzing Urban Service
Distributions (Lexington, Mass.: Lexington Books, 1982);
and Frank S. Levy, Arnold Meltsner, and Aaron Wildavsky,
Urban Outcomes (Berkeley, Cal.: University of California
Press, 1974). A general review oriented toward local
officials can be found in Richard C. Rich, "Neglected
Issues in the Study of Urban Service Distributions: A
Research Agenda," Urban Studies, 16, 1979. Recent
empirical analyses, in which reference to much of these
earlier empirical works can be found, would include:
Brian McDonald, "Educational Equity and the Fiscal
Incidence of Public Education," National Tax Journal,
33:1, March 1980; John Packer, "Equity in Transit
Finance," Journal of the American Planning Association
47, October 1981; Kenneth R. Mladenka, "The Distribution
of Benefits in an Urban Environment: Parks and Libraries
in Houston," Urban Affairs Quarterly, 13, September
1977; George E. Antunes and John P. Plumlee, "The
Distribution of an Urban Public Service: Ethnicity,
Socioeconomic Status and Bureaucracy as Determinants of
the Quality of Neighborhood Streets," Urban Affairs
Quarterly, 12, March 1977; Bryan D. Jones, Service
Delivery in the City: Citizen Demand and Bureaucratic
Rules (New York: Longman, 1980); Goldberg and Scott,
"Fiscal Incidence..."
    18. The economic analysis has its origins in the
same principles as the public choice literature (see
Note 16). The more specific economic analysis, however,
focuses on the optimal provision of public goods. See,
for example, Michael J. Boskin, "Local Government Tax
and Product Competition and the Optimal Provision of
Public Goods," Journal of Political Economy, 81, 1973;
Michael E. Burns and Cliff Walsh, "Market Provision of
Price-excludable Public Goods: A General Analysis,"
Journal of Political Economy, 89:1, February 1981; David
A. Starrett, "Land Value Capitalization in Local Public
Finance," Journal of Political Economy, 89, April 1981;
Sam Bucovetsky, "Inequality in the Local Public Sector,"
Journal of Political Economy, 90, February 1982. Two
additional strains can be identified in this literature.
One strain can be called the efficiency strain. This
strain asks the question of how to provide services at
the minimum cost. See for example, Robert W. Poole, Jr.
Cutting Back City Hall (New York: Universe Books, 1980);
Selma Mushkin (ed.), Public Prices for Public Goods

(Washington, D.C.: Urban Institute, 1972); Donald Fisk, Herbert Kiesling, and Thomas Muller, Private Provision of Public Services: An Overview (Washington, D.C.: Urban Institute, 1978). A second strain in this analysis focuses on the implications of optimal provision of services and the geographic distribution of services. See, for example, Cowing and Holtman, The Economics...; Wallace E. Oates, E.P. Howrey, and W.J. Baoumal, "The Analysis of Public Policy in Dynamic Urban Models," Journal of Political Economy, 79, January 1971; Odland and Balzer, "Localized Externalities...;" Yung-Mei Tsai, Otoman Bartos, and Lee Sigelman, "The Urban Dynamics Model: A Validation Study," Urban Affairs Quarterly, 17, December 1981.

19. Two simplifying assumptions in this analysis render the extraction of these generalizations relatively easy. First, we make no effort to assess whether expenditures for each service were too large or too small prior to the energy price shock. This avoids a difficult qualitative question. J. Fred Giertz, "Centralization, Collective Choice and Public Expenditure," Publius, Winter 1981, makes the point that avoiding qualitative questions about whether expenditures are "too large or too small," renders the analysis much simpler.

Second, we are fairly certain what the direction of change will be -- i.e., reductions in service and increases in revenues. Therefore, we can orient our discussion in one direction. Howard Glennerster, "Prime Cuts: Public Expenditure and Social Services Planning in a Hostile Environment," Policy and Politics, 8:4, 1981, has argued that there is no guarantee that processes of contraction and processes of expansion will be the same. Therefore, being able to focus on one likely direction of change simplifies matters significantly.

20. Miller and Roby, The Future..., pp. 84-87, identify five fundamental issues in the analysis of basic services:

1. Public versus private delivery of services.
2. Definition of basic services as investments or amenities.
3. Delivery of objective minimum services versus adequate levels of service.
4. Connection between services and well-being.
5. Availability of services versus actual utilization of services.

It can readily be seen that the first two issues fall essentially in the areas of public goods analysis, while the latter three fall in the area of equity of distribution.

21. Vincent Ostrom and Elinor Ostrom, "Public Goods

and Public Choices," in Savas (ed.), Alternatives for....
   22. Ibid., pp. 10-11.
   23. Dimond et al., A Dilemma....
   24. Ibid., p. 17.
   25. Dimond, et al., A Dilemma..., argue these points with reference to John Rawls, A Theory of Justice (Cambridge, Mass.: Harvard University Press, 1971), p. 75.
   26. Ibid. Dimond, et al., A Dilemma..., do not endorse equality as the basis for the distribution of services, even though they identify it as a principle.
   27. It is useful to note here that even more conservative analyses recognize categorical distinctions between types of services. Moreover, these distinctions provide the leverage for distinguishing carefully between efficiency considerations as such and choice about which services to deliver. That is, the choice of whether to deliver a service must be separated from the choice of (1) who to deliver it to, (2) how to deliver it, and (3) at what price. The issues of how and at what price can easily be confused with the much more fundamental issues of whether and to whom.
   For example, Poole, Cutting Back..., identifies a very restricted set of genuine public goods at the local level:

> About the only local services that come close to looking like classical public goods are mosquito abatement and other public health measures and certain preventive aspects of police and fire protection. (p. 26).

At the same time, however, he argues that even for non-public goods which require user fees, equity considerations can lead to provision of the services for free. Thus, the first principle of establishing user fees is the principle of fairness which, in Poole's argument, includes the notion that:

> It would be far more equitable to provide such services on a user-pays basis, so that only those who benefit directly end up paying. To the extent that some members of the community may be too poor to afford these charges, it is quite possible to provide free passes or other forms of explicit subsidy only for them. (p. 33).

   28. These are the strains identified in Note 18 above.
   29. We do not mean to belittle the study of efficient delivery of services and choices about public versus private (contractual) service delivery. There is

280

a growing and increasingly sophisticated literature on
the relative efficiency of various delivery mechanisms.
However, we are also convinced that efficiency improvements are not the real issue. After all efficiency
improvements have been made, there will still be fiscal
stress due to the magnitude of the impact of rising
energy prices. Thus, more than efficiency improvement
will have to be made to cope with the impact. Real
reductions in service will be necessary.

30. Boskin, "Local Government...," p. 204.
31. Muth, <u>Urban Economic Problems</u>, p. 364.
32. In a sense, we are suggesting that the pattern
of expenditure changes which Muth documents for the
1960-1970 period will be reversed in the 1972-1980
period.
33. Thomas S. Arrington and David D. Jordan,
"Willingness to Pay Per Capita Costs as a Measure of
Support for Urban Services," <u>Public Administration
Review</u>, 42, March/April 1982. See also, Michael R.
Fitzgerald and Robert F. Durant, "Citizen Evaluations
and Urban Management, Service Delivery in an Era of
Protest," <u>Public Administration Review</u>, 40,
November/December 1980.
34. Liebert, <u>Disintegration...</u>, p. 22.

Bibliography

Abelson, Peter W. "Some Benefits of Small Local
Government Areas." Publius (Winter 1981).

Abt Associates. "Evaluation of the Performance Funding
System." Cambridge, Mass.: draft prepared for the
U.S. Department of Housing and Urban Development,
July 1981.

American Gas Association. Gas Facts, 1979. Arlington,
Va.: 1980.

Anderson, C. Dennis and Gordon H.C. McDougall. Consumer
Energy Research: An Annotated Bibliography. Canada:
Consumer Research and Evaluation Branch of Consumer
and Corporate Affairs, July 1980.

Antunes, George E. and John P. Plumlee. "The Distribution of an Urban Public Service: Ethnicity,
Socioeconomic Status and Bureaucracy as Determinants
of the Quality of Neighborhood Streets." Urban
Affairs Quarterly 12 (March 1977).

Arrington, Thomas S. and David D. Jordan. "Willingness
to Pay Per Capita Costs as a Measure of Support for
Urban Services." Public Administration Review 42
(March/April 1982).

Askin, A. Bradley, ed. How Energy Affects the Economy.
Lexington, Mass.: Lexington Books, 1978.

Baily, Martin Neil. "Productivity and the Services of
Capital and Labor." Brookings Papers on Economic
Activity 1 (1981).

Beebout, Harold, Gerald Peabody, and Pat Doyle. "The
Distribution of Household Energy Expenditures and
the Impact of High Prices," in Hans H. Landsberg,
ed., High Energy Costs -- Assessing the Burden.
Washington, D.C.: Resources for the Future, 1981.

Bish, Robert L. The Public Economy of Metropolitan
Areas. New York: Markham, 1971.

Boskin, Michael J. "Local Government Tax and Product
Competition and the Optimal Provision of Public
Goods." Journal of Political Economy 81 (January

282

1973).

Bradbury, Katharine L., Anthony Downs, and Kenneth A.
Small. Urban Decline and the Future of American
Cities. Washington, D.C.: The Brookings Institution,
1982.

Bridges, Jr., Benjamin and Michael D. Packard. "Price
and Income Changes for the Elderly." Social Security
Bulletin 44:1 (January 1981).

Buchanan, James M. and Robert D. Tollison, eds. The
Theory of Public Choice. Ann Arbor: University of
Michigan Press, 1972.

Bucovetsky, Sam. "Inequality in the Local Public
Sector." Journal of Political Economy 90 (February
1982).

Burns, Michael E. and Cliff Walsh. "Market Provision of
Price-excludable Public Goods: A General Analysis."
Journal of Political Economy 89:1 (February 1981).

Cambridge Reports, Inc. Electricity Pricing: Choices for
the 1980s. N.D.

Coe, Richard D. "A Comparison of Utility Payments and
Burdens Between 1971 and 1979," in James N. Morgan
and Greg S. Duncan, eds., Five Thousand American
Families: Patterns of Economic Progress, Vol. VIII.
Ann Arbor: Institute for Social Research, 1980.

Committee for Economic Development and The Conservation
Foundation. Energy Prices and Public Policy. New
York: Committee for Economic Development, July 1982.

Consumer Energy Council of America. Energy Conservation
in New Buildings: A Critique and Alternative
Approach to the Department of Energy's Building
Energy Performance Standards. Washington, D.C.:
April 1980.

---- "Questions and Answers on Crude Oil Decontrol."
Washington, D.C.: April 30, 1979.

Consumer Energy Council of America Research Foundation.
A Comprehensive Analysis of the Costs and Benefits
of Low Income Weatherization and its Potential
Relationship to Low Income Energy Assistance.
Washington, D.C.: June 2, 1981.

---- A Comprehensive Analysis of the Impact of a Crude
Oil Import Fee: Dismantling a Trojan Horse.
Washington, D.C.: April 1982.

---- Natural Gas Decontrol: A Case of Trickle-Up
Economics. Washington, D.C.: January 28, 1982.

---- "Oil Price Decontrol and the Poor: A Social Policy
Failure." Washington, D.C.: for the U.S. Congress,
Joint Economic Committee, February 2, 1981.

---- The Past as Prologue I: The Underestimation of
Price Increases in the Decontrol Debate: A Compar-
ison of Oil and Natural Gas. Washington, D.C.:
February 1982.

---- The Past as Prologue II: The Economic Effects of
Rising Energy Prices: A Comparison of the Oil Price

Shock and Natural Gas Decontrol. Washington, D.C.:
March 1982.
Cooper, Mark. "Comment on the Impact of High Prices," in
Hans H. Landsberg, ed., High Energy Costs --
Assessing the Burden. Washington, D.C.: Resources
for the Future, 1981.
---- "Energy Policy and Jobs: The Conservation Path to
Fuller Employment." A paper presented to the
Conference on Energy and Jobs, Industrial Union
Department, AFL-CIO, May 5, 1980.
Cowing, Thomas and A.G. Holtman. The Economics of Local
Public Service Consolidations. Lexington, Mass.:
Lexington Books, 1976.
Curtin, Richard T. "Consumer Adaptation to Energy
Shortages." Journal of Energy and Development 2:1
(Autumn 1976).
Danziger, James W. and Peter Smith Ring. "Fiscal Limi-
tations: A Selective Review of Recent Research."
Public Administration Review (January/February
1982).
"The Decaying of America." Newsweek. August 30, 1982.
"Decontrol of Oil Prices Expected Today." The Wall
Street Journal. January 28, 1981.
Denison, E. "Explanations of Declining Productivity
Growth." Survey of Current Business 59 (1979).
Dimond, Paul R., Constance Chamberlain, and Wayne
Hillyerd. A Dilemma of Local Government. Lexington,
Mass.: Lexington Books, 1978.
Dohner, Robert S. "Energy Prices, Economic Activity, and
Inflation: A Survey of Issues and Results," in Knut
Anton Mork, ed., Energy Prices, Inflation, and
Economic Activity. Cambridge, Mass.: Ballinger,
1981.
Downs, Anthony. Neighborhoods and Urban Change.
Washington, D.C.: The Brookings Institution, 1981.
---- "The Successes and Failures of Federal Housing
Policy." The Public Interest 34 (Winter 1974).
Duffy, Martin, et al. Inflation and the Elderly: Summary
Report. Lexington, Mass.: Data Resources, Inc.,
April 1980.
Duncan, Greg. "Some Equity Aspects of Gasoline Price
Inflation," in James N. Morgan and Greg S. Duncan,
eds., Five Thousand American Families: Patterns of
Economic Progress, Vol. VI. Ann Arbor: Institute for
Social Research, 1978.
Eckstein, Otto. The Great Recession: With a Postscript
on Stagflation. New York: North Holland, 1978.
---- "Shock Inflation, Core Inflation, and Energy
Disturbances in the DRI Model," in Knut Anton Mork,
ed., Energy Prices, Inflation, and Economic
Activity. Cambridge, Mass.: Ballinger, 1981.
Egan, John, John Carr, Andrew Mott, and John Roos,
Housing and Public Policy: A Role for Mediating

284

Structures. Cambridge, Mass.: Ballinger for the American Enterprise Institute, 1981.

The Energy Policy Project of the Ford Foundation. A Time to Choose. Cambridge, Mass.: Ballinger, 1979.

Eribes, Richard A. and John S. Hall. "Revolt of the Affluent: Fiscal Controls in Three States. Public Administration Review 41 (Speecial Issue, January 1981).

Fahrar, Barbara C., et al. Public Opinion About Energy: A Literature Review. Washington, D.C.: U.S. Department of Commerce, National Technical Information Service, June 1979.

Faith, Roger L. "Local Fiscal Crises and Intergovernmental Grants: A Suggested Hypothesis." Public Choice 34 (1979).

Feldstein, Martin, ed. The American Economy in Transition. Chicago: Chicago University Press, 1980.

Fellner, William. "The Declining Growth of American Productivity: An Introductory Note," in William Fellner, ed., Essays on Contemporary Economic Problems. Washington, D.C.: American Enterprise Institute, 1979.

---- ed. Essays on Contemporary Economic Problems. Washington, D.C.: American Enterprise Institute, 1979.

---- Essays on Contemporary Economic Problems. Washington, D.C.: American Enterprise Institute, 1981.

Fenoalta, Stefano. "The Discipline and Theory: Notes on Contrafactual Methodology and the New Economic History." Journal of European Economic History 2:3 (1975).

Fisher, Ronald C. and Janet Kohlase. "Local Government Revenue: Tax Reliance, Revenue Diversification, and Metropolitan Finance." Presented at the Conference on Urban Development and Public Finance: The Decade Ahead. Washington, D.C.: University of the District of Columbia and U.S. Department of Housing and Urban Development, April 5-6, 1982.

Fisk, Donald, Herbert Kiesling, and Thomas Muller. Private Provision of Public Services: An Overview. Washington, D.C.: Urban Institute, 1978.

Fitzgerald, Michael R. and Robert F. Durant. "Citizen Evaluations and Urban Management: Service Delivery in an Era of Protest." Public Administration Review 40 (November/December 1980).

Foster Associates, Inc. A Comparison and Appraisal of Ten Natural Gas Deregulation Studies. Washington, D.C.: Chemical Manufacturers Association, February 16, 1982.

Friede, Edward R. and Charles L. Schultze, eds. Higher Oil Prices and the World Economy: The Adjustment Problem. Washington, D.C.: The Brookings Institution, 1975.

Gelb, Bernard A. and Everson W. Hall. Revenue and
Macroeconomic Impacts of an Oil Import Tax: A Brief
Review. Washington, D.C.: Congressional Research
Service of the Library of Congress, April 6, 1982.
Giertz, J. Fred. "Centralization, Collective Choice and
Public Expenditure." Publius (Winter 1981).
Gilderbloom, John Ingram. "Moderate Rent Control: Its
Impact on the Quality and Quantity of the Housing
Stock." Urban Affairs Quarterly 17:2 (December
1981).
Glassberg, Andrew. "The Urban Fiscal Crisis Becomes
Routine." Public Administration Review 41 (Special
Issue, January 1981).
Glennerster, Howard. "Prime Cuts: Public Expenditure and
Social Services Planning in a Hostile Environment."
Policy and Politics 8:4 (1980).
Goldberg, Kalman and Robert C. Scott. "Fiscal Incidence:
A Revision of Benefits Incidence Estimates." Journal
of Regional Science 21:2 (1981).
Goodwin, Craufurd D., et al. Energy Policy in Perspec-
tive: Today's Problems, Yesterday's Solutions.
Washington, D.C.: The Brookings Institution, 1981.
Gordon, Robert J. "Alternative Responses of Policy to
External Supply Shocks." Brookings Papers on
Economic Activity 1 (1975).
Gordon, Robert S. "Postwar Macroeconomics: The Evolution
of Events and Ideas," in Martin Feldstein, ed., The
American Economy in Transition. Chicago: Chicago
University Press, 1980.
Gramlich, Edward M. "Macro Policy Responses to Price
Shocks." Brookings Papers on Economic Activity 1
(1979).
Gravitz, Alisa. DOE Report on the Rental and Multi-
Family Housing Energy Efficiency Workshop: Memor-
andum for DOE Multi-Family Task Force. Washington,
D.C.: U.S. Department of Energy, Office of Conser-
vation Policy and Evaluation, January 30, 1981.
Greene, Kenneth V. and Thomas J. Parliament. "Political
Externalities, Efficiency, and the Welfare Losses
from Consolidation." National Tax Journal 33:2 (June
1980).
The Grier Partnership. Too Cold...Too Dark. Washington,
D.C.: for the Community Services Administration,
1981.
Hagemann, Robert P. Inflation and Household Characteris-
tics: An Analysis of Group Specific Price Indexes.
BLS Working Papers, No. 10. Washington, D.C.: U.S.
Bureau of Labor Statistics, December 1980.
Harris, Jeffrey P. and Jack M. Hollander, eds. Improving
Energy Efficiency in Buildings: Progress and
Problems. Proceedings of the 1980 Summer Study
organized by the American Council for an Energy-

286

Efficient Economy. University of California, Santa
Cruz: August 10-22, 1980.

Hayes, William L. Statistics. New York: Holt, Rinehart
and Winston, 1963.

Hemphill, Robert and Robert L. Owens. "Burden Allocation
and Electric Utility Rate Structures Issues and
Options in the TVA Region." Presented at A Confer-
ence on Higher Energy Costs: Assessing the Burden,
Organized by Resources for the Future and the
Brookings Institution, October 9-10, 1980.

Herendeen, R. and J. Tanaka. "Energy Costs of Living."
Energy (June 1976).

Herendeen, Robert, B. Hannon, and C. Ford. "An Energy
Consuming Tax: How Large Should Rebates Be?"
Unpublished.

Hicks, Daniel A., ed. Urban America in the Eighties:
Perspectives and Prospects. New Brunswick, N.J.:
Transaction Books, 1982.

Hill, Daniel. "The Relative Burden of Higher Gas
Prices," in James N. Morgan and Greg S. Duncan,
eds., Five Thousand American Families: Patterns of
Economic Progress, Vol. VIII. Ann Arbor: Institute
for Social Research, 1980.

Hirst, Eric, et al. Residential Energy Use and
Conservation Actions: Analysis of Disaggregate
Household Data. Oak Ridge, Tenn.: Oak Ridge National
Laboratory, March 1981.

Hogan, W. and Alan Manne. "Energy-Economic Interactions:
The Fable of 'The Elephant and the Rabbit'," in
Robert S. Pindyck, ed., Advances in the Economics of
Energy and Resources: The Structure of Energy
Markets, Vol. I. Greenwich, Conn.: JAI Press, 1979.

Hudson, E.A. and D.W. Jorgenson. "Energy Prices and the
U.S. Economy 1972-1976." Natural Resources Journal
18 (1978).

ICF Inc. Preliminary Analysis of the Macroeconomic
Impacts of Natural Gas Decontrol: The Structure and
Behavior of the DRI and Wharton Models. Draft, April
20, 1981.

Ihlanfeldt, Keith Ray. "The Incidence of the Property
Tax on Homeowners." National Tax Journal 32:4
(December 1979).

Inside Energy. June 11, 1982, p. 6.

International City Management Association. An Assessment
of Local Government Energy Management Activities.
Washington, D.C.: August 1980.

Jones, Bryan D. Service Delivery in the City: Citizen
Demand and Bureaucratic Rules. New York: Longman,
1980.

Jorgenson, Dale W. "Energy Prices and Productivity
Growth." Data Resources Inc. (1979).

Journal of Social Issues. 37:2 (1981).

Judd, Dennis R. and Robert E. Mendelson. The Politics of

Urban Planning. Chicago: University of Illinois Press, 1973.

Kalt, Joseph. The Economics and Politics of Oil Price Regulation: Federal Policy in the Post Embargo Era. Cambridge, Mass.: MIT Press, 1981.

Kan, James B. and Paul H. Rubin. "The Size of Government." Public Choice 36 (1981).

Kendrick, John. "International Comparisons of Recent Productivity Trends," in William Fellner, ed., Essays in Contemporary Economic Problems. Washington, D.C.: American Enterprise Institute, 1981.

Khadduri, Jill, Katherine Lyall, and Raymond Struyk. "Welfare Reform and Housing Assistance: A National Policy Debate." Journal of the American Institute of Planners 44:1 (1978).

Khadduri, Jill and Raymond Struyk. "Improving Section 8 Rental Assistance, Translating Evaluation into Policy." Evaluation Review 5:2 (1981).

Landsberg, Hans H., ed. High Energy Costs -- Assessing the Burden. Washington, D.C.: Resources for the Future, 1981.

---- et al. Energy: The Next Twenty Years. Cambridge, Mass.: Ballinger, 1979.

---- and Joseph M. Dukert, eds. High Energy Costs -- Uneven, Unfair, Unavoidable? Baltimore: Johns Hopkins Press for Resources for the Future, 1981.

"The Leverage of Lower Oil Prices." Business Week. March 22, 1982, pp. 66-73.

Levy, Frank S., Arnold Meltsner, and Aaron Wildavsky. Urban Outcomes. Berkeley, Cal.: University of California Press, 1974.

Liebert, Roland J. Disintegration and Political Action: The Changing Functions of City Governments in America. New York: Academic Press, 1976.

Lindsay, David Scott and Ira S. Lowry. Rent Inflation in St. Joseph County, Indiana, 1974-78. Santa Monica, Cal.: The Rand Corporation for the U.S. Department of Housing and Urban Development, November 1980.

Lineberry, Robert L. Equality and Urban Policy. Beverly Hills: Sage, 1977.

---- ed. The Politics and Economics of Urban Services. Beverly Hills: Sage, 1978.

Los Angeles. Action Report prepared under the Comprehensive Community Energy Management Program, N.D.

Loury, Glenn C. An Analysis of the Efficiency and Inflationary Impacts of the Decontrol of Natural Gas Prices. Washington, D.C.: Natural Gas Supply Association, April 1981.

Lovell, Catherine H. "Evolving Local Government Dependency." Public Administration Review 41 (Special Issue, January 1981).

---- "Revenue-Raising Limitations on Local Government: A

288

Focus of Alternative Responses." Public Administration Review Special Issue (January 1981).

Lowry, Ira S. Rental Housing in the 1970s: Searching for
the Crisis. Santa Monica, Cal.: The Rand Corporation
for the U.S. Department of Housing and Urban
Development, January 1982.

MacKenna, David W., Jacilyn Walker and P.D. Creer, Jr.
Energy and Local Government: The Price of Crisis.
Arlington, Texas: Institute of Urban Studies, The
University of Texas at Arlington, 1975.

Mackenzie, J. "Summary: Institutional Issues," in
Jeffrey P. Harris and Jack M. Hollander, eds.,
Improving Energy Efficiency in Buildings: Progress
and Problems. Proceedings of the 1980 Summer Study
organized by the American Council for an Energy-
Efficient Economy. University of California, Santa
Cruz: August 10-22, 1980.

Masotti, L.H. and Robert L. Lineberry. The New Urban
Politics. Cambridge, Mass.: Ballinger, 1976.

McCaffery, Jerry. "Revenue Budgeting: Dade County Tries
a Decremental Approach." Public Administration
Review 41 (Special Issue, January 1981).

McDonald, Brian. "Educational Equity and the Fiscal
Incidence of Public Education." National Tax Journal
33:1 (March 1980).

McKinney, Jerome B. "Process Accountability and the
Creative Use of Intergovernmental Resources." Public
Administration Review 41 (Special Issue, January
1981).

Meehan, Eugene J. The Quality of Federal Policymaking:
Programmed Failure in Public Housing. Columbia, Mo.:
University of Missouri Press, 1979.

Meerman, Jacob. "Are Public Goods Public Goods?" Public
Choice 35 (1980).

Miller, S.M. and Pamela Roby. The Future of Inequality.
New York: Basic Books, 1970.

Mladenka, Kenneth R. and Kim Quaile Hill. "The Distribution of Benefits in an Urban Environment: Parks
and Libraries in Houston." Urban Affairs Quarterly
13 (September 1977).

Mogull, Robert G. "Jurisdictional Spending for Public
Welfare." Journal of Regional Science 21:3 (August
1981).

Morgan, James N. and Greg S. Duncan, eds. Five Thousand
American Families: Patterns of Economic Progress.
Vol. VI. Ann Arbor: Institute for Social Research,
1978.

Morgan, James N. and Greg S. Duncan, eds. Five Thousand
American Families: Patterns of Economic Progress.
Vol. VIII. Ann Arbor: Institute for Social Research,
1980.

Mork, Knut Anton, ed. Energy Prices, Inflation, and
Economic Activity. Cambridge, Mass.: Ballinger,

1981.

---- and Robert E. Hall. "Macroeconomic Analysis of Energy Price Shocks and Offsetting Policies: An Integrated Approach," in Knut Anton Mork, ed., Energy Prices, Inflation, and Economic Activity. Cambridge, Mass.: Ballinger, 1981.

Murray, Michael P. "Tenant Benefits in Alternative Federal Housing Programmes." Urban Studies 17 (February 1980).

Musgrave, Richard A. and Peggy B. Musgrave. Public Finance in Theory and Practice. New York: McGraw Hill, 1980.

Mushkin, Selma, ed. Public Prices for Public Products. Washington, D.C.: Urban Institute, 1972.

Muth, Richard. Urban Economic Problems. New York: Harper and Row, 1975.

National Academy of Sciences, National Research Council. Energy in Transition 1985-2010: Final Report of the Committee on Nuclear and Alternative Energy Systems. San Francisco: W.H. Freeman and Co., 1980.

National Council of Senior Citizens, Project Energy Care. Seared Hopes and Frozen Promises. Washington, D.C.: June 30, 1982.

Newton, Kenneth. Urban Political Economy. New York: St. Martin's Press, 1981.

Nolan, John R. "Reexamining Federal Housing Programs in a Time of Fiscal Austerity: The Trend Toward Block Grants and Housing Allowances." The Urban Lawyer 14:2 (1982).

Nordhaus, William D. "Oil and Economic Performance in Industrial Countries." Brookings Papers on Economic Activity 2 (1980).

Oates, Wallace E., E.P. Howrey, and W.J. Baoumol. "The Analysis of Public Policy in Dynamic Urban Models." Journal of Political Economy 79 (January 1971).

Odland, John and Blanche Balzer. "Localized Externalities, Contagious Processes and the Deterioration of Urban Housing: An Empirical Analysis" Social and Economic Planning Sciences 13 (1979).

Ohio. Office of Consumers' Counsel. Characteristics of Residential Electric and Gas Customers. Columbus, Ohio: June 1979.

Okun, Arthur. Prices and Quantities: Macroeconomic Analyses. Washington, D.C.: The Brookings Institution, 1981.

Olsen, Edgar O. "Housing Programs and the Forgotten Taxpayer." The Public Interest 66 (Winter 1982).

Olson, Jr., Mancur. The Logic of Collective Action. Cambridge, Mass.: Harvard University Press, 1965.

Ostrom, Vincent and Elinor Ostrom. "Public Goods and Public Choices," in E.S. Savas, ed., Alternatives for Delivering Public Services. Boulder, Col.: Westview Press, 1977.

Packer, John. "Equity in Transit Finance." Journal of
the American Planning Association 47 (October 1981).
Pascal, Anthony. "The Post Municipal City." Presented at
the Conference on Urban Development and Public
Finance: The Decade Ahead. Washington, D.C.: Univer-
sity of the District of Columbia and U.S. Department
of Housing and Urban Development, April 5-6, 1982.
Pennsylvania State University, College of Human Develop-
ment, The Community Development Program for the
Bureau of Consumer Services of the Public Utility
Commission of the Commonwealth of Pennsylvania.
Residential Utility Consumer Payment Problems: A
Study of Customer, Company and PUC Interactions,
Vol. II: Consumer and Company Responses to Impending
Utility Terminations. May 1982.
Perry, George. "The United States," in Edward R. Friede
and Charles L. Schultze, eds., Higher Oil Prices and
the World Economy: The Adjustment Problem.
Washington, D.C.: The Brookings Institution, 1975.
Perry, George L. "Potential Output: Recent Issues and
Present Trends." Brookings Reprint 336 (1978).
Phelps, Edmund S. "Commodity-Supply Shocks and Full-
Employment Monetary Policy." Journal of Money,
Credit and Banking 10:2 (May 1978).
Pierce, James L. and Jared J. Enzler. "The Effects of
External Inflationary Shocks." Brookings Papers on
Economic Activity 1 (1974).
Pindyck, Robert S., ed. Advances in the Economics of
Energy and Resources: The Structure of Energy
Markets, Vol. I. Greenwich, Conn.: JAI Press, 1979.
The Pollyana Institute. Rental Housing: Two Decades of
Progress. Washington, D.C.: 1980.
Poole, Robert W., Jr. Cutting Back City Hall. New York:
Universe Books, 1980.
Power, Meg and Joel Eisenberg. Low Income Energy
Assistance in the 1980s: The Needs and the Choices.
Washington, D.C.: Northeast Coalition for Energy
Equity, March 1, 1982.
Pucher, John, Chris Henderson, and Sue McNeil. "Socio-
economic Characteristics of Transit Riders: Some
Recent Evidence." Traffic Quarterly 35:3 (July
1981).
Rasche, R. and J. Tatom. "The Effects of the New Energy
Regime on Economic Capacity, Production and Prices."
Federal Reserve Bank of St. Louis Review (1977).
---- ---- "Energy Prices and Potential GNP." Federal
Reserve Bank of St. Louis Review (1977).
Rawls, John. A Theory of Justice. Cambridge, Mass.:
Harvard University Press, 1971.
Reischauer, Robert D. "Federal Budget Reveals Political,
Economic Costs of Housing Assistance." Journal of
Housing 38 (March 1981).
Remmie, C. "Focusing on the Market for Residential

Retrofit: Present Opportunity and Future Prospects,"
in Jeffrey P. Harris and Jack M. Hollander, eds.,
Improving Energy Efficiency in Buildings: Progress
and Problems. Proceedings of the 1980 Summer Study
organized by the American Council for an Energy-
Efficient Economy. University of California, Santa
Cruz: August 10-22, 1980.
Rich, Richard C. Analyzing Urban Service Distributions.
Lexington, Mass.: Lexington Books, 1982.
---- "Neglected Issues in the Study of Urban Service
Distributions: A Research Agenda." Urban Studies 16
(1979).
Sadaca, Robert, Morton Isler, and Joan DeWitt. The
Development of a Prototype Equation for Public
Housing Operating Expenses. Washington, D.C.: An
Urban Institute Paper, June 1975.
Salins, Peter D. The Ecology of Housing Destruction:
Economic Effects of Public Intervention in the
Housing Market. New York: New York University Press
for the International Center for Economic Policy
Studies, 1980.
Sanders, M. Elizabeth. The Regulation of Natural Gas
Policy and Politics, 1938-1978. Philadelphia: Temple
University Press, 1981.
Savas, E.S., ed., Alternatives for Delivering Public
Services. Boulder, Col.: Westview Press, 1977.
Sayre, William P. "Subsidized Housing -- Costs and
Benefits." Federal Reserve Bank of Chicago 111:3
(1979).
Schelling, Thomas C. Thinking Through the Energy
Problem. New York: Committee for Economic Develop-
ment, 1979.
Schneider, Mark and John R. Logan. "Fiscal Implications
of Class Segregation: Inequalities in the
Distribution of Public Goods and Services in
Suburban Municipalities." Urban Affairs Quarterly 17
(September 1981).
Schurr, Sam, et al. Energy in America's Future: The
Choices Before Us. Baltimore: Johns Hopkins Press
for Resources for the Future, 1979.
Serot, David E. "The Energy Crisis and the U.S. Economy,
1973-1975," in A. Bradley Askin, How Energy Affects
the Economy. Lexington, Mass.: Lexington Books,
1978.
Slavet, Joseph, Katherine Bradbury, and Philip I. Moss.
Financing State-Local Services. Lexington, Mass.:
Lexington Books, 1975.
Starrett, David A. "Land Value Capitalization in Local
Public Finance." Journal of Political Economy 89
(April 1981).
Sternlieb, George. The Tenement Landlord. New Brunswick,
N.J.: Rutgers University, 1969.
---- and James W. Hughes. "Rent Control's Impact on the

292

Community Tax Base," in George Sternlieb and James
W. Hughes, eds., America's Housing: Prospects and
Problems. New Brunswick, N.J.: Rutgers University,
Center for Urban Policy Research, 1980.
---- ---- eds. America's Housing: Prospects and
Problems. New Brunswick, N.J.: Rutgers University,
Center for Urban Policy Research, 1980.
Stobaugh, Robert and Daniel Yergin, eds. Energy Future:
The Report of the Energy Project at the Harvard
Business School. New York: Random House, 1979.
Stockton State College. A Survey of the Psychosocial and
Economic Effects of Inflation and Natural Gas
Deregulation on Residential and Commercial
Customers. November 1981.
Straussman, Jeffrey D. "More Bang for Fewer Bucks? Or
How Local Governments can Rediscover the Potentials
(and Pitfalls) of the Market." Public Administration
Review 41 (Special Issue, January 1981).
Strucker, J.P. and T.F. Kirkwood. The Economic Impact of
Automobile Travel Cost Increases on Households.
Santa Monica, Cal.: The Rand Corporation, July 1977.
Strucker, James P. "The Impact of Energy Price Increases
on Households: An Illustration." Rand Paper Series
No. P-5585. Santa Monica, Cal.: The Rand Corpora-
tion, 1976.
---- Rent Inflation in Brown County, Wisconsin, 1973-79.
Santa Monica, Cal.: The Rand Corporation for the
U.S. Department of Housing and Urban Development,
August 1978.
Struyk, Raymond J. and Jill Khadduri. "Saving the
Housing Assistance Plan: Improving Incentives to
Local Governments." Journal of the American Planning
Association 46:4 (October 1980).
Tatom, J. "Energy Prices and Capital Formation." Federal
Reserve Bank of St. Louis Review (1979).
---- "The Productivity Problem." Federal Reserve Bank of
St. Louis Review (1979).
Therndenson, Stephen. Poverty, Planning and Politics in
the New Boston: The Origins of ABCD. Boston: Basic
Books, 1969.
Thurman, Stephan and Berner, Richard. "Analysis of Oil
Price Shocks in the MPS Model," in Knut Anton Mork,
ed., Energy Prices, Inflation, and Economic
Activity. Cambridge, Mass.: Ballinger, 1981.
Tsai, Yung-Mei, Otoman Bartos, and Lee Sigelman. "The
Urban Dynamics Model: A Validation Study." Urban
Affairs Quarterly 17 (December 1981).
U.S. Congress. Crude Oil Windfall Profit Tax Act of
1980, Conference Report. 96th Cong., 2nd sess., May
7, 1980.
---- Congressional Budget Office. The Decontrol of
Domestic Oil Prices: An Overview. Washington, D.C.:
May 1979.

———— ———— The Economic and Budgetary Consequences of an
Oil Price Decrease: A Preliminary Analysis, March
1983. Washington, D.C.
———— ———— Indexing with the Consumer Price Index:
Problems and Alternatives. Washington, D.C.: June
1981.
———— ———— Low Income Energy Assistance: Issues and
Options. Washington, D.C.: June 1981.
———— ———— Memorandum: Oil Import Fees. Washington, D.C.:
March 22, 1982.
———— ———— Oil Import Tariff: Alternative Scenarios and
their Effects. Washington, D.C.: April 1982.
———— House. Government Operations Committee. Manpower
and Housing Subcommittee. Statement of John Simon,
General Manager, New York City Housing Authority.
97th Cong., 1st sess., May 19, 1981.
———— ———— ———— ———— Testimony of Phillip Winn, HUD
Assistant Secretary for Housing. 97th Cong., 1st
sess., May 19, 1981.
———— ———— Interstate and Foreign Commerce Committee.
Testimony of Gorman Smith. 94th Cong., 2nd sess.,
June 22, 29, 1976.
———— Joint Economic Committee. Energy Subcommittee.
Testimony of Charles L. Schultze, Chairman, Council
of Economic Advisors. 96th Cong., 1st sess., April
25, 1979.
———— Office of Technology Assessment. Energy Efficiency
of Buildings in Cities. Washington, D.C.: 1982.
———— ———— Residential Energy Conservation. Washington,
D.C.: 1979.
———— Senate. Banking, Finance and Urban Affairs
Committee. Housing and Urban Affairs Subcommittee.
Testimony of Lewis Spence, Council of Large Public
Housing Authorities. 97th Cong., 2nd sess., March
30, 1982.
———— ———— Special Committee on Aging. Hearings on the
Impact of Rising Energy Costs on Older Americans.
95th Cong., 1st sess., April 1977.
U.S. Department of Commerce. Bureau of the Census.
Characteristics of the Population Below the Poverty
Level: 1979. Washington, D.C.: December 1981.
———— ———— Census of Housing: 1960, HC 1-1: United States
Summary. Washington, D.C.
———— ———— Census of Housing: 1970, HC 7-4. Washington,
D.C.: 1973.
———— ———— City Government Finances. Washington, D.C.:
various dates.
———— ———— Money Income in 1978 of Households in the
United States. Washington, D.C.: 1980.
———— ———— Money Income of Families and Persons in the
United States: 1979. Washington, D.C.: 1981.
———— ———— Money Income of Households in the United
States: 1979. Washington, D.C.: 1981.

294

———— ———— U.S. Department of Housing and Urban
Development (Sponsor). Annual Housing Survey:
Current Housing Report Series H-150, Parts A-F.
Washington, D.C.: various dates.

U.S. Department of Energy. A Study of Alternatives to
the NGPA Appendix A: Two Market Analyses of Natural
Gas Decontrol Appendix C: Macroeconomic Consequences
of Natural Gas Decontrol. Washington, D.C.: November
1981.

———— Energy Information Administration. Annual Report to
Congress, 1978. Washington, D.C.

———— ———— A Distributional Analysis of the 1985 Energy
Projections for the Annual Report to Congress of the
Energy Information Administration. Washington, D.C.:
June 1978.

———— ———— Monthly Energy Review. Washington, D.C.:
various issues.

———— ———— The National Interim Energy Consumption Survey: Exploring the Variability in Energy Consumption. Washington, D.C.: July 1981.

———— ———— Residential Energy Consumption Survey:
Characteristics of the Housing Stock and Households.
Washington, D.C.: February 1980.

———— ———— Residential Energy Consumption Survey:
Consumption and Expenditures, April 1978 through
March 1979. Washington, D.C.: July 1980.

———— ———— Residential Energy Consumption Survey: 1979-
1980 Consumption and Expenditures, Part I: National
Data. Washington, D.C.: April 1981.

———— ———— Residential Energy Consumption Survey: 1978-
1980 Consumption and Expenditures, Part II: Regional
Data. Washington, D.C.: May 1981.

———— ———— Residential Energy Consumption Survey:
Consumption Patterns of Household Vehicles, June
1979 to December 1980. Washington, D.C.: April 1982.

———— ———— Residential Energy Consumption Survey: Housing
Characteristics, 1980. Washington, D.C.: June 1982.

———— ———— Residential Energy Consumption Survey:
Consumption and Expenditures, April 1980 through
March 1981, Part I: National Data. Washington, D.C.:
September 1982.

———— ———— State Energy Data Report: 1960 through 1980.
Washington, D.C.: July 1982.

———— Fuel Oil Marketing Advisory Committee. Low Income
Energy Assistance Programs. Washington, D.C.: July
1979.

———— Fuel Oil Marketing Advisory Committee. Low Income
Energy Assistance Programs. Washington, D.C.: July
1980.

———— Office of Hearings and Appeals. Fuel Oil Evidentary
Hearing. Washington, D.C.: August 1978.

———— Office of Policy, Planning and Analysis. The Interrelationships of Energy and the Economy. Washington,

D.C.: July 1981.

---- Technical Information Center. Energy Abstracts for
Policy Analysis. Washington, D.C.: first published
November 1974.

U.S. Department of Health and Human Services. Social
Security Administration. Income of the Population 55
and Over, 1978. Staff Paper No. 41. Washington,
D.C.: December 1981.

U.S. Department of Housing and Urban Development.
"Adjustment to the PFS Allowable Utilities Consumption Levels." Memorandum from Philip Abrams. Washington, D.C.: March 16, 1982.

---- Alternative Operating Subsidy System for the Public
Sector. Washington, D.C.: May 1982.

U.S. Department of Labor. Bureau of Labor Statistics.
Consumer Expenditure Survey: Interview Survey,
1972-73 Average Annual Income and Expenditures for
Commodity and Service Groups Classified by Family
Characteristics. Report No. 455-4. Washington, D.C.:
1977.

---- ---- Consumer Expenditure Survey: Interview Survey,
1972-73 Inventories of Vehicles and Selected
Household Equipment, 1973. Report No. 455-5.
Washington, D.C.: 1978.

U.S. Department of Transportation. Federal Highway
Administration. Office of Highway Planning. Home-
to-Work Trips and Travel: Report 4, 1977 Nationwide
Personal Transportation Study. Washington, D.C.:
December 1980.

---- ---- ---- Household Vehicle Ownership: Report 2,
1977 Nationwide Personal Transportation Study.
Washington, D.C.: December 1980.

---- ---- ---- Household Vehicle Utilization: Report 5,
1977 Nationwide Personal Transportation Study.
Washington, D.C.: April 1981.

---- ---- ---- Purposes of Vehicle Trips and Travel:
Report 3, 1977 Nationwide Personal Transportation
Study. Washington, D.C.: December 1980.

---- ---- ---- Vehicle Occupancy: Report 6, 1977
Nationwide Personal Transportation Study.
Washington, D.C.: April 1981.

U.S. Executive Office of the President. Economic Report
of the President. Washington, D.C.: January 1981.

---- Economic Report of the President. Washington, D.C.:
February 1982.

---- Economic Report of the President. Washington, D.C.:
February 1983.

---- Council of Economic Advisors. Office of Management
and Budget. Report on Indexing Federal Programs.
Washington, D.C.: January 1981.

U.S. General Accounting Office. A CPI for Retirees is
not Needed now but Could be in the Future.
Washington, D.C.: June 1, 1982.

---- Rental Housing: A National Problem that Needs
    Immediate Attention. Washington, D.C.: November
    1979.
Versel, Mark J. "Zero-base Budgeting: Setting Priorities
    through the Ranking Process." Public Administration
    Review 38 (November 1978).
The Washington Post. June 26, 1982.
Yergin, Daniel. "America in the Strait of Stringency,"
    in Daniel Yergin and Martin Hillenbrand, eds.,
    Global Insecurity: A Strategy for Energy and
    Economic Renewal. Boston: Houghton Mifflin, 1982.
---- "Crisis and Adjustment: An Overview," in Daniel
    Yergin and Martin Hillenbrand, eds., Global
    Insecurity: A Strategy for Energy and Economic
    Renewal. Boston: Houghton Mifflin, 1982.
---- and Martin Hillenbrand, eds. Global Insecurity: A
    Strategy for Energy and Economic Renewal. Boston:
    Houghton Mifflin, 1982.

Index